**amazon.in**

**Tax Invoice/Bill of Supply/Cash Memo**
(Triplicate for Supplier)

**Sold By :**
Facsimile Publishers
C2/12 Pragati Market, Ashok Vihar Phase 2
NEW DELHI, DELHI, 110052
IN

**PAN No:** AAACG4699N
**GST Registration No:** NotApplicable

**Billing Address :**
Vennila
4/450, New housing board colony, Srivilliputhur road
SIVAKASI, TAMIL NADU, 626123
IN
**State/UT Code:** 33

**Shipping Address :**
Vennila
Vennila
4/450, New housing board colony, Srivilliputhur road
SIVAKASI, TAMIL NADU, 626123
IN
**State/UT Code:** 33
**Place of supply:** TAMIL NADU
**Place of delivery:** TAMIL NADU

**Order Number:** 405-1326193-0916317
**Order Date:** 07.12.2025

**Invoice Number :** IN-4217
**Invoice Details :** DL-132759261-2526
**Invoice Date :** 07.12.2025

| Sl. No | Description | Unit Price | Qty | Net Amount | Tax Rate | Tax Type | Tax Amount | Total Amount |
|---|---|---|---|---|---|---|---|---|
| 1 | India and Her Neighbours \| 9357228829 ( PB11110334002 64 ) HSN 49011010 | ₹311.00 | 1 | ₹311.00 | 0% | IGST | ₹0.00 | ₹311.00 |
| | | | | | 0% | IGST | ₹0.00 | |
| | | | | | 0% | None | ₹0.00 | |
| TOTAL: | | | | | | | ₹0.00 | ₹311.00 |

**Amount in Words:**
Three Hundred Eleven only

**For Facsimile Publishers:**

**Authorized Signatory**

Whether tax is payable under reverse charge - No

# India and Her Neighbours

# India and Her Neighbours

*Editor*

**Dr Rani Desai**

*Published by*

Kalpaz Publications
C-30, Satyawati Nagar,
Delhi – 110052
Ph.: 011-47034999, 9811692060
www.kalpazpublications.com
E-mail: kalpaz@hotmail.com

*Distribution Network*
gyanbooks.com
India, USA, Canada, UK, Australia, France



ISBN: 978-93-5722-810-7 (HB)
First Published, 2024

*Printed at:* Gyan Press, Delhi.



**INDIA AND HER NEIGHBOURS**

Editor: Dr Rani Desai

# Contents

# Preface

VPM's Centre for International Studies (Regd), Mulund, Mumbai organised a two-day National Seminar on INDIA AND HER NEIGHBOURS on 11$^{th}$ & 12$^{th}$ February 2023. The seminar was sponsored by the Ministry of External Affairs, Government of India.

The Keynote address was delivered by Mr Anup Singh, Under Secretary, Foreign Policy Planning, Ministry of External Affairs, New Delhi. He reiterated the principles of Samman (Respect), Samvad (Dialogue), Shanti (Peace), Samriddhi (Prosperity) and Sanskriti (Culture).

Amb. A.R. Ghanshyam, IFS, (Retd) Former High Commissioner of India to Nigeria gave a background to India's contribution to World economy over centuries and the need to reduce the distance between India and its neighbours during his Special address.

Shri Seshadri Chari, Executive Director, Forum for Strategic and Security Studies, who delivered the Presidential address referred to India's extended neighbourhood that spans across Central Asia and spoke about 'India's Civilisational Neighbourhood'. During his address, he denounced the use of the term POK while advocating the term POI, because our neighbour has occupied a part of India.

Mr Chetan Shah, Chairman and Managing Director of Marathon Nextgen Realty Ltd. delivered the Inaugural Address. He spoke about the need for strengthening our collaboration in infrastructure and research technologies, tourism and energy with India's neighbouring countries.

Dr Sarup Prasad Ghosh, Director-Member Secretary, MAKAIAS, Kolkata, highlighted the need for cultural diplomacy and spiritual diplomacy, among others at the Valedictory session. The two-day session witnessed academic papers presented by reputed scholars from India and Nepal with over 27 presentations. The seminar of such intellectual quality would not have been possible without the continued support of the Ministry of External Affairs to VPM's CIS.

The seminar would not have been a success without the support and able chairing of the sessions by Prof Chintamani Mahapatra, Mr Sarosh Bana, Prof Arvind Kumar and Amb. A.R. Ghanashyam, IFS. We are grateful to all the eminent and esteemed Speakers, the scholars who contributed to the success of the seminar.

Whilst we express our deep gratitude once again to the Ministry of External Affairs, New Delhi we are also highly appreciative of the support from the Trustees, the faculty members of VPM, the student volunteers and the office staff who worked in the background to make the seminar a success.

**Dr Rani Desai**

Hon.Director, VPM's Centre for
International Studies (Regd)

# List of Contributors

**Dr Pramod Kumar**, Associate Professor, Centre for Russian and Central Asian Studies, School of International Studies, Jawaharlal Nehru University, New Delhi.

**Brig Rahul K. Bhonsle**, Director, Security Risks Asia, New Delhi.

**Mr Sarosh Bana,** Executive Editor, *Business India.*

**Ms Meera Atul Bhadre**, Ph.D. Scholar, Dept. of Political Science, SNDT Women's University, Mumbai.

**Dr Kavita Sharma**, Asst. Professor, VPM's R Z Shah College of Arts, Science and Commerce.

**Mr Pradeep V. Kamat**, Management Educator, Mumbai & Senior Fellow, Forum for Integrated National Security (FINS), Mumbai.

**Dr Nitin S. Kulkarni**, Associate Professor, MET's Institute of Management, Mumbai.

**Ms Dharmistha Gala**, Assist. Prof., MET's Institute of Management, Mumbai & Ph.D. Scholar.

**Dr B. Krishnamurthy**, Professor (Retd.), Department of Politics & International Studies, Centre for European Studies, Pondicherry University.

**Dr Anup Shekhar Chakraborty**, Associate Professor, Department of Political Science, North-Eastern Hill University (NEHU).

**Prof Dhan Prasad Pandit**, Professor, Tribhuvan University, Kathmandu, Nepal.

**Dr R. G. Gidadhubli**, Former prof. & Director, Centre for Soviet Studies, University of Mumbai.

**Mr Pulind Samant**, Ph.D. Scholar, VPM's Centre for International Studies.

**Mr Prakash Ignatius Almeida**, Director, Institute for South Asian Peace Studies.

**Prof Chintamani Mahapatra,** Founder Chairperson, Kalinga Institute of Indo-Pacific Studies Formerly Professor at School of International Studies, Jawaharlal Nehru University, New Delhi.

**Prof Rajiv Gupte**, Associate Professor, MET Institute of Management.

**Prof Anand Limaye**, Faculty, MET-Institute of Management.

**Prof Prashant Shamrao Amrutkar**, Dean, Faculty of Humanities, Dr Babasaheb Ambedkar Marathwada University, Aurangabad.

**Note:** The papers carry the names and designation of officials, representatives and speakers who had been serving in those posts at that time.

# Introduction

VPM's Centre for International Studies hosted a two-day National Seminar on **'INDIA AND HER NEIGHBOURS'** on 11th & 12th February 2023. Despite India's vast diversity, its functions as a cohesive geopolitical entity with robust economic inter-dependencies among its diverse constituents with many a challenge in maintaining unity would like to maintain its unity and separate identity.

Drawing parallels, we can regard African nations such as Kenya, South Africa, Nigeria and Ghana as distant neighbours. Similarly, East Asian countries like Japan, Korea, China and Taiwan constitute our distant neighbour when identifying certain commonalities like cultural relations, economic ties, political dynamics.

This Compendium encompasses the papers presented at the seminar delving into the preliminary categorisation of nations as immediate neighbours and distant neighbours, and the numerous issues that emerge for discussion as we explore the complexities of our relationship with neighbouring countries.

Dr Pramod Kumar in his paper "Mapping India's Extended Neighbourhood: India and Central Asia Relations in Modi Government" highlights the emergence of the five Soviet Central Asian states on the world map after the disintegration of the Soviet Union in 1991. India and Central Asia share centuries old historical and civilisational bonds making them part of India's extended neighbourhood. Indian engagements in Central Asia are guided by various official considerations including the extended neighbourhood are guided by "look north policy". And 'connect Central Asia Policy' which will open new ways in India Central Asia in international geopolitical dynamics.

In Brig. Rahul Bhonsle's paper "The Relevance and Irrelevance of Borders," the focus is on the evolving definition of India's neighbourhood, ranging from the Indian Sub-Continent to South and Southern Asia. Despite rich cultural diversity, borders gain significance in the twenty-first century due to identity preservation, differentiation from neighbours based on religion, language, ethnicity, and social factors, and accountability for state responsibilities. In South Asia, India's size inequality with neighbouring states is unique, making borders crucial as barriers to the spread of Indian influence. However, well-defined borders, a post-1947 phenomenon, have become contested areas, fostering conflicts. The author suggests that for regional prosperity, it is essential to make borders irrelevant through contextual integration, particularly as India's economic strength rises. Seamless integration in trade, tourism, and socio-cultural exchanges can lift the region out of underdevelopment. The paper explores this dichotomy and examines whether resolving border issues can bring about regional advantages.

Mr Sarosh Bana gave the critiques view in his paper, "China seeking to geopolitically circumscribe India", it concerns arise over China's potential military use of the Maldivian island of Feydhoo Finolhu, acquired by a Chinese company in 2016 on a 50-year lease for $4 million. The island's substantial expansion to 100,000 $m^2$ fuels suspicion of a Chinese military base, potentially for nuclear submarines and as a listening post to monitor Indian naval activities in the strategic Indian Ocean region. Despite being just 623 km from India's southern tip, Kanyakumari, the Maldives faces a substantial debt, estimated at $6.4 billion by Q1 2022, constituting 113 percent of its GDP. The escalating regional tensions prompt the suggestion that India should prioritize diplomatic efforts alongside military upgrades to navigate the complex geopolitical landscape.

Ms Meera Bhadre's paper on "Geopolitics of Immediate and Extended Neighbourhood: A case study of Indo-Myanmar and Indo-Maldives ties", focuses on examining India's foreign policy in its 'immediate' and 'extended' neighbourhoods. The research aims to address two key questions: the extent of geopolitical influence on theoretical aspects of 'neighbourhood' in International Relations (IR) and how India is navigating its 'neighbourhood' policy in the subcontinent. Central to India's approach is the 'neighbourhood first' policy, primarily a strategy for regional security and stability. The paper's objective is to identify the nature and scope of 'neighbourhood' from both bilateral and regional analytical perspectives, emphasising their interdependence. While positive bilateral relationships and increased cooperation drive regional collaboration, an effective regional treaty or organisation unifies neighbours for the purpose of fostering a peaceful and prosperous shared neighbourhood.

Dr. Kavita Sharma in her paper on "Maritime Prowess enhancement in the Interest of India's Maritime Neighbourhood Policy" has raised certain point on the India's foreign policy on Maritime and its impact. India's peninsular shape has historically fostered extensive maritime connections with both immediate and distant neighbours, driven by trade, religion, and culture. These historical ties continue to shape contemporary interactions. In the current era, India's foreign policy places significant emphasis on navigating maritime challenges, both immediate and distant. Post-Cold War, economic liberalisation prioritised trade and commerce, predominantly conducted via sea routes, showcasing the enduring maritime dimension of India's engagements. The paper argues for a focused shift in India's maritime strategy to address contemporary challenges, laying the groundwork for a resilient maritime neighbourhood. Enhancing India's maritime capabilities not only addresses immediate concerns but also contributes to elevating its global identity. India's unique maritime position presents an opportunity to fortify regional influence and project itself as a global player adept at addressing maritime challenges on an international scale. By strategically navigating contemporary challenges and leveraging its historical maritime legacy, India can fortify regional standing and enhance its global identity in the intricate web of international relations.

Prof Pradeep Kamat in his paper, "India and Gulf-Extended Neighbourhood" examines the deepening relationship between India and the Gulf Cooperation Council (GCC), comprising six Arab Gulf States. Historically rooted in cultural ties, India's Look West Policy since 2005 has accelerated political, economic, and human relations with the GCC. The region is crucial for India due to its strategic location, energy resources, and a substantial Indian diaspora. Economic ties amount to $160 billion, including significant remittances from 7.5 million Indians. With a focus on a balanced strategic environment, India and the GCC share mutual interests, particularly in the context of India's growing influence in Asia. The paper highlights the evolving dynamics and the GCC's recognition of India's emerging political and economic power, emphasising India's renewed focus on the GCC.

Dr B. Krishnamurthy in his paper, "India, 'France of Asia'. Convergence in or Influence on Foreign Policies?" explores the enduring relationship between India and France. Despite the geographical distance, France has remained one of India's immediate neighbours since 1947, officially until 1962. Over 10,000 French nationals reside in the Union Territory of Pondicherry, with around 7,000 participating in French National and EU Parliamentary elections. France's overseas territories, including Mayotte and La Réunion islands in the Western Indian Ocean, contribute to its engagement in regional organisations such as the Indian Ocean Commission, Indian Ocean Rim Association (IORA), Quadrilateral Defence Coordination Group, and Indian Ocean Naval Symposium (IONS). This positions France as a distant but significant neighbour of India. The noteworthy convergence in foreign policies and political understanding between India and France is emphasised, inspiring France to act as an immediate neighbour despite the physical distance. Both nations prioritize strategic autonomy in foreign policy, with India historically following non-alignment and France claiming genuine non-alignment and practicing un-alignment. This commitment to strategic autonomy is evident in their political, diplomatic, economic, and defence cooperation, leading scholars to characterise India as the "France of Asia."

Dr Anup Shekhar Chakraborty, in his paper Bootlegging in South Asia's Neighbourhood: The Eastern Himalayas and India's Northeast in focus" delves into the dynamic and complex relationships within South Asia's neighbourhood. Amidst the constant shifts in ties and varying notions of friendship, particularly in Nepal, Bhutan, and India's Northeast, the paper examines the transition from monarchy to democracy and the resulting intricacies in geo-political, geo-cultural, and geo-economics spaces. Focusing on bootlegging engagements, the study explores China's influence in Nepal and Bhutan and its impact on the disgruntled geographies of India's Northeast. The paper employs the "Bootleggers and Baptists" concept from regulatory economics to understand how interest groups influence favourable rules. The interdisciplinary micro-analysis offers insights into the intricate engagements in bootlegging, revealing China's subtle presence in South Asia's neighbourhood.

In his paper, "Rise of Modi and Nepal–India Relations" Prof Dhan Prasad Pandit explores the deep and friendly ties between Nepal and India, characterised by historical and cultural links, an open border, and extensive people-to-people connections. The relationship has gained renewed momentum with increased political exchanges and meetings across various sectors, fostering economic, developmental, and cooperative initiatives in water resources, hydropower, defence, and security. Despite occasional government-level tensions, the unique interdependence based on people-to-people relations ensures prompt resolution. Prof Pandit cautions against complacency, recognising the potential threat posed by vested interest groups to these amicable relations.

In their paper on "Geopolitical Risk pertaining to India's Immediate & Distant Neighbours: A Review of Geopolitical Risk Management

Practices of Selected Indian Listed Companies", Dr Nitin S. Kulkarni and Ms Dharmishta Gala discusses India's remarkable economic growth over the past three decades, transforming from an underdeveloped economy to the sixth largest globally, driven by Economic Reforms in 1991. India's integration into the global economy, evidenced by a rising Trade to GDP ratio (17% in 1991 to 43.68% in 2021), has led to the emergence of Indian companies operating in diverse regions. However, the turbulent global geopolitical landscape, marked by conflicts, climate change, and the recent impact of COVID-19, has posed challenges for these companies. The paper addresses a literature gap in understanding how Indian companies, particularly those listed on the National Stock Exchange (NSE) and part of the Nifty-50 Index, recognise and manage geopolitical risks. The Nifty-50 Index represents a significant portion of the Indian economy. The study focuses on companies within this index as of January 9th, 2023, reviewing their risk management practices through an examination of their annual reports for the Financial Year 2022. The paper aims to evaluate these companies' responses to geopolitical risks related to India's immediate and distant neighbours, providing insights into the risk mitigation strategies adopted by these entities.

Dr R. G. Gidadhubli's paper on "India-Russia Multifaceted Cordial Strategic Partners," underscores the enduring and comprehensive nature of bilateral relations. Over decades, the countries have fostered political, security, energy, social, and economic ties. Both nations actively support regional organisations like BRICS and SCO. While Russia has been a key source of oil for India, challenges have impacted this aspect. The collaboration in nuclear energy, evident in the construction of 25 nuclear plants, demonstrates a strong partnership. The 'Special and Privileged Strategic Relationship' has propelled India's progress in defence. Social and political ties are reinforced through summit meetings. Despite being major trading partners, challenges must be addressed to expand trade and reinforce economic partnerships. Both nations share common constraints and challenges, and resolving them can enhance bilateral ties and contribute to solving regional and global issues.

In his paper on "Indonesia: Not Distant Neighbour but Brother of India, a Member of the Indic Family," Mr Pulind Samant examines the intricacies of India's relations with both immediate and distant neighbours. He deliberates on the factors influencing these relations and questions whether physical proximity should be the sole determinant in shaping India's foreign policy. While the terminology of 'immediate and distant neighbours' may not be prevalent in international relations, the concept of 'neighbourhood' gained prominence, as seen in India's 'Neighbourhood First' policy in 2014. Prime Minister Modi further expanded this perspective in 2020 by introducing the notion of the 'extended neighbourhood,' acknowledging nations like Indonesia, which may not be geographically proximate but share historical ties disrupted by colonial divisions. Despite not fitting conventional perceptions of proximity, Indonesia has a rich and longstanding civilisational relationship with India, encompassing culture, religion, and ethnicity. Despite a brief deviation in the early 1960s, Indonesia has consistently maintained healthy bilateral relations with India in the post-independence period.

Mr Prakash Almeida emphasises in his paper on "Climate Change and Action", the global nature of the threat, requiring a collective response beyond political borders. He notes the inevitability of climate change and its severe impact on less developed and developing countries, particularly in South Asia. The region, vulnerable due to geological and demographic factors, faces imminent threats like extreme weather events and devastating floods. The paper advocates for a united and planned response in South Asia to address climate change, disaster mitigation, and rehabilitation. It stresses the need for innovative systems to achieve carbon-neutral and sustainable economic development. Despite challenges within SAARC, the paper urges India, under Prime Minister Narendra Modi's leadership, to take initiative in leading the region's collective response to climate change.

In his paper on 'Education as a Factor in Promoting Good Neighbourliness in South Asia,' Prof Chintamani Mahapatra underscores the crucial role of trade, investment, defence cooperation, and political understanding in fostering positive relations between India and its South Asian neighbours. He identifies the historical narrative as a key factor shaping these relationships, particularly how it is taught in neighbouring countries, often leading to anti-India sentiments. The paper highlights the impact of early education on individuals who later become leaders, bureaucrats, diplomats, or business professionals, influencing their actions and behaviors in regional dynamics. Prof Mahapatra suggests that India can promote better understanding among its neighbours through education, positioning it as a key component of national security. Drawing on examples from Western developed countries, he explores how education can be used to foster trade, business, and international cooperation. The paper raises questions about India's current policies on education, evaluates the success of initiatives like the South Asian University, and considers the potential for improvement. Prof Mahapatra advocates for a dynamic and innovative approach, urging the government to use education as a tool to advance a policy of good neighbourliness in the region.

In the paper on "India's Vaccine Diplomacy and Regionalism", Dr Rajiv Gupte and Prof Anand Limaye explores India's role as the "Pharmacy of the World," particularly during the COVID-19 pandemic and India's significant contribution by delivering approximately 163 million vaccine doses to 96 countries, emphasising the Maitri Initiative and vaccine diplomacy. The paper analyzes the impact of this diplomacy in alignment with India's Neighbourhood First policy, focusing on countries like Bangladesh, Myanmar, Nepal, Bhutan, Maldives, Sri Lanka, and Afghanistan. Examining public opinion changes pre and post COVID-19, the paper asserts India's potential to supply a "Malaria Vaccine" to 55 African countries, with plans to extend the same to South Asian neighbours. Addressing the regional context, Dr Gupte argues for a strengthened regionalism approach in trade, considering disruptions in the supply chain. The paper advocates for a robust regional framework, examining a Game-theory model to assess the inclusion of trade partners such as Japan and the United States. As India assumes a leadership role in the Global South, the paper discusses new initiatives like the "Global Pandemic Treaty" and "Indo-Pacific Charter," contextualised against the backdrop of the COVID-19 pandemic.

Prof Prashant Amrutkar discusses in his paper on "India's Cultural Diplomacy: An Effort towards Strengthening Neighbourhood Ties", cultural diplomacy as a longstanding form of international engagement, emphasizing the exchange of ideas, values, and traditions to bolster relationships and promote national interests. India's rich cultural diversity, democratic ethos, and non-aligned foreign policy have traditionally constituted key elements of its soft power. The paper notes the resurgence of the concept of "Civilisation" in global discussions, positioning India as a civilisation state, particularly under Prime Minister Narendra Modi's leadership. Post-2014, the Modi administration actively integrates soft power into foreign policy, introducing the "Panchamrita" label that encompasses dignity, dialogue, prosperity, security, culture, and civilisation. The paper underscores the administration's commitment to employing soft power to complement traditional diplomacy, enhance global perception, foster international relations and drive economic development and foreign investment. The paper aims to analyze how cultural diplomacy contributes to achieving India's foreign policy objectives and strengthening bonds with immediate neighbours.

# 1

# Mapping India's Extended Neighborhood: India and Central Asia Relations

**Dr Pramod Kumar**

## Introduction

The five Soviet Central Asian Republic says appeared on the map of the world after the Soviet Union's disintegration. The name of these republics are Kazakhstan Kyrgyzstan Tajikistan Turkmenistan and Uzbekistan. These countries are landlocked and not having any access to the international trade routes through the sea. India and Central Asia are having historical and civilizational links through the centuries. The India and Central Asia relations have been given a different official names like extended neighborhood, immediate and strategic neighborhood, look North Policy and Connect Central Asia Policy. The Soviet breakup and afterwards changes in the global orders influenced India's Central Asia policy. After disintegration of Soviet Union, a power vacuum emerged and major international powers were searching scope to influence these republics. The emergence of these newly independent countries in the space of former Soviet Union is one of the most dramatic changes in the geopolitical and geostrategic landscape in the region.(Ivan Campbell, 2013, p. 6).

The Central Asia is a pivot of Asia. 'These countries sometimes known as Middle Asia or inner Asia. Central Asia is very important for not only Asia and Europe but also for the major powers of the world for their strategic locations and security concerns. This region is also more significant for energy security For India'. (Freire & Kanet, 2010, p. 32).

After 1991 this region has 'witnessed the New Great Game' because of its strategic location energy competition for pipelines. This region is full of natural resources especially oil and gas.(Patnaik, 1995, pp. 2–7).

Historically, 'Central Asia is closely linked with the nomadic people and the Silk Road, which act as a crossroad between West Asia, south Asia, east Asia and Europe for movement of goods and services ideas and people'. Geographer Alexander Von Humboldt Introduce the concept of 'Central Asia' for the first time in 1843. Many historical textbooks still refer to this region as 'Turkistan as the name used during Stalin's period'. The geography of landlocked Central Asia ranges from vast plain areas to the high mountains that have a great importance to its topographical condition and different many types of climates. (Hiro, 2011, p. 18). As Some of the scholars have stated that throughout history central Asia has been divided red divided conquered and fragmented time to time. Central Asia had served more as the battleground for external powers then as a power in its own right. (Levitin, 2001, p. 51). Historically central Asia became the epi-Centre of for the New great game. The modern version is being played out even today among Russia, China, USA, Turkey Iran and EU.

## Central Asia: Geo Political Significance

Central Asian republics are having considerable security and economic interest in the region. To maximize the geopolitical lead and to protection of their own national interest these countries are trying to play a important role in the region. 'These five Central Asian republics are looking for building relations and connectivity to the global markets'.(Kort, 2004, pp. 2–4). Central Asia Republics willing to revive the ancient Silk Road which became one of the most feasible trade routes at the present time. 'Their connectivity with Russia remains the most dominant feature of this region. China has built multilateral as well as bilateral relations with these central Asian republics'(Alam, 2005, p. 81).

All Central Asian States gifted with minerals, oil and gas as well as hydroelectric resources. Kazakhstan has the 'world's second largest reserves and is the world's largest producer 23,000 tons of uranium in 2014'(Athar Zafar, 2015). It has almost all kinds of minerals including iron-ore, coal, oil, gas, gold, lead, zinc, molybdenum and so on. Uzbekistan has large and proven reserves of gas, uranium and gold. Turkmenistan blessed with world's fourth largest reserves of natural gas. Due to the geographical terrain Tajikistan is having with huge hydroelectric potential. Kyrgyzstan being a mountainous country is rich in gold and hydroelectric power. (Stobdan, 2016).

However, 'India has already assisted Tajikistan to rehabilitate and modernize the Varzob-1 hydropower Plant through the Indian Public sector Company BHEL (Bharat Heavy electrical Limited) and National Hydro Power Corporation (NHPC). The hydro power station was inaugurated in 2012 and it is operational' . (Eelke P. Kraak, 2012).

## India and Central Asia's Historical Links

India and Central Asia region having historical civilization links which date backs to 2500 years ago. The reference about these countries found in 'Mahabharata'. However 'partition of India and the subsequent Pakistani occupation of part of Kashmir caused a direct physical cut off on India's northern border'.(P. Stobdan, 2015).

Ambassador Ashok Sajjanhar talks about on India Central Asia links that relations between India and Central Asia are ancient and civilizational. 'India was connected closely with Central Asia through the Silk Route from approximately 3rd century BC until 15th century AD when the sea route from Europe to India was discovered. The ancient silk route connects India with Central Asia for not only transportation of goods and commodities like silk, textile, spices but also it was an effective channel of exchange of thoughts ideas religion, tradition and philosophy. Buddhism has travelled over this route from India to Central Asia and up to China'. (Sajjanhar, n.d.-a). However, in the mediaeval time Emperor Babar came from Fergana Valley after losing his kingdom to try his fortune in foreign lands.

During the Soviet period culture, dance, music, movies, literature bound the Central Asian Republics closely with Indian culture. Visit by 'Pandit Jawaharlal Nehru the first Prime Minister of India along with his daughter Indira Gandhi to Almaty Tashkent, Ashgabat in 1955 brought the region close to India. Bollywood actors like Nargis, Mithun Chakraborty and others brought India into homes and hearts of common people of this Central Asian region'. (Sajjanhar, n.d.-b). India was the first country to open a consulate in the Central Asia region after the Soviet disintegration. Indian Embassy in Tashkent played a very significant role in facilitating people to people contact, cultural diplomacy between India and broader Central Asian region (Kavalski, 2009, p. 36).

## Indian initiatives in Central Asia

For the last three decades Indian government has taken lots of initiatives to show the presence in the Central Asian region. Indian government have officially started some of the policies towards Central Asian region to have a better presence in the geopolitical scenario. It was regarded as extended neighborhood, Strategic and immediate neighborhood, Look North policy and finally in 2012 connect Central Asia Policy.

Prime Minister Narendra Modi's visit to Central Asian countries leads India's attention in the region. In the context of BRICS and SCO summits held at Ufa, Russia, India's membership in the Shanghai Cooperation Organization (SCO) has larger scope for cooperation, especially in security matters ("Evolving Geopolitics in Eurasia," n.d.). However, Energy security will be the key motive for his visits. ("Prime Minister Modi in Central Asia," 2015). India's objectives 'to increase its share of electricity generated through nuclear energy from 3.5% to 25% by 2050, but it has inadequate reserves of uranium. It needs constant supplies of the fuel from republics such as Kazakhstan, Uzbekistan and Russia, with whom it has signed deals for supplying uranium. Pipeline arrangements, on the other hand, are more complex. The Turkmenistan-Afghanistan-Pakistan-India (TAPI) gas pipeline project, that was likely to bring natural gas from Turkmenistan to Afghanistan, Pakistan and India, has stuck due to India-Pakistan disagreements'(Stobdan, 2016). Until these disagreements are resolved, it is unlikely that the TAPI pipeline project will materialize. It is necessary for Indian Government to discuss alternative methods for India to receive natural gas from Turkmenistan. 'Bringing Turkmenistan's gas to a port through a pipeline via Iran and then shipping it to India as LNG is only possible when economic sanctions on Iran are lifted'("Prime Minister Modi in Central Asia," 2015).

As P Stobdan writes "three ground-breaking developments in the nuclear and oil sectors will finally smooth India's entry into the Central Asian energy sector. Firstly, the most significant takeaway from the Prime Minister's visit is President Nursultan Nazarbayev's bold decision to sign a major contract renewing the long-term supply of uranium to India". 'Secondly, India's ONGC-Videsh Ltd (OVL) finally achieved its first breakthrough when Prime Minister Modi launched drilling operations for oil exploration in the Satpayev block on July 7, 2015'(Stobdan, 2016, p. 14). He further stressed, "the Ufa summit followed by the prime minister's visit to Turkmenistan may possibly have cleared the way for the realization of the Turkmenistan- Afghanistan-Pakistan-India (TAPI) pipeline". In Ashgabat, the prime minister named the "TAPI project a 'key pillar' and stressed that it should be realized 'quickly'. He added: 'TAPI could transform regional economic cooperation and bring prosperity along the route . . . .I convey our interest in long-term investment in the energy sector in Turkmenistan'(Stobdan, 2016, p. 14).

As Prof C Raja Mohan talks about "Prime Minister Modi will find that shifting tectonic plates have changed the regional balance of power and are threatening the internal stability of its regimes. Modi will need much diplomatic skill and even more purposeful policies to seize the new geopolitical opportunities that are coming India's way, and overcome the many traditional constraints on Delhi's regional engagement"(C.Raja Mohan, n.d.).

In the geopolitical scenario the visits of Indian Prime Minister to Iran very significant. It generated momentum to India-Iran relations, taking them to a newer height. The Chabahar port of Iran can now offer India a gateway to Central Asia and Europe also reinvigorating India's 'Connect Central Asia' policy(Vaid, n.d.). However, Chabahar port pact was the centerpiece of India-Iran talks, and was described as 'strategic' by Iranian President Rouhani as "Chabahar port has connecting points between India and Afghanistan, Central Asia, Caucasus and Eastern Europe". If the trade is routed through this port, the cost of importing urea and dry fruits can come down significantly, along with the cost of oil imports("Raising the Stakes with Chabahar," 2016). India has also expressed its interest in setting up LNG plant, gas cracker and LPG extraction unit in Chabahar. (Vaid, n.d.).

Another significant area where India can leverage its rich Soft Power resources to strengthen its image and influence in Central Asia. 'New Education Policy and projecting India as an ancient civilization and education Hub. Education has always been a significant factor in enhancing India's soft power outreach. It is used to improve the nation's cultural diplomacy, international relations, and economic progress'. In addition to that 'Education also helps foster greater understanding between countries by improving the knowledge of foreign cultures and languages, thus strengthening India's presence on the global stage'(Какимжанов et al., 2023). In the context of 'Kazakhstan, signing of Memorandum of Understanding in November 2022 between South Kazakhstan Medical Academy, Shymkent, Kazakhstan and JSS Academy of Higher Education & Research, Mysore to promote pharma education and research is a good example of soft power diplomacy for mutual benefit'. However, the major salient features of the academic collaboration that offers 'Twin Degree, Joint Degree and Dual Degree Programmes to foreign institutions are aimed to pave the way for meaningful academic collaboration between well-performing Indian Universities and top-ranked foreign higher educational institutions'. (Какимжанов et al., 2023).

## Challenges for India in Central Asian Region

When we talk about the challenges in India and Central Asia relations it is necessary to see ‘major challenges are geographical, New Great Game, Influence of China and Russia’s big brother Role’. Rohit Unnikrishnan discussed ‘India must also recognize its limitations in Central Asia. It lacks geographic access. Internal development is equally important if it is to give India a space to enlarge in the region’ (“Evolving Geopolitics in Eurasia,” n.d.). ‘It is time for India to reconnect with a rapidly changing Central Asia increasingly the focus of world attention, and rivalry among the great powers over security and energy stakes’(P. Stobdan, 2015).

The OBOR project later called as BRI is an approach for ‘China to establish a greater role for itself in geopolitics, especially in a region it considers its “strategic backyard”. It is also a way to expand ‘China’s trade routes and reduce its dependency on the Straits of Malacca and sea routes, as well as a firm land connection to mainland Europe’.(McDermott, 2012). However, there is no doubt that ‘as a way to project China’s supremacy through non-confrontation and hope, OBOR is very effective’(“Evolving Geopolitics in Eurasia,” n.d.). China is already a ‘major trading partner of the Central Asian countries, and Chinese investment could be used to meet its infrastructural shortfalls. It is a continuation of China’s “Go West” policy, aimed at overcoming regional disparities in its development and reallocating its plenty of resources throughout the region, thereby integrating it more closely with its economy’(“Evolving Geopolitics in Eurasia,” n.d.).

## Conclusion

It is true that ‘there is no permanent friend or enemy in international relations’. In his speech at Nazarbayev University in Kazakhstan, PM Modi emphasized ‘the role Central Asia plays in connecting various regions. ‘The shortest route to Central Asia is through Pakistan, and this could be the reason for increased cooperation or increased tension between the two countries. Both countries have been approved for SCO membership, and that is one avenue where cooperation could be possible’(“Evolving Geopolitics in Eurasia,” n.d.).

A C Raja Mohan has pointed out ‘a long-term strategy to overcome the continuing limitations on India’s role in Central Asia. One of them is the lack of physical connectivity to the region. Delhi’s recent engagement with Iran on developing its port infrastructure and the transport corridor to inner Asia are important first steps’(C.Raja Mohan, n.d.).

As P Stobdan is focusing ‘in terms of connectivity, while the over-land route through Iran and Afghanistan or the International North-South Transport Corridor are important pursuits, any connectivity to Eurasia is logically more directly possible through the northern parts of India, along the traditional India-Central Asia route that went across the Himalayan passes and the Xinjiang steppes. By accessing Eurasia, India can seek interlocking regional economic integration with its northern neighbors, including China. In fact, it may be the only realistically possible option worth pursuing'(P. Stobdan, 2015).

It is also necessary to see the 'membership of the Shanghai Cooperation Organization (SCO) presents a very good opportunity for India. In 2019, the first India-Central Asia dialogue was organized jointly by India and Uzbekistan in Samarkand'(Reykandeh & Falarti, 2023) (Gupta, 2020). It was a significant step taken by 'India in a direction to establishing its ground in Central Asian region'. In addition to this, 'India initiated "India-Central Asia Business Council (ICABC)" to promote business and economic diplomacy in the region. Thus, India is engaging with them by providing assistance in the field of transportation, agricultural, information technology and military training to build a strong and long lasting relationship with the region. The withdrawal of American soldiers from Afghanistan and the resurgence of Taliban in Afghan will have direct impact on the CARs peace and stability, which will, further, have an impact on India's national security. China, on the other hand, is trying to create its dominance in Central Asian region with its economy'(Singh & Rani, 2022).

Ayjaz Wani expressed in his article 'India has strengthened its diplomatic ties and intellectual capital while also advocating a progressive agenda on connectivity, counterterrorism, and Afghanistan. Despite several Western scholars terming the SCO as a China-created and China-dominated grouping, India's presidency served as an invaluable platform for the country to gain recognition as a crucial regional power and establish itself as a constructive, reliable, and trusted partner for all SCO member states'. (Ayjaz, n.d.).

'Iran is extremely important to India - geo-strategically in terms of entry into Afghanistan and because of India's energy dependency. With western sanctions on Iran and pressure on India to review its relations with Iran, a subsea natural gas pipeline would find few financers. However, India needs to cultivate and maintain independent relations with Iran and exploit the option of a natural gas pipeline if the opportunity presents itself'(Khan et al., 2023). We need a proactive approach to deal with Central Asian Region and India has already started at bilateral and multilateral platforms.

## References


Alam, M. M. (2005). *Central Asia: Present challenges and future prospects.* Knowledge World.

Arvind Gupta. (n.d.). *India and Central Asia: Need for a Pro-active Approach | Institute for Defence Studies and Analyses*. Retrieved June 28, 2016, from http://www.idsa.in/policybrief/IndiaandCentralAsia_agupta_141013

Athar Zafar. (2015). *India-Central Asia: Finding New Synergies for Greater Engagement*. ICWA, New Delhi. www.icwa.in/pdfs/PB/2014/IndiaCentralAsiaPB09072015.pd

Ayjaz, W. (n.d.). *SCO under India's presidency*. Orfonline.Org. Retrieved January 10, 2024, from https://www.orfonline.org/expert-speak/sco-under-indias-presidency

C.Raja Mohan. (n.d.). *A passage to inner Asia | ORF*. Retrieved March 2, 2017, from http://www.orfonline.org/research/a-passage-to-inner-asia/

Eelke P. Kraak. (2012, April 9). The Geopolitics of Hydropower in Central Asia: The Syr Darya. *Gateway House*. http://www.gatewayhouse.in/geopolitics-hydropower-central-asia-syr-darya/

Evolving geopolitics in Eurasia: Implications for India. (n.d.). *ORF*. Retrieved March 2, 2017, from http://www.orfonline.org/research/evolving-geopolitics-in-eurasia-implications-for-india/

Foltz, R. C. (1999). Mughal India and Central Asia. *Harvard International Review*, *21*(2), 79.

Freire, M. R., & Kanet, R. E. (2010). *Key players and regional dynamics in Eurasia*. Springer. http://link.springer.com/book/10.1057/9780230290754

Heijmans, A., Simmonds, N., & van de Veen, H. (2004). *Searching for peace in Asia Pacific: An overview of conflict prevention and peacebuilding activities*. Lynne Rienner Publishers. https://www.rienner.com/search/dezeeuw?page=113

Hiro, D. (2011). *Inside Central Asia: A Political and Cultural History of Uzbekistan, Turkmenistan, Kazakhstan, Kyrgyz stan, Tajikistan, Turkey, and Iran*. The Overlook Press. https://books.google.co.in/books?hl=en&lr=&id=bG0jCQAAQBAJ&oi=fnd&pg=PT8&dq=dilip+hiro+inside+central+asia&ots=KmpkYypftd&sig=o3U0kGpU1iOJik7veRICvJuabe4

Ivan Campbell. (2013). *India's role and interests in Central Asia*. SAFERWORLD. www.saferworld.org.uk/downloads/.../indias-role-and-interests-in-central-asia.pdf

Kavalski, E. (2009). *India and Central Asia: The International Relations of a Rising Power*. IB Tauris. https://books.google.co.in/books?hl=en&lr=&id=2XcAAwAAQBAJ&oi=fnd&pg=PP7&dq=India+and+Central+Asia+Relations&ots=rgdWHZoDfC&sig=Ju1FHLlY97UIXCVgr3IVL-C0dJc

Khan, A., Singh, S., Singh, B., & Kaur, A. (2023). Eurasia Factor in India's Energy Diplomacy: Paradigmatic Shifts in Corridor Approach to Connectivity. In A. Khan, S. Singh, B. Singh, & A. Kaur (Eds.), *India's Energy Diplomacy in Eurasia: Geopolitical and Geo-economic Perspectives* (pp. 141–177). Springer Nature. https://doi.org/10.1007/978-981-99-8281-3_4

Kort, M. (2004). *Central Asian Republics*. Facts On File.

Levitin, L. I. (2001). *Uzbekistan on a Historical Treshold: Critical Observations by a Supporter of President Karimov*. Granta Ed.

McDermott, R. N. (2012). The Shanghai Cooperation Organization's Impact on Central Asian Security. *Problems of Post-Communism*, *59*(4), 56–65. https://doi.org/10.2753//PPC1075-8216590405

P. Stobdan. (2015, May 7). Central Asia: Back in India's sight. *Gateway House*. http://www.gatewayhouse.in/central-asia-back-into-indias-lens/

Patnaik, A. (1995). *Commonwealth of Independent States: Problems and prospects*. Konark Publishers.

Prime Minister Modi in Central Asia. (2015, July 24). *Gateway House*. http://www.gatewayhouse.in/prime-minister-modi-in-central-asia/

Raising the stakes with Chabahar. (2016, May 25). *The Hindu*. http://www.thehindu.com/opinion/editorial/india-raising-the-stakes-with-chabahar/article8641709.ece

Reykandeh, K. B., & Falarti, M. M. (2023). Central Asian Republics: India's Shifting Foreign Policy Landscape under Narendra Modi. *Journal of Iran and Central Eurasia Studies*, *6*, 1.

Sajjanhar, A. (n.d.-a). India-Central Asia relations: Expanding vistas of partnership. *ORF*. Retrieved March 2, 2017, from http://www.orfonline.org/expert-speaks/india-central-asia-relations-expanding-vistas-of-partnership/

Sajjanhar, A. (n.d.-b). India-Central Asia relations: Expanding vistas of partnership. *ORF - Ideas. Forums. Leadership. Impact*. Retrieved June 28, 2016, from http://www.orfonline.org/expert-speaks/india-central-asia-relations-expanding-vistas-of-partnership/

Singh, S., & Rani, N. (2022). Geopolitics in Central Asian Region: Implications for India. *INDIAN STUDIES REVIEW*, 115.

Stobdan, P. (2016). India and Central Asia: Untying the Energy Knot. *Strategic Analysis*, *40*(1), 14–25.

Vaid, M. (n.d.). Chabahar pact: A potential game changer. *ORF*. Retrieved March 2, 2017, from http://www.orfonline.org/research/chabahar-pact-a-potential-game-changer/

Какимжанов, А., Ахмедьянова, Д., & Веди, С. (2023). INDIA'S SOFT POWER OUTREACH STRATEGY: CULTIVATING ITS CULTURAL INFLUENCE IN CENTRAL ASIA (THE CASE OF KAZAKHSTAN). *CENTRAL ASIA'S AFFAIRS*, *1*(89). https://journal-caa.kisi.kz/index.php/caa/article/view/111

# 2

# The Relevance and Irrelevance of Borders in India's Neighbourhood

**Brig Rahul Bhonsle**

## Introduction

Borders are an important marker defining identity of modern states. Even as globalisation and regionalism may have rendered borders less relevant in some parts of the World such as in Western Europe. Yet the outbreak of hostilities in Ukraine in February 2022 denotes how borders are important frames of reference which can even lead to a war between two state entities which were unitary as part of the Soviet Union three decades ago. And then there is, "Brexit"[1] where the United Kingdom decided to exit the European Union (EU) despite having varied border laws. Suffice to say the borders remain one of the complexities of inter-state relations requiring extensive deliberations.

In the context of "India's Neighbourhood," borders have a contested dimension as well given that the modern state structure has evolved over the last seven and a half eight decades or so and is regarded by some as an artificial construct. The Neighbourhood which has transited from being the Indian Sub-Continent to South Asia and has also been referred to in some context as Southern Asia which includes China and Iran is characterised as the least integrated amongst regional security complexes across the World.

While politico-economically the grouping of states as the SAARC (South Asian Association of Regional Cooperation) as a reference identity, even when the organisation was active the integration was limited. Explaining this phenomenon in context, India's former National Security Adviser Shivshankar Menon writes lack of physical geographic boundaries in what he calls as Southern Asia is limited to the North with Tibet due to the Himalayan massif. Absence of physical barriers has meant that the region is open to migration, trade, economic, social and cultural contacts through the millennium.[2] If this is the experience of the past, pre- partition and pre-British legacy, a way to integrate the region could be to make the borders of states in the region irrelevant given the historical, socio-cultural and ethno-religious realities. This may also overcome the challenge of integration. Yet how pragmatic can this be or is it an utopian framework in the context of an understanding of nationhood, nationalism and South Asian region needs to be discussed and is thus being attempted in this Paper.

## Defining India's Neighbourhood

The focus of India's foreign policy is South Asia and thus "Neighbourhood First,"[3] is the mantra that defines the same which has been oft repeated and quoted in the context of support by New Delhi to states in the region. Commonly identified as states from the west -Afghanistan, Pakistan, Nepal, Bhutan, Myanmar[4], Bangladesh leading to the Oceanic countries of Sri Lanka and Maldives, one commonality of these is that these have geographic contiguity only with India. This provides a singular significance for India as a frame of reference particularly being the largest state in the region be it area-wise, politically and certainly economically. While Indian-sub-continent was popularly used before Partition for the South Asian region, scholars in the United States have for the first time identified the region as South Asia given the post-British colonial era resulted in new and independent states as India, Pakistan, Myanmar and Sri Lanka. South Asia is thus seen as an all-inclusive and more appropriate designation of the region by these.[5]

An important facet of India as the centre piece of South Asia that is evident not flagged prominently is that the communities in the states on the periphery have very strong roots with people in the country which comes in many forms. Ethnically speaking linkages between the Tamils in India and Sri Lanka is well established. Multiple communities in the North East have their connections across the border in Myanmar, the Tharus and Madhes have a significant footprint in Nepal as well as in India while despite the political and violent divide the Punjab in Pakistan and India have a likeness. Given that, South Asia is an artificial construct this peculiarity is quite relevant and is also not unique to this regional complex. Not just ethnically, but socially, religious and linguistically there are multiple linkages between India and states in the region which in fact renders creating borders extraneous, yet these have become "lines written in stone," not just metaphorically say and thus the reasons for relevance needs to be understood.

Another facet of India's centrality arises from India's size geographic, demographic and economic which is also amplified by structural advantages with 72 percent of the land surface, 77 percent of population and 75 percent of economic output of the South Asia India naturally assumes salience. This is a unique phenomenon in South Asia with one state dominating the region which is not found in other regional complexes where there is a degree of parity except in North America. This has its own nuances which will be discussed in subsequent parts of the Paper. Whatever be the definition of this arc of humanity in South Asia with some of the richest cultural heritage of multiple hues, ethnicity and shared history, borders have become relevant in the Twenty-first Century due to several factors which will be examined now. What may emerge is a necessity for South Asia to adopt centrifugal direction away from reflexive nationalism.[6]

## Part I – Relevance of Borders in India's Neighbourhood

### Why Borders are relevant in India's Neighbourhood?

Apart from boundary defining a state as per international relations theory, borders are particularly relevant as an expression and preservation of one's identity to differentiate oneself from one's neighbour be it from the religious, linguistic, ethnic or social perspective. Religion alone cannot unite countries as the example of Pakistan denotes. At the same time language and culture also cannot be a unifying factor as division between India and Bangladesh shows. While this may have occurred due to an artificial construct the possibility of unifying the people of West Bengal in India and Bangladesh is not practical as the boundaries have not only been solidified on the ground in the form of pillars and fencing but in the national psyche. This also denotes the characteristic of relevance of borders in terms of creation of a unique nationality. The nationalities that have been created post-Partition in 1947 – India and Pakistan and Bangladesh in 1971 have been defined by the border and even where the same is contested in the form of Line of Control in the context of Jammu and Kashmir, relevance of the boundary has assumed importance.

Relevance of borders is also a factor in fixing accountability of state responsibility for security and welfare of people residing within. Where the accountability is defused such as in Pakistan Occupied Jammu and Kashmir while Pakistani state is preserving the security dimension it is a well-known fact that the people of Kashmir in the areas which have been occupied by Pakistan have suffered. Is part of the problem the lack of clear definition of the boundary and thus accountability in the mind of the Pakistan state who continues to flag Jammu and Kashmir as a disputed entity and thus feels lesser responsibility for welfare of the people in this part. This dimension needs some exploration.

Significantly emerging from the above is a deduction that clear definition of boundary provides for harmonious relations between states. India has contentious borders at present with China and Pakistan. These are "hot," borders in the sense they have become flashpoints for conflicts between the three nuclear armed states. With Pakistan a tenuous cease fire agreement is holding on the Line of Control since February 2021 prior to which thousands of rounds of artillery and mortar were fired for some years before the tension was quelled but is not climinated.

While India and China Line of Actual Control or the border as is known in Sikkim and Arunachal Pradesh was under negotiations the process of delimitation, delineation and demarcation was some way off. The Line of Actual Control however had not seen violence for decades until June 2020 in Galwan in Eastern Ladakh even though there were transgressions happening since 2013 with a notable one in 2017 in Doklam in Sikkim sector. On 7 December 2022 again an attempt to seize a high altitude post in the Tawang sector was made by the People's Liberation Army (PLA). Clearly demarcated borders assume relevance.

However, it is state polity and ambitions that defines conflict on borders. This is evident from the resolution of the much contentious India Bangladesh land boundary issue through a mutually accepted agreement in 2015. The large number of so called, "adverse possessions" had defined the border then but was smoothly settled. The Parliament of India passed the 100th Constitutional Amendment with unanimity on May 6th and May 9th 2015 to implement the Bangladesh-India Land Border Agreement of 1974 and the 2011 Protocol. [7] This could be seen as a defining development in inter-boundary relations in South Asia but one that is difficult to be replicated in other contexts for example China and Pakistan.

In the context of the maritime boundary settlement through arbitration was achieved by India with Bangladesh as well as by Myanmar with the latter in 2012. The outcome is much peace for people on both sides of the land boundary giving a certainty of daily existence.[8]

Another significance of boundary is preservation of territorial integrity of small states in the South Asian region. In South Asia borders also assume significance as a barrier for pervasion of influence of India the only state which has common geographic congruity with others and only through which they can link with their counterparts in the regional context. The inequality of size between India and other states in the region is unique to South Asia when compared to other regional complexes in the world be it South East Asia or Europe. This is particularly so in terms of India's domineering presence in the region as the largest state entity as has been brought out earlier. While as per the UN Charter all states in the international system enjoy sovereign equality, but geopolitics of large and small pervades thus pervade into asymmetry.[9] There is a constant contest between the smaller states to achieve 'notional' parity with India in reality which acts as another factor which makes borders relevant.

India's immediate neighbours are concerned over a possible dominating role of their large and subsuming regional-cum-global power which has ambitious agenda for leadership in the World if not the region. These neighbours are certainly highly skeptical of India's domination and at times aggressive approach. Settled boundaries gives them a degree of assurance of prevention of their territorial integrity.

In this context China has emerged as a new actor in the neighbourhood as some of India's neighbours are also China's immediate neighbours to include Afghanistan, Pakistan, Nepal, Bhutan and Myanmar. In addition, China is also active with Indian Ocean states Sri Lanka and Maldives. China takes advantages of any differences that arise between India and its neighbours. For instance, in 2015 when India placed a blockade on goods transit to Nepal, China inked a trade and transit agreement.[10] In this context boundaries assume relevance as exploitation of any differences by an adversarial state as China can be a touch point.

Importantly this assumes much significance in the wake of recent aggressive moves by China to assert and expand territorial limits from South China Sea in the Pacific to the Sakteng sanctuary in Bhutan. While China and Bhutan had two defined boundary disputes known as the Western Sector [269 square kms] near the India-China-Bhutan trijunction, and the Jakarlung and Pasamlung valleys in the Northern Sector [495 square kms][11], China added the Sakteng sanctuary in 2020.[12] In this context while India is a status quo power, there are indications that China is a revisionist one to preserve usurping of land by larger states in the region, well defined boundary is essential. An Ironically ill-defined borders have led to rise of competitive influences and conflict thus making the same more relevant.

Boundaries also express nationalism in terms of various forms be it religious, sociocultural, linguistic or reflexive. There is an intrinsic sentiment in people to carve out distinct land for this purpose. The Nagas in North East India for instance have been insisting on a Nagolim or Naga

Homeland with and insurgency followed by a cease-fire and talks which is continuing since 1997. The aspirations of the Naga insurgent groups the NSCN IM and Working Committee of Naga National Political Groups the other main antagonist has boiled down to a Constitution and a Flag within the Indian State.[13] Boundary thus acts as a mechanism for preservation of the sub-identity and though it may not result in an internationally recognised state but the aspiration for distinction remains.

States may also make some compromise in terms of boundaries by allowing a Free Movement Regime (FMR)[14] that exists between India and Myanmar allowing people to travel for fixed periods on the other side within 16 kms of the border, yet a delineation remains. The phenomenon of boundary as an expression for national identity and aspiration of a state is not only relevant to South Asia but is also one of the fact that led to the UK breaking up with the European Union though by a very small margin opting for the same in 2020.[15]

## Part II – Irrelevance of Borders

### Irrelevance of Borders

Even as factors which relate borders to be relevant in the context of India's neighbourhood have been covered, that the South Asian regional complex is the least integrated is well established. The political reasons for the same aside for prosperity within a region which has very strong geographical connectivity be it with India or through India integration is essential and for this it may appear that borders have become burdens of division. The significance for integration in the case of South Asia is more relevant as it is one of the most impoverished in terms of human development.[16] By sharing prosperity through seamless integration of trade, tourism, experiences of growth, people to people interaction and socio-cultural impulses, India has the potential for accelerating the region out of the underdevelopment trap. In many ways the boundary has acted as a barrier for promotion of the same.

Globalisation is the central theme that seeks to unite countries in a mutually beneficial matrix of engagement which is well established as a paradigm in international relations. No doubt there has been a setback to globalisation in the recent past due to COVID-19 and the outcome of what can be called as the "Trump effect," or the isolationist policies adopted by former US President Donald Trump. Despite the setback globalisation remains the way ahead and thus a conceptual framework for making border contextually relevant for South Asia.

Context of soft borders needs to be highlighted here. India has a soft border with Nepal and Bhutan. There is a free movement of people both countries to and fro. This has strengthened people to people relations while being mutually beneficial economically. While the benefits of the free border regime between India and Nepal can also be quantified in terms of facilitating of trade to the land locked country. India has provided 22 transit points to Nepal along with port facilities in Kolkata, Mumbai and Kandla. Vishakhapatnam has also been added to this recently.[17]

Similarly, the soft border regime with Bhutan has also led to special relations between the two countries. Interestingly, India and Bhutan are coordinating in terms of boundary talks with China even as Thimpu has adopted an independent stance in negotiations, New Delhi's concerns of the Siliguri corridor which falls south of the Western sector that is claimed by China has been accepted.[18]

Converting the soft borders into free trade and transit movement through the Bangladesh, Bhutan, India and Nepal [BBIN][19] agreement has had limited success, here the inability to pursue the project with resolution to a successful conclusion overcoming inhibitions in Thimpu remains of significance.

As a factor of religion the agreement between India and Pakistan to open the Kartarpur corridor was in November 2019 to mark the 550th Birth anniversary of Guru Nanak Dev at a time when relations between the two sides had assumed a new low after India removed Article 370 in Jammu and Kashmir is another landmark event that shows that barriers of the border can be overcome selectively.[20] While India and Pakistan went on to inaugurate the Kartarpur Corridor separately the understanding to provide the Sikh community which is predominantly located in Indian state of Punjab and the North spiritual solace denotes that states can if the issue is recognised as important for the people at large come to favourable conclusions.[21]

In this context, economic factors assume much importance. The emergence of strong unions such as the European or Association of South East Asian Nations (ASEAN) indicates that opening borders through trade, travel, tourism and exploration of cultures can be beneficial for individual countries as well. South Asia has remained a laggard in this respect.

Energy is an important factor for development today. South Asia's energy demand has grown substantially but two-thirds energy use in South Asia is imported. This has resulted in volatility of the situation subject to global fluctuations in oil and gas prices. South Asia is also heavily dependent on fossil fuels, which account for about 80 percent of total primary energy production in the region. Greenhouse gas (GHG) emissions from power generation in South Asia are the largest (68 percent) compared to emissions from other sectors as per the World Bank.[22]

To resolve the same, a South Asia Regional Electricity Market in the form of "One Sun One World One Grid Initiative", launched by the governments of India and the United Kingdom at COP26 in Glasgow in November 2021 could be the way ahead.[23] The initiative envisages the interconnection of all forms of renewable energy across continents via a trans-continental power transmission grid and is supported by the World Bank. The Bank is also willing to support a regional power market to facilitate greater integration through cross-border transmission infrastructure. [24] Such a grid can be supported by energy storage for effective exploitation of low levels of generation during lean periods in some countries, adjustment of demands in peak periods and thus creating a mutually beneficial network with shared resources which is self-financed. Several global bodies as the World Bank are willing to support the same.

Smaller countries can benefit as India's economic strength rises for this making the borders less relevant assumes significance. In the South Asian economic panorama, it would be relevant to see that those countries as Bangladesh which have established strong linkages with India in the past one and a half decade of rule of the Awami League government in Dhaka has considerably benefited from India's prosperity. Thus, India and Bangladesh have both shown an uniform growth in GDP of an average of over 6 percent consistently in the last decade or so. On the other hand, countries as Pakistan which have sutured the links have suffered and today are knocking at the doors of the International Monetary Fund (IMF) for an External Fund Facility arrangement to avoid a default. In fact, Sri Lanka which hitched to China in the past decades finds itself in just such a predicament of having defaulted in 2022 with tumultuous outcomes in the political dimension with a President having to flee to a neighbouring country fearing siege by ugly mobs.[25]

## Conclusion - Making Borders Contextually relevant

South Asia's challenges in integration are many – borders are not the only facet but can become a facilitator. India as the largest state in the region has in the past taken initiatives to make borders less relevant. One such doctrine was known as the Gujral Doctrine, a soft power non-reciprocal approach emphasising cooperation, negotiated settlements and economic collaboration. The aim was to shift the image of India as a regional bully to India as a facilitator for the growth of small states without expecting reciprocity.[26]

It would be nobody's case that South Asia should move towards dismantling of borders, these remain highly relevant given the various factors that have been covered in Part I of the paper. On the other hand, economic and energy integration should not be hindered by the barriers of boundaries. Towards this end making the borders contextually relevant or irrelevant assumes important and South Asian countries need to work towards the same.

In this context in the South Asian region may have to move away from 'reflexive nationalism' apart from the sustained anti-India narrative that has been floated by antagonist states as Pakistan and increasingly India.[27] As per Neil Walker, "Reflexive nationalism", involves flexibility in relations between states where collective goals are not absolute but self-adjusting which are pre-determined. Reflexive nationalism claims a standing right to decide - 'sovereignty of choice' rather than 'sovereignty of outcome,' and has resulted in movements away from centrality in Europe.[28] This entails a tendency to move away from the centrality of a union to sustain individual national goals and objectives which may be perceived by a narrow minority but form a dominant theme in regional engagement. Borders are a defining element in this discourse on national sovereignty in terms of territory at the cost of benefit to the people at large.

## Notes

1. Government of Netherlands. What is Brexit? Available at https://www.government.nl/topics/brexit/question-and-answer/what-is-brexit. Accessed on February 052023
2. Shivshankar Menon. Brace Yourself, South Asia's Geopolitics Is Becoming More Complex, Less Stable. Available at https://thewire.in/diplomacy/india-south-asia-geopolitics-shivshankar-menon accessed on 28 January 2023.
3. Neighbourhood First Policy: India continues to prioritize its neighbours in intl activities. Available at Neighbourhood First Policy: India continues to prioritize its neighbours in intl activities. Accessed on 02 Feb 2023
4. Myanmar though not a part of SAARC but essentially remains geographically and with linkages with India and Bangladesh is included in the Paper.
5. Prof Baljit Singh, Dr Mamta Sharma. India's Neighbourhood, Extended Neighbourhood And Near Abroad. University Of Jammu. Available at https://www.distanceeducationju.in/pdf/402%20INDIA'S%20NEIGHBOURHOOD.pdf Accessed on January 30. 2023.
6. Neil Walker. Teleological and reflexive nationalism in the new Europe. Changing Borders in Europe. Edition1st Edition. First Published, 2019. Imprint Routledge.

https://www.taylorfrancis.com/chapters/edit/10.4324/9780429492044-10/teleological-reflexive-nationalism-new-europe-neil-walker

7. Prof Baljit Singh, Dr Mamta Sharma. India's Neighbourhood, Extended Neighbourhood And Near Abroad. University Of Jammu. Available at https://www.distanceeducationju.in/pdf/402%20INDIA'S%20NEIGHBOURHOOD.pdf Accessed on January 30. 2023.
8. Bay of Bengal Maritime Boundary Arbitration between Bangladesh and India (Bangladesh v. India). Available at https://pca-cpa.org/en/news/bay-of-bengal-maritime-boundary-arbitration-between-bangladesh-and-india-bangladesh-v-india/. Accessed on February 02.
9. Prof Baljit Singh, Dr Mamta Sharma. India's Neighbourhood, Extended Neighbourhood And Near Abroad. University Of Jammu. Available at https://www.distanceeducationju.in/pdf/402%20INDIA'S%20NEIGHBOURHOOD.pdf Accessed on January 30. 2023.
10. Biswas, Baral. India's 'Blockade' Has Opened the Door for China in Nepal. Available at https://thewire.in/diplomacy/indias-blockade-has-opened-the-door-for-china-in-nepal Accessed on February 05.
11. Bhutan China Boundary Talks - EGM and Beyond. Available at https://www.security-risks.com/post/bhutan-china-boundary-talks-egm-and-beyond. Accessed on February 05.
12. Bhutan China Boundary Talks - EGM and Beyond. Available at https://www.security-risks.com/post/bhutan-china-boundary-talks-egm-and-beyond. Accessed on February 05.
13. Nagaland Set for Elections Before Accord. Available at https://www.security-risks.com/post/nagaland-set-for-elections-sans-accord. Accessed on 02 February 2022.
14. Infiltration of Terrorists. Available at https://pib.gov.in/Pressreleaseshare.aspx?PRID=1559107. Accessed on 05 Feb 2023.
15. Government of Netherlands. What is Brexit? Available at https://www.government.nl/topics/brexit/question-and-answer/what-is-brexit. Accessed on February 052023
16. Human Development Index South Asia: A review. Available at https://www.security-risks.com/post/human-development-index-2022-south-asia-a-review Accessed on 01 February 2023.
17. Prof Baljit Singh, Dr Mamta Sharma. India's Neighbourhood, Extended Neighbourhood And Near Abroad. University Of Jammu. Available at https://www.distanceeducationju.in/pdf/402%20INDIA'S%20NEIGHBOURHOOD.pdf Accessed on January 30. 2023.
18. Prof Baljit Singh, Dr Mamta Sharma. India's Neighbourhood, Extended Neighbourhood And Near Abroad. University Of Jammu. Available at https://www.distanceeducationju.in/pdf/402%20INDIA'S%20NEIGHBOURHOOD.pdf Accessed on January 30. 2023.
19. BBIN Motor Vehicles Agreement Regains Momentum. Available at https://pib.gov.in/newsite/PrintRelease.aspx?relid=175638. Accessed on 02 February 2023.

20. Pilgrimage to Kartarpur Sahib. Available at https://prakashpurb550.mha.gov.in/kpr/. Accessed on 03 February 2023.
21. Prof Baljit Singh, Dr Mamta Sharma. India's Neighbourhood, Extended Neighbourhood And Near Abroad. University Of Jammu. Available at https://www.distanceeducationju.in/pdf/402%20INDIA'S%20NEIGHBOURHOOD.pdf Accessed on January 30. 2023.
22. Guangzhe Chen. An integrated electricity market in South Asia is key to energy security JULY 19, 2022. Available at https://blogs.worldbank.org/endpovertyinsouthasia/integrated-electricity-market-south-asia-key-energy-security. Accessed on 02 February 2023
23. Guangzhe Chen. An integrated electricity market in South Asia is key to energy security JULY 19, 2022. Available at https://blogs.worldbank.org/endpovertyinsouthasia/integrated-electricity-market-south-asia-key-energy-security. Accessed on 02 February 2023
24. Guangzhe Chen. An integrated electricity market in South Asia is key to energy security JULY 19, 2022. Available at https://blogs.worldbank.org/endpovertyinsouthasia/integrated-electricity-market-south-asia-key-energy-security. Accessed on 02 February 2023
25. Sri Lanka Instability, Chaos etc. Available at https://www.security-risks.com/post/sri-lanka-instability-crisis-chaos-to-feral-state. Accessed on 01 February 2023.
26. Pratip Chattopadhyay. The Politics of India's Neighbourhood Policy in South Asia. South Asian Survey. 18(1) 93–108. SAGE Publications. Los Angeles, London, http://www.dcac.du.ac.in/documents/E-Resource/2020/Metrial/422CihnnitaBaruah2.pdf
27. Pratip Chattopadhyay. The Politics of India's Neighbourhood Policy in South Asia. South Asian Survey. 18(1) 93–108. SAGE Publications. Los Angeles, London, http://www.dcac.du.ac.in/documents/E-Resource/2020/Metrial/422CihnnitaBaruah2.pdf
28. Neil Walker. Teleological and reflexive nationalism in the new Europe. Changing Borders in Europe. Edition1st Edition. First Published 2019. Imprint Routledge. https://www.taylorfrancis.com/chapters/edit/ 10.4324/978042949

# 3

# China seeking to geopolitically circumscribe India

**Mr Sarosh Bana**

Germane to China's regular transgressions at our borders has been its vigorous outreach, whereby it is seeking to deflate New Delhi's sphere of influence across its neighbourhood by buying influence with Pakistan, Nepal, Bhutan, Bangladesh, Myanmar, Sri Lanka and the Maldives.

In November 2022, the PRC's foreign aid agency, China International Development Cooperation Agency (CIDCA), held a meeting in Kunming, Yunnan province, with 19 Indian Ocean Region (IOR) countries in which India was conspicuously absent. The theme of the meeting was *Shared Development: Theory and Practice from the Perspective of the Blue Economy*.

In its annual report to the Congress, titled *Military and Security Developments Involving the People's Republic of China [PRC] 2022*, the US Department of Defense (DoD) sees the PRC's foreign policy as seeking to build a "community of common destiny" that supports its strategy to realise "the great rejuvenation of the Chinese nation". Beijing's revisionist ambition for the international order derives from the objectives of its national strategy and its political and governing systems.

India has apparently devised a counter-strategy, where Prime Minister Narendra Modi has, since coming to power in 2014, formulated a *Neighbourhood First* policy to signal India's commitment to regional connectivity. He has also invested heavily in fostering personal relationships with global leaders, including with Chinese President Xi Jinping.

Xi has evidently not reciprocated, as China looms menacingly over

India at the 3,488 km Line of Actual Control (LAC), the Himalayan frontier that divides the two nuclear powers.

Despite three agreements - in 1993, 1996 and 2013 - for maintaining peace and tranquility at the border, Beijing has consistently disputed the demarcations.

Apart from its border with China, India shares another 11,619 km of its land frontiers with six other countries: 3,323 km along Pakistan, 106 km along Afghanistan, 1,751 km along Nepal, 699 km along Bhutan, 4,097 km along Bangladesh, and 1,643 km along Myanmar.

China is closely allied with Pakistan, also a nuclear power that too is positioned against India. India has had one full-fledged war with China that lasted a month in 1962, while it and Pakistan have gone to war four times, at the time of Partition in 1947, and in 1965, 1971 and 1999.

In pursuit of its "string of pearls" strategy - for establishing a network of military and commercial facilities in the IOR encircling India - China has built the Gwadar port in Pakistan's Baluchistan province that links to Kashgar in far western China's Xinjiang region via the $62 billion China-Pakistan Economic Corridor (CPEC). This massive joint infrastructure project is a flagship component of China's ambitious Belt and Road Initiative (BRI), which, in turn, is a $1 trillion sequence of infrastructure projects spanning 70 countries.

Beijing has lavished generous loans to many of its beneficiary countries as part of the BRI enterprise, only to assume control over the infrastructure projects created by it by way of compensation in case of defaults on repayments. Drawing from World Bank data, Forbes reckons 97 countries as being under Chinese debt, with Sri Lanka, Pakistan and the Maldives among the biggest debtors.

Though Beijing insists the BRI is largely a commercial rather than a military initiative, naval basing appears very much part of an unspoken agenda.

Gwadar port will gain China a maritime gateway to the Arabian Sea on India's west and on to the Persian Gulf, the gulfs of Oman and Aden, and the Indian Ocean. India opposes the CPEC, as the project runs through Gilgit-Baltistan and Pakistan-occupied Kashmir (PoK) that it disputes.

China is nonetheless the biggest weapons supplier for the Pakistani military. It has partnered with the Pakistan Air Force to build the JF-17 Thunder fighter aircraft, and in November 2021, delivered its largest and most technologically advanced warship, the first of four such Type 054A/P frigates that have enormous surface-to-surface, surface-to-air and underwater firepower, besides superior surveillance potential. Pakistani Ambassador to China Moin ul-Haque was quoted as saying that these 3,963 tonne multi-mission platforms will ensure balance of power in the IOR and will form the mainstay of the Pakistan Navy.

In December 2022, Karachi Shipyard & Engineering Works laid the keel for the first - and concurrently started steel cutting work on the second - of the four modified Type 041 Yuan class (renamed Hangor class) diesel-electric attack submarines it will be assembling under a technology transfer agreement with China. Under a $5 billion order that Islamabad placed with Beijing in 2017, these four will join Pakistan Navy by 2028, while four more under construction at China's Wuchang Shipbuilding Industry Group will be delivered by the end of 2023. This fleet of eight submarines will form the core of Pakistan's sea-based nuclear second-strike triad.

Pakistan is feared to go bankrupt, as it owes $77.3 billion of its external debt to China alone, according to Forbes.

In January 2023, Pakistan Prime Minister Shehbaz Sharif extended an olive branch to India, expressing a desire for peace talks, saying that "conflicts brought nothing good to any side but misery and poverty". This is not the first time a Pakistani political or military leader was extending a hand of friendship, but New Delhi has consistently clarified that it would brook no reference to Kashmir and cross-border terrorism would first need to end.

An anti-India undercurrent has always existed in Nepal, but like several neighbouring countries, governments there have alternately leaned towards India and China, depending upon which party is ruling. Five times Prime Minister Sher Bahadur Deuba is President of the Nepali Congress, a party regarded close to India, while three times PM K.P. Sharma Oli's Communist Party of Nepal supports China.

Despite its historical ties with India, this Hindu idyll in the Himalayas soured relations in 2020 when it amended its Constitution to include the areas of Kalapani, Lipulekh and Limpiyadhura that India claims are part of its border state of Uttarakhand that adjoins Nepal in the west. The three contested areas cover about 370 $km^2$ and the strategic Lipulekh pass connects Uttarakhand with the Tibet Autonomous Region (TAR), where Indian pilgrims visit the sacred Mansarovar lake and Mount Kailash.

Kathmandu was possibly incited by New Delhi's redrawing of its map in 2019 following its downsizing of the politically-sensitive state of J&K into the two UTs of Ladakh and J&K. The map incorporates certain territories disputed by both Nepal and China.

Nepal also took umbrage at India's construction in 2020 of an 80 km road from Dharchula to Lipulekh by the Defence Ministry's Border Roads Organisation (BRO), while China has resented India's construction of the 290 km road linking Darcha in Himachal Pradesh with Ladakh that will criss-cross a number of high-altitude snow-bound passes, and will provide vital access for troops and heavy weaponry to the frontier bases in Ladakh, including the Kargil region. It will be the third road link to Ladakh after the Manali-Leh and Srinagar-Leh highways.

India is now concerned by the Regional International Airport built by China's CAMC Engineering Company in the tourist town of Pokhara, central Nepal, through a $216 million loan from the Export–Import Bank of China, one of two institutional banks in China chartered to implement state policy on other developing countries. The airport, which was inaugurated by Nepal Prime Minister Pushpa Kamal Dahal on 2023 New Year's day, is part of the BRI and can provide Beijing strategic depth, as it lies close to India's most populated state of Uttar Pradesh, with the key Indian Air Force (IAF) base in Gorakhpur town located a little over 300 km by road, less than 20 minutes by commercial flight and under 10 minutes by fighter aircraft. Besides, a Pokhara-New Delhi commercial flight would take under an hour, while a Chinese PLA Air Force (PLAAF) jetfighter, if stationed in Pokhara, could reach India's capital far quicker.

Pokhara airport's commercial viability has been questioned, given its limited ability to cater to only smaller aircraft with less fuel and passenger load. It is feared that if Nepal consequently defaults on the Chinese loan, China could well wrest the air facility away on long lease for its exclusive use, possibly as a PLAAF airbase. China is besides seeking to develop hotels, resorts and holiday-homes in Pokhara exclusively for Chinese citizens.

The tiny 38,394 km$^2$ Buddhist Himalayan kingdom of Bhutan, located at the tri-junction with India and China, has a Treaty of Friendship with India since 1949, while it has had historically tense relations with China with which it has no diplomatic ties. Their relations have been primarily stressed by their long-standing differences on the 477 km border that divides them, but Beijing is now determinedly reaching out to Thimphu. Both sides have held 11 rounds of expert group meetings and 24 rounds of talks on the issue since 1984, but have yet to reach an agreement, though both recently announced reaching a "positive consensus".

China lays claims to 764 km$^2$ of Bhutanese territory, including Doklam, Sinchulung, Dramana and Shakhatoe in Bhutan's northwest, Pasamlung and Jakarlung valleys in north-central, and, since 2020, the Sakteng wildlife sanctuary near Bhutan's eastern border with Arunachal Pradesh. It was at Doklam in 2017 that Indian troops challenged Chinese personnel furtively building roads there, leading to a 73-day military standoff.

China has also repeatedly violated the spirit of its 1998 agreement with Bhutan for maintaining peace and tranquility at the border, by systematically encroaching on Bhutanese territory, building roads as well as villages in the border areas, especially near Doklam. This trijunction is of immense strategic significance for India, which continues to deploy its forces in the area to deter any advance of the PLA ranged against it.

Bhutan is now negotiating with China on a three-step roadmap for resolving the border impasse. China's roadmap, which has not been made public, reportedly seeks a territorial swap, where Doklam and other enclaves in Bhutan's west will be exchanged for areas in the north.

The 18-20 January 2023 visit to Bhutan of India's Foreign Secretary Vinay Mohan Kwatra was reportedly intended to gauge the outcome of the latest Bhutan-China border talks held in Kunming, in China, on 13 January. Kwatra was apparently assured by Bhutanese authorities that they would not allow Indian strategic interests to be compromised. New Delhi's principal concern is that if Bhutan accedes to the Chinese proposal, not only will India's security interests be vastly compromised, but China could well try subsequently to subjugate Bhutan, whereby India would lose a vital buffer between itself and China.

If China gains control over Doklam, it will be able to acquire strategic oversight of the Siliguri corridor, also known as the Chicken's neck that is a mere 17 km wide strip of land in West Bengal that squeezes between Nepal, Bhutan and Bangladesh to provide a crucial road and rail transportation link between the rest of India and its far north-eastern states. Bhutan had almost agreed to ink a similar territory exchange agreement in 2001, but a recalcitrant India had foiled the move.

India has traditionally served the economic and security interests of Bhutan, which has pointedly spurned any such help from the Chinese. Beijing might well be provoked to adopt a more forceful approach to bring Bhutan within its fold.

In Sri Lanka too, the authoritarian brother-trio Mahinda, Gotabaya and Basil Rajapaksa are known to be in the Chinese camp, while Prime Minister Ranil Wickremesinghe, who took office after the Rajapaksa's stepped down amidst economic and political turmoil in the country in 2022, is inclined towards India.

In 2022 alone, India extended aid worth $3.8 billion to Sri Lanka, including lines of credit, a currency swap and deferring of loan repayments at the height of the crisis.

When Sri Lanka defaulted on its $1.26 billion deal with China for developing its southern seaport of Hambantota, Beijing deemed it more opportune to take over the port it created rather than relax the repayment norms that Colombo pleaded for. China may prospectively use this port it acquired in 2017 on a 99-year lease, as also Gwadar port, as PLA Navy (PLAN) bases in order to bolster its maritime profile in the Indo-Pacific. The World Bank estimates Chinese loans to Sri Lanka to total $6.8 billion, or 10.8 percent of the island state's $63 billion external debt. Last May, Sri Lanka was the first country in two decades to default on its sovereign debt.

In August 2022, Colombo disregarded New Delhi's remonstrations to allow the docking at Hambantota of a Chinese military survey ship, Yuan Wang 5, which was known to be fitted with various tracking and surveillance devices.

China's string of pearls blueprint delineates a chain of ports through Sonadia, in Bangladesh, Kyaukphyu, in Myanmar, and Laamu Atoll, in the Maldives. The Sonadia deep-sea port deal was to be signed during Prime Minister Sheikh Hasina's China visit in 2014, but was shelved on speculation that it was blocked by India. However, it could be revived, with Hasina lauding China for being "a key development partner", with Bangladesh's 2017 purchase of two Chinese-made Type 035G Ming Class submarines worth $204 million that upgraded its navy into a "three-dimensional force."

China is developing a deep-sea port and Special Economic Zone in Kyaukphyu (KPSEZ) in Myanmar's western state of Rakhine as a key module of its BRI and as part of China-Myanmar Economic Corridor (CMEC). Naypyidaw is anxious to expedite the project, concessions and shareholders' agreements on which had been signed during President Xi's visit to Myanmar in 2020.

The three-phase project will be mutually beneficial as China will access natural gas from Myanmar whose economy all but collapsed since the junta overthrew the democratically elected government in a military coup in February 2021. The country earned $800 million from natural gas exports mainly to China and Thailand between April and July 2022, with oil and gas pipelines already functioning between Kyaukphyu and Kunming in the landlocked Yunnan province that borders Myanmar.

India finds KPSEZ potentially challenging as the port is but 105 km from the deepwater port that it constructed in 2016 at Sittwe, Rakhine's capital, on the Bay of Bengal. Indian Minister Sarbananda Sonowal said in January 2023: "Sittwe port is developed and ready for operation. This project is monitored by the Ministry of External Affairs. We were entrusted with building infrastructure and also dredging, which we did splendidly."

Sittwe port connects to Paletwa town in Myanmar's Chin state and onward to India's Mizoram, where 30,000 refugees from Myanmar have taken shelter since the military coup there. The port, at the mouth of Kaladan river, will make the river navigable year-round and additionally provide an alternative route to India's landlocked north-eastern states like Mizoram. India is also developing a 117 km two-lane highway from near Lawngtlai in Mizoram to the Myanmar border to provide road linkage to Sittwe port. Transportation from Sittwe port to Paletwa will be by waterway and from Paletwa to the India-Myanmar border, by road.

It is suspected that China will double KPSEZ as a military facility, apart from providing it direct access to the Indian Ocean via the Bay of Bengal, while spurring development in Yunnan province. The Indian Navy's Eastern Naval Command at Visakhapatnam abuts Bay of Bengal and a nuclear submarine base code named *Project Varsha* is being developed adjoining it.

The Indian Ocean idyll of the Maldives is raising anxieties in both India and China as it heads for presidential elections this September 2023. The two dominant political parties there are divided between the two Asian giants. The Ibu Solih administration has been a staunch supporter of India ever since his Maldivian Democratic Party (MDP) came to power in November 2018, overthrowing the Progressive Party of Maldives-People's National Congress (PPM-PNC) coalition of Abdullah Yameen that had come under Chinese influence.

Yameen is now serving an 11-year sentence after he was convicted in December 2022 by a criminal court in a $1 million money laundering case. His conviction disqualifies him from contesting the September polls. India is, however, mindful of the fact that this former Maldivian President was acquitted by the island nation's Supreme Court in 2021 in a similar graft case in which he had been sentenced by a lower court to five years in November 2019, following his 2013-2018 presidential term, for embezzling $1 million in government funds using a private company. After his present conviction, Yameen's lawyers told media persons that they will appeal the case and expressed confidence that he will be released by March.

The Solih government is beholden to India for its unflinching support and has implemented the 'India First' policy. India has executed several infrastructure projects in the Maldives to curb China's rising profile there, and wants the island nation to play a crucial role under New Delhi's 'Neighbourhood First Policy' and 'SAGAR' (Security and Growth for All in the Region) vision for the IOR, but Malé, is also prized by China owing to its strategic location.

Yameen had once proclaimed at a PPM-PNC rally that he claimed full ownership of the 'India Out' campaign that seeks to oust Indian military personnel from Maldivian soil. Maldives was invited by China to its IOR countries' meeting in Kunming last November, but confirmed later that it did not attend the conference in its "official capacity".

On his India visit in August 2022, Solih, together with Prime Minister Modi, presided over the signing of six documents on areas like cyber security, disaster management, and police infrastructure development. They also launched the Greater Malé Connectivity Project (GMCP), the largest infrastructure project to be ever undertaken in the Maldives and one of India's largest in the neighbourhood. GMCP will be built under India's $100 million grant and $400 million Line of Credit, with an additional $100 million Line of Credit extended for other development projects in the Maldives.

Maintaining that Maldives-India relations went beyond diplomacy, Solih told reporters, "This visit is an affirmation of the close bond between our two countries."

China, in turn, had opened its 2 km-long China-Maldives Friendship Bridge in 2018 as a landmark BRI project that was the Maldives' first cross-sea bridge connecting the islands of Malé, Hulhule and Hulhumale. Hailing the bridge in 2021, on the third anniversary of its opening, as "a true symbol of China-Maldives everlasting friendship", Malé Mayor Mohamed Muizzu had said, "This bridge has been the most important transformational development that the Maldives has seen for a very long time." China has also been swamping the Maldivian markets with Chinese goods.

India suspects that the massive expansion – from 38,000 $m^2$ to 100,000 $m^2$ - of the Maldivian island of Feydhoo Finolhu that a Chinese company acquired in 2016 on 50-year lease for $4 million, has been for establishing a Chinese military base, possibly for nuclear submarines, and may also be used as a listening post to track Indian naval movements in this strategic part of the Indian Ocean.

Maldives lies but 623 km away from Kanyakumari, the southernmost tip of India. Maldives' Finance Ministry reportedly estimated the island country's debt at $6.4 billion by end Q1 2022, 113 percent of its GDP.

With the neighbourhood becoming vitiated, New Delhi needs to invest as much in its diplomatic efforts as in bolstering its defences.

After all, the challenge is enormous.....and imminent.

# 4

# Examining Geopolitics of Immediate and Extended Neighbourhood: A case study of Indo-Myanmar and Indo-Maldives ties

**Ms Meera Bhadre**

## Introduction

Indian Foreign Policy has witnessed a remarkable transition at the turn of the century; from non-alignment to multi-alignment (Raghavan, PS), from *panchsheel* to *vasudhaiva kutumbakam*, from sea-blindness to *SAGAR* and from Look East to Look West and Act East (Kumar, Y.). A striking transformation in India's attitude towards neighbouring countries is best reflected in Prime Minister Modi's gesture of inviting heads-of-the-states of the SAARC members to his swearing-in ceremony in 2014 (Swami) including Pakistan, sowing the germinal seed of India's 'Neighbourhood First' policy.

Generally speaking, 'neighbourhood' has a geographic and spatial dimension. The conceptualisation of 'neighbourhood' in land-use and urban planning has brought up various aspects of its origin. Research has also exposed dynamics of the concept discussing how the concept has changed over time, geography, culture and economics. Neighbourhoods are produced by the same actors that consume them (Galster, G.); is an assertion of its utility both as 'means' and 'ends'.

In politics, the theoretical concept of 'neighbourhood' relies essentially on geography. It is based on borders. A neighbouring country is therefore, a country with whom one shares territorial or maritime borders. Instead of a simple empirical understanding; a normative and conceptual framework will reveal what lies beneath the veneer of territories and borders. It illuminates a deeper notion of neighbourhood based on shared history, culture and economy. Thus, a broader and more nuanced understanding of neighbourhood is mandated to exhibit its two-pronged approach as a means of foreign policy and an end of regional peace and stability.

South Asia has been a theater of global power politics (McGarr, Paul M.) The South Asian subcontinent is one of the most politically volatile and culturally diverse regions of the world. India plays an indispensable role in South Asia's geopolitics of energy (Kaplan, Robert D.) and water (Scott, David). The Indian subcontinent happens to be a major actor in the regional political and economic space of South Asia. India accounts for 72 percent of the total area, 77 percent of the total population, and 78 percent of the regional national gross product (Mohan C.R.). India is the largest country in the subcontinent and shares territorial and maritime boundaries with almost all the SAARC members; thus serving as a bellwether state in the region. In a post-cold war and post-pandemic world, Indian foreign policy faces both unique challenges and opportunities. Notwithstanding, it has continued to be a stable democracy with a robust economy compared to others in the region. This lends India a certain amount of pre-eminence to influence conduct of other states in the region and in turn in regional cooperation and stability.

## Research Objective

The research paper studies the geopolitics of 'immediate' and 'extended' neighbourhood in India's foreign policy. It aims to answer two important research questions. One, what is the degree of geopolitical influence on the theoretical aspects of 'neighbourhood' in IR? And how is India navigating the theory and practice of 'neighbourhood' policy?

## Literature Review

Kautilya's Arthshastra presents not only a historical account of India's earliest neighbourhood policy (Ramaswamy T.N.) but also reveals the geopolitical relevance in statecraft through the chief tenets of Kautilyan *rajamandala*, or 'circle of states' – a concentric, geopolitical conception of the inter-state realm typifying friend-foe relationships (Lt Gen. Menon and Kamal). Kautilya suggested establishing hierarchical military officialdom as well as diplomatic relations with neighbouring states for safeguarding frontiers and national security (Sahoo, P, 2016).

The British also used the policy of neighbouring states as buffer states to resist the West Asians, Russians and Chinese (Mahajan S). A notable development was Panchsheel; one of the major principles of India's earliest neighbourhood policy (Singh S.). It was extended by Indira Gandhi and came to be known as India's Monroe Doctrine. '*She believed that India's vicinity was its exclusive zone of supremacy and dominance and no foreign power would be allowed to interfere*' (Mohan C.R., Beyond India's Monroe doctrine); a realist perspective displaying disposition of a regional hegemon.

A valuable addition in India's foreign policy under Prime Minister Inder Kumar Gujral was Gujral Doctrine emphasizing on smaller neighbours. It focused on facilitation of free trade, cooperation on common problems like disease, insurgency, terrorism, trafficking, distribution of natural resources, free movement of ideas, people, techniques, technologies and thoughts, intelligence sharing, regional development and so on (Murthy P.,1999). Unfortunately the nuclear tests carried out by India created tension in the region and in more ways than one contributed to the rather unimpressive take-off expected for the policy. Neighbours saw it as an Indian plan to gain regional hegemony and prompted them to invite regional and extra-regional powers into the area to counter India (Perkovich G, 2003).

## Methodology

To compare and contrast the two 'neighbourhood' concepts used in India Foreign Policy, the paper employs a case study of the bilateral ties between India and its 'neighbours' viz. Myanmar and Maldives. Secondary sources were used for data collection including official websites of external affairs, documents, briefs, archives, journals and magazines, excerpts from published interviews and telecasts etc.

## Key Findings

The study of Indo-Maldives and Indo-Myanmar relations illuminates the strategic use of the concept of 'immediate' and 'extended' neighbourhood within Indian Foreign Policy.

Myanmar shares both territorial and maritime border with India while Maldives is a maritime neighbour of India; the eight degree channel separating Indian island of Minicoy from Maldives. India established diplomatic ties with Myanmar in 1948 and with Maldives after its independence in 1965. The initiative to reach out to both the countries seems to emanate as much from geography as historical, ethnic, religious and cultural factors. Myanmar borders China, Bangladesh, Thailand and Laos and the strategically sensitive north-eastern states of India (Ashraf Fahmida, 2008).Maldives is an island state in the Indian Ocean Region.

IOR has earned its due recognition in India's foreign policy at the turn of the 21st century. The application of the neighbourhood paradigm has been shaped by the IOR immensely.

Historically, Maldives had an India-first foreign policy, where it did rely on India for political and economic stability. '*An example of which can be the refusal to let the US use the Gan base as it would have thrown the regional security of South Asia off-balance. India also helped Maldives handle a coup against the then president Maumoon Gayoom in 1988. The warm relations that had been maintained over the decades weakened in the last five years and then surged again. With the termination of the lucrative $500 million contract with India under President Yameen, tensions between the countries increased. They further sank when India refused entry to a member of the Maldivian parliament wanting to visit the country for a health check-up and Maldives began to deny Indians work in their state, proudly advertising 'Indians need not apply'. These incidents do confirm the political leverage of smaller neighbours in the wake of rising China ready to replace India as the regional partner*' (Shabbir Fatima, 2021).

Maldives plays a crucial role in the regional security of South Asia and the Indo-Pacific region. Political instability has been a bone of contention in Indo-Maldives relations. However, since 2019 and especially in 2020, the relations between the two states have significantly improved. '*New Delhi had understood that the entire region needs to develop simultaneously for the larger common good and collective human security impinging oftentimes on the traditional security of the region as a whole*' (N. Sathiya Moorthy, 2022). *'In August 2020, India offered $500 million in aid to Maldives and proposed a connectivity project. Covid-19 crisis saw India extending aid, health facilities, and other important requirements to the Maldives which improved its ability to tackle the virus. Numerous researchers have noted a shift in the Maldivian foreign policy inclining towards an 'India first' notion once again and bilateral ties between the two states have improved significantly'* (Shabbir Fatima, 2021). Democracy in South Asia is crucial for long-term and sustainable projects. Political stability in Maldives has allowed India to step in with development assistance and also take up the 'Responsibility to Protect' (R2P). *'Thus, India's new-found slogan of being the 'Net Security Provider' in South Asia included human security as much as traditional security, which also included international terrorism as among the key concerns of the region'* (N. Sathiya Moorthy, 2022).

While political ties between Myanmar and India go back as early as 1948, the bilateral relationship did not transcend the political challenges until 2004 with the Look East Policy (Ashraf Fahmida, 2008). Though India established diplomatic ties with Myanmar and Maldives early on, the bilateral engagement has been fraught with challenges, predominantly owing to domestic politics in Maldives and Myanmar ("Indo-Myanmar Brief," 2020). The democratic deficit in Maldives and Myanmar is a major reason for lack of fruition of neighbourly ties with India. Geopolitics plays a key role in the subcontinent's political and economic power dynamics. Indian ties with Myanmar can be studied in three phases; 1948-1962, 1962-1992, 1992-2012, 2012 till date. The case study reveals that Indian foreign policy towards Myanmar in the first three phases was dictated by morals and principles of democracy, compromising national interests for a long time. While Myanmar's martial law created distance between two immediate neighbours; coupled with India's heavy loss to China in the 1961 war, the Sino-Burmese axis seem to be strengthening. Myanmar's opposition government NCGUB, opened office on Indian soil in 1992 further straining the ties (Shabbir Fatima, 2021).

Indian foreign policy towards Myanmar post 2012 under the BJP-led government has shown foresight and vigour by proactively engaging Naypidaw. It seems New Delhi would not want to repeat history that created a vacuum in the region; easily exploited for strategic purposes by other powers in the region and outside. The key to a sustained relationship with Myanmar is improved connectivity infrastructure that will promote greater integration of the north eastern region. The ORF research indicates prevailing challenges in the form of lack of coordination, difficult terrain, security concerns and flawed feasibility studies. In addition, rise of resistance groups, new equation among insurgent groups and failure of military operations, engagement of local subcontractors and no formal links with govt-in-exile pose new challenges in a post-coup Myanmar (Bannerjee Sreeparna, 2023). It is wishful for India to expect growth and sustainability of democratic ecosystem in its neighbours; however an effective neighbourhood policy can help expedite project implementation, engage all stakeholders and provide fillip to people-to-people contacts despite political divergences. Thus, despite sharing borders, democratic deficit made Myanmar an extended neighbour while in present times, the potential of an immediate neighbour is being tested and utilized. Maldives is a maritime neighbour yet has been relatively closer to India than Myanmar with political, economic and strategic defence ties.

The following three tables present a brief overview of the case study. While Myanmar and Maldives both have close bilateral ties with India; India shares regional aspirations with them through the platforms of

SAARC, BIMSTEC and track two initiatives like BCIM shown in Table 1.0. Table 3.0 summarizes the nature of geopolitics observed in the conduct of bilateral relations among India, Myanmar and Maldives that have resonance in the region. Table 4.0 lists India's large-scale Development Partnership with Maldives.

**Table 1.0: Key factors of India's neighbourhood policy in context of Maldives and Myanmar**

| Key Factors in India's Neighbourhood policy | Indo-Myanmar | Indo-Maldives |
|---|---|---|
| Geopolitics of IOR | Maritime interests in Bay of Bengal<br>Littoral State<br>Maritime Partner in Bay of Bengal | Maritime Interests in Western Indian Ocean<br>Littoral State |
| Geopolitics of Energy | Rich in Natural Resources (Oil & Gas reserves)<br>Investments by ONGC Videsh Limited, IOCL and GAIL | - |
| Geoeconomics | Bilateral trade, Grant Projects, Line of credit Projects, MOUs, JWG s Indian exports to Myanmar US$839.04 Million(United Nations COMTRADE database) | FTA with India<br>Indian exports to Maldives US$591.79 Million(United Nations COMTRADE database) |
| Chinese Influence | BRI endorsement Highest FDI<br>CMEC (Sittwe, Coco, Hianggyi, Khaukphyu, Mergui and Zadetkyi Kyu)<br>Debt Trap (40% of foreign debt) | BRI endorsement<br>FTA with China<br>Infra projects<br>Over a billion$ debt to Chinese lenders |
| Geopolitics of Climate Security | - | Maldives is an SIDS facing threat of climate change<br>Proposal for renewable power transfer under One Sun, One World & One Grid initiative Coastal, Environmental collaboration and cooperation |
| Regional factors | For greater and deeper engagement with ASEAN | For ensuring rule based order in IOR including freedom of navigation, security, sustainability of maritime interests |

| | | |
|---|---|---|
| Geopolitics of Security | Land Border Crossing Agreement with Myanmar/ Insurgents in North East/ Spillover of prevailing ethnic strife | India as 'first responder' in the IOR and 'preferred security partner' |
| Domestic issues | Democratic Transition Military Junta Human Trafficking Six JF-17 light-weight multi-role fighter jets from Pakistan | Anti-India parties Political insecurity Indian-funded dockyard for the Maldivian coast guard Presence of Indian military |

*Source:* The official website of MEA, India; https://mea.gov.in/Portal/ForeignRelation/India-Maldives_2022.pdf; https://mea.gov.in/Portal/ForeignRelation/Bilateral_Brief_-latest.pdf,)

**Table 2.0 Participation in Regional Fora**

| Forum | India | Maldives | Myanmar |
|---|---|---|---|
| SAARC | Yes | Yes | No |
| BIMSTEC | Yes | No | Yes |
| IORA | Yes | Yes | No |
| ASEAN | Summit Level-Partner | No | Yes |
| EAS | Yes | No | Yes |
| BRI | No | Yes | Yes |
| IONS | Yes | Yes | Yes |

*Source*: Official websites of SAARC, BIMSTEC, IORA, ASEAN, EAS, BRI, IONS.

**Table 3.0 India's Development Partnership with Maldives (World News, 2021)**

| **High-Impact Community Projects funded by India with a total financial outlay of MVR 200 million (USD 13 million)** | | |
|---|---|---|
| Ekuveni Running Track and Cricket Ground (Completed and Inaugurated) | Setting up 3 fish-processing plants, and a | Setting up a bottled-water plant in Hoarafushi |
| Installation of Streetlights in Kolhufushi (Completed) | Setting up 5 eco-tourism zones | Classrooms in Lhohi and Kinolhas schools. (completed) |
| Development of Vaani Police Centre (Completed) | Setting up a Drug-Detoxification Centre in Addu. | Setting up a soil-testing lab at the Hanimaadhoo Agricultural Research Centre. |
| Providing 'Vehicles and machinery' to the Male' City council (Completed) | Providing equipment for setting up Outdoor gyms on 61 islands (completed) | Central Park and renovated Jetty in Hulhumale |

| | | |
|---|---|---|
| Goidhoo-Fehendhoo school ferry(completed) | Wetland Park in Faresmathoda | A refurbished 'My Home -Fiyavathi' orphanage in Hulhumale |
| Rasdhoo Coastal protection project | Convention Centre in Ukulhas | Providing equipment for setting up 67 Children's Parks spread across the Atolls (completed) |

**Table 4.0 Infra Projects of India in Myanmar (Bannerjee Sreeparna, 2023)**

| Project | Details | Status |
|---|---|---|
| Kaladan Multimodal Transit Transport Project | Kolkata port- Sittwe port- Paletwa-Zorinpui | Phase 1&2 completed |
| India-Myanmar-Thailand Trilateral highway project | Moreh, India to Mae Sot, Thailand via Myanmar | Ongoing |
| India-Myanmar Border Area Development | Roads, bridges, and schools in Chin State and the Naga Self-Administered Area | Ongoing |
| Rakhine State Development Program | Pre-fabricated housing for displaced Rohingyas; development of schools and roads | Ongoing (partly handed) |

In the last decade, India's neighbourhood policy seems to be relying more on realpolitik. India's neighbourhood policy towards both Myanmar and Maldives post 2004 can be summed up as being proactive and constructive despite political challenges towards leveraging India's position as a regional power in south asia. Within the context of great-power dynamics in the region, it is clear that India and China are competing for relative gains in both Maldives and Myanmar (Shabbir Fatima, 2021). There are massive scale Chinese investments in both Maldives (SD 210 million Friendship Bridge, Facelift of Maldivian island of Feydhoo Finolhu etc) (Prasad Manish, 2022) and Myanmar (New Yangon City project, Mandalay-Tigyaing-Muse Expressway, Kyaukphyu Special Economic Zone (KPSEZ), Kyaukphyu-Naypyidaw Highway projects and more) (Bannerjee Sreeparna, 2023). However, the five years from 2014 to 2019 left Maldives in a Chinese debt trap, a state of emergency, as well as large scale human rights violations including targeted killing of journalists who dared to expose the situation on ground (Prasad Manish, 2022). India has a huge advantage over China, especially in view of its increasing debt-trap victims. Indian neighbourhood policy should not be a zero-sum game with China but in fact create conditions for a rule-based order, greater democratization and better connectivity in the region.

## Views and Discussion

Research seems to show that a 'neighbor' in the parlance of Indian foreign policy seems to have a few defining features as shown in Table 5.0. Neighbourhood concept cannot be limited to borders alone. India is reimagining the concept using empirical and normative methods to formulate an effective and inclusive foreign policy that can foster close ties with regional and extra-regional partners and garner their support at various platforms/fora. The demands of regional consensus on trade and connectivity pan-Asia (read BRI), the global deliberation and debate on climate change at UNCED, world trade and commerce at WTO, addressing concerns of the global south at G20 etc. has proved that multilateralism reaps higher and greater dividends in international relations.

**Table 5.0 Characteristic features of India's Immediate and Extended Neighbours**

<table>
<tr><th>Feature</th><th>Definition</th><th>Maldives</th><th>Myanmar</th><th>Immediate neighbor</th><th colspan="3">Extended Neighbour (West Asia, Central Asia, South East Asia)</th></tr>
<tr><td>F1</td><td>Sharing territorial/maritime border</td><td>✓</td><td>✓</td><td>✓</td><td colspan="3">×</td></tr>
<tr><td>F2</td><td>Number of Countries separating each other/Geographically distant region.neighbour of a neighbour</td><td>×</td><td>×</td><td>none</td><td colspan="3">✓</td></tr>
<tr><td>F3</td><td>Political Sameness</td><td>✓</td><td>×</td><td>✓</td><td>✓</td><td>×</td><td>×</td></tr>
<tr><td>F5</td><td>Shares Bilateral Ties</td><td>✓</td><td>✓</td><td>✓</td><td>✓</td><td>✓</td><td>✓</td></tr>
<tr><td>F6</td><td>Historic, Cultural and Ethnic links</td><td>✓</td><td>✓</td><td>✓</td><td>✓</td><td>✓</td><td>×</td></tr>
<tr><td>F7</td><td>Collaboration and engagement in regional fora</td><td>✓</td><td>✓</td><td>✓</td><td>✓</td><td>×</td><td>✓</td></tr>
<tr><td>F8</td><td>Capable of sharing and shaping India's regional interests/regional partners</td><td>✓</td><td>✓</td><td>✓</td><td colspan="3">✓</td></tr>
</table>

A pertinent concern is the political heritage of the subcontinent. The frequency of coups, wars, martial law, political assassinations etc. there seems to be a quasi-geographical conception of the region as a political region. Therefore, neighbourhood paradigm failed in the context of Indo-Myanmar ties between 1948-2012. With the advent of globalization and information and communication technology, one may assume borders are turning invisible. Yet there is a certain 'virtual geography' at play. There will remain certain aspects of the distance factor, relating to culture and to local geographic conditions, that are likely to ensure geopolitical influence on foreign policy.

Geopolitics of the Indian subcontinent also seems to reveal growing dependencies in the region. Trade and commerce is India's primary strategy of regional cooperation. Afghanistan, Bangladesh, Bhutan, Maldives, Myanmar, Nepal, Pakistan, and Sri Lanka, collectively referred to as 'South Asia' or N8 are major trading neighbours of India (Sinha, R and Sareen, N). There exists a dependency of smaller nations on India for security, trade and commerce, energy and power. This is swiftly changing with China surpassing India as the largest (Sinha, R and Sareen, N) trading partner to majority of the N8. Defying the logic of proximity, most of India's neighbours are now largely reliant on China for their imports; raising challenges to the conventional wisdom on 'neighbourhood policy'.

Finally, geopolitics is simply one framework to understand the concept of 'neighbourhood' in International relations. To promote a circle of countries with whom to enjoy cordial ties and cooperative relations which will ultimately lead to establishment of an area of prosperity and good neighbourliness'. The concern lies in the nature of politics and governance among the 'neighbours'; immediate or extended. Critical theories reveal (Smith, K. E) that neighbourhood policy can be an attempt to create good neighbours; to be precise the kind who conform to 'your values', 'standards and laws' in specific economic and social areas. This raises questions of toleration and diversity about the legitimacy of a 'neighbourhood' policy.

## Conclusion

Francis Sempa in his work on geopolitics addresses its ubiquitous reference to describe, explain, or analyze specific foreign policy issues and problems. The 'neighbour and neighbourhood' vocabulary predominantly emerges from a geopolitical thought. However, it can be argued that the concept has transcended geopolitics to include market, economics, culture and converging national and international interests. Though, post-cold war scholars have predicted that economics would replace geopolitics as the driving force in international politics; however International relations have never been about permanence. Lord Palmerstone, British Home Secretary blamed the regional imbalance on national interests; "*[w]e have not eternal allies and we have not perpetual enemies. Our interests are eternal and perpetual and those interests it is our duty to follow*" (Maoz et al.) At the core of it, India's 'neighbourhood first' policy is essentially a regional security and stability strategy (Muni, SD). The immediate and extended neighbourhood strategy of India serves well in engaging near and far neighbours who are likely to shape and impact both a dyadic and regional cooperation with India.

India, as the new G20 president has adopted the mantra 'One Earth, One Family, One Future". This development only complements the paper's research objective. It clearly exhibits India's belief in multilateralism and how India espouses efforts and initiatives that promote solidarity, cooperation and confidence-building among immediate and extended neighbours as well as distant partners. Based on India's gradual expansion of 'neighbourhood'; one can surmise that the concept of 'extended' neighbourhood is a derivative of the geopolitical construct of 'sphere-of-influence'; either a quest to create one or fear of losing one.

## References


Ashraf Fahmida. (2008). INDIA-MYANMAR RELATIONS. *Strategic Studies, 28*(1(Spring issue)), 223-233. Retrieved Dec, 2023, from https://www.jstor.org/stable/45242456

Bannerjee Sreeparna. (2023, Feb 22). *India's connectivity Projects with Myanmar post-coup: A stocktaking*. ORF. Retrieved Feb, 2023, from https://www.orfonline.org/research/indias-connectivity-projects-with-myanmar-post-coup/#_edn26

Brewster, D. (2020, Nov 24). *Maldives - India first or India out*. the interpreter. Retrieved Jan, 2023, from https://www.lowyinstitute.org/the-interpreter/maldives-india-first-or-india-out)

Galster, G. (2001). On the nature of neighbourhood. *Urban studies, 38*(12), 2111-2124.

Henrikson, Alan K. (2022). Distance and Foreign Policy: A Political Geography Approach. *International Political Science Review/ Revue Internationale de Science Politique, 23*(4), 437–66. http://www.jstor.org/stable/1601543.

Htwe,Thein. (2022, Nov). *China's influence in Myanmar*. The Conversation Journal. Retrieved Jan, 2023, from https://theconversation.com/chinas-influence-in-myanmar-could-tip-the-scales-towards-war-in-the-south-china-sea-189780

Indo-Myanmar Brief [pdf]. (2020, Oct). In *The Official Website of MEA, GoI*. MEA. Retrieved Jan, 2023, from https://mea.gov.in/Portal/ForeignRelation/Myanmar_2020_oct.pdf

Kaplan, Robert D. (2014). The Geopolitics of Energy. *Stratfor Global Intelligence, 2*.

Kumar, Y. (2021). Indian Foreign Policy: Challenges And Modi Doctrine. *Quit India To New India: History And Society, 225*.

LALL, M. (2006). Indo-Myanmar Relations in the Era of Pipeline Diplomacy. *Contemporary Southeast Asia, 28*(3), 424–446. http://www.jstor.org/stable/25798799

Lt Gen. Menon, P., & Kamal, K. (2021, Mar 9). Why China is the Kautilya of international politics? *The Print*. Retrieved Jan, 2023, from https://theprint.in/opinion/why-china-is-the-kautilya-of-international-politics/618044/

Mahajan, S. (2003). *British foreign policy 1874–1914: The role of India*. Routledge.

Mitra, R. (2022, Jan 19). *The China-India Cold War in Maldives*. The Diplomat. Retrieved Jan 21, 2023, from https://thediplomat.com/2022/01/the-china-india-cold-war-in-maldives/

Muni, S. D. (2017). *Modi's 'neighbourhood first'initiative*. MODI AND THE WORLD: (RE) CONSTRUCTING INDIAN FOREIGN POLICY.

Murthy, P. (1999). The Gujral doctrine and beyond. *Strategic Analysis*, *23*(4), 639-652.

N. Sathiya Moorthy. (2022, Oct 04). India-Maldives ties: Extending additional credit lines. *ORF*. https://www.orfonline.org/expert-speak/india-maldives-ties-extending-additional-credit-lines/

Prasad Manish. (2022, Jan 22). Enter the dragon – Chinese entrenchment proving costly for Maldives. *India TV*. https://www.indiatvnews.com/opinion/news-enter-the-dragon-chinese-entrenchment-proving-costly-for-maldives-abdulla-yameen-pro-chinese-ppm-pnc-coalition-752327

Raghavan, P.S. (2017). The Making of India's Foreign Policy: From NonAlignment to Multi-Alignment. *Indian Foreign Affairs Journal*, *12*(4), 326-341. Retrieved Jan, 2022, from http://www.associationdiplomats.org/publications/ifaj/Vol12/12.4/IFAJ-12.4-Article%201-(F).pdf

Shabbir Fatima. (2021, July). *Sino-Indian Competition in the Maldives: Implications for Regional Security*. Focus. Retrieved Feb, 2023, from http://irs.org.pk/Focus/11FocusJuly21.pdf

Singh, S. (1998). Three agreements and five principles between India and China. In *Across the Himalayan Gap* (pp. 505-518).

Sinha, R, & Sareen, N. (2020). *India's limited trade connectivity with South Asia*. Brookings. Retrieved Jan 21, 2023, from https://www.brookings.edu/research/indias-limited-trade-connectivity-with-south-asia/

Swami, P. (2014, May 21). In a first, Modi invites SAARC leaders for his swearing-in. *The Hindu*. Retrieved Jan 24, 2023, from https://www.thehindu.com/news/national/in-a-first-modi-invites-saarc-leaders-for-his-swearingin/article6033710.ece World News. (2021, Jan 16). India implements community projects worth $13 million in the Maldives. *The Hindustan Times*. https://www.hindustantimes.com/world-news/india-implements-community-projects-worth-13-million-in-the-maldives-101610810693030.html

# 5

# Maritime Prowess Enhancement in the Interest of India's Maritime Neighbourhood Policy

**Dr Kavita Sharma**

## Introduction

India is a grand old maritime nation and had a glorious maritime heritage since ancient times. A study of India's maritime history has been indicative of India had a great maritime prowess. India exercised maritime supremacy over not only in its immediate neighbouring seas or oceans but even in its extended neighbouring seas or oceans. India has been engaged in ocean trading since time immemorial. Shipping from India was well developed and the country was a world leader in the ancient past. It had trade relations with number of countries in West-Asia, Africa and Europe. Maritime history of India also brings out that India thrived on trade relations with countries in East Asia, namely Java and Sumatra. There are even evidence of India having trade relations with number of countries in the Pacific and Indian Ocean. Trades of such level could not have been possible without appropriate maritime security measures. Rulers from Peninsula India especially in the coastal States such as the Pallavas, the Cholas, the Pandyas, and the Cheras had maintained naval forces for protection of their Ports and trading ships trade from enemies. Such capabilities have been evident from the Indian expeditions to East Asian countries. Thus, it is evident that the Indian rulers from pre-historic times had a strong navy and maintained considerable maritime influence in the region. Such a strong navy had ensured flourishing maritime trade for the benefit of the all nations in the region. However, maritime history of India also narrates an opposite scenario where India's maritime prowess was neglected and led to decline of maritime power from thirteenth century onwards. This led to colonisation of not only India but also other countries in the region. Post-Independence India has been very much aware of developing strong Navy and has made significant progress towards enhancing its maritime prowess. In the era of globalisation, sea trade remains the backbone of the world economy. However, globalisation and technological advancement have also made the maritime space that much more insecure with the involvement of non-state actors in a big way. India being one of the largest nations and strong maritime power in the region is looked upon by other nations in the region for support. In the changed security environment, India has onus of ensuring safe and secure maritime environment for the wellbeing of the region at large. This has been one of the critical parts of its foreign policy and in turn necessitates further enhancement of its maritime prowess which will not be in the interest of India alone but even for the other countries in the maritime neighbourhood and international community at large.

## India's Foreign Policy

India has been following ethos of 'Vasudhaiva Kutumbakam' in her foreign policy. Vasudhaiv Kutumbkam is a Sanskrit phrase meaning "The world is one family". Soon after independence, India adopted its Constitution and Article 51 of the Constitution provided guidelines for its foreign policy. Such guidelines have been for promoting international peace and security. Accordingly, over a period of 75 years since independence India has practiced its foreign policy based on the principles of Panchsheel and Non-alignment. It opposed colonialism and racism, believed in peaceful settlement of disputes, stood for the international law. It believed in support to United Nations and maintaining an equal world order. Since independence, India has always tried to maintain friendly relations with all the nations and especially with the countries in the neighbourhood.

After 75 years of independence, India has grown noticeably and with that has to define its relationship with the world in the changed international environment. The world has changed considerably since India got its independence. The bi-polar world of USA and Soviet Union has vanished with a unipolar world under USA and is once again inching towards bipolar competition to some extent with China in the contemporary times. Further, the changed scenario is also been distracted with multipolar illusions. Under such circumstances, India faces numerous challenges at this juncture in defining its own foreign policy and shaping its actions in engaging with the world.

Today, India has been confident in reflecting its national interest in the forefront besides standing firm on its moral values. There is clear reflection of a confident India standing for "India First" foreign policy. Today, India is the most populous country, the fifth largest economy and fourth largest military power. India has to have its own standing and its voice in the global space. Twenty-first Century India is very pragmatic in its approach and same is even reflected from its foreign policy in which national interests are paramount. India has been pursuing realistic diplomacy keeping its priorities foremost. Pursuance of such policy has been evident from the acts like taking on China's Belt and Road Initiative since 2014, responding to China's military aggression with a strong military pushback, working with USA without entering into any formal alliance, deepening economic interdependence with the world, maintaining time tested relationship with Russia, becoming part of Quadrilateral Security Dialogue (QUAD) as well as of BRICS, etc.

However, another important aspect of India's foreign policy has been the concept of Vasudhaiva Kutumbakam. It is based on the concepts of **Sabka Saath, Sabka Vikas, Sabka Vishwas**, which means "The whole world is one family where members live in harmony, work and grow together and have trust in one another." India believes in democratic values and stands for promoting democracy, building consensus on global issues like terrorism, climate change, health hazards etc.

India being a grand maritime nation has a large maritime neighbourhood. Being a peninsular country, India had rich maritime history reflective of its maritime linkages with the Indian Ocean Rim countries and beyond. India had historically involved trade, religion and culture relationships as maritime linkages and same goodwill continues even today. However, soon after independence more emphasis was laid on continental issues and accordingly foreign outreach had become more of continental. It is only after the liberalisation reforms in 90s that maritime outreach started getting priority and development of maritime assets became important part of national agenda. In the recent times, the focus on building maritime capability and maritime outreach has seen significant growth with dedicated national policies in developing maritime infrastructure.

## India's Maritime Neighbourhood

Peninsula geography divides Indian Ocean into two halves and India sits in the centre. This geostrategic location significantly influences the country's policy approaches, strategic calculations and naval posturing on both sides of peninsula. India has a vast maritime neighbourhood and in the contemporary times maritime neighbourhood is being considered in two categories – Immediate Neighbourhood and Extended Neighbourhood. As part of Immediate neighbourhood, India shares maritime boundaries with Pakistan, Maldives, Sri Lanka, Bangladesh, Myanmar, Thailand, and Indonesia. Besides this Seychelles and Mauritius are also considered as part of Immediate Neighbourhood. Indian Ocean Rim countries and some countries in the Pacific become part of extended neighbourhood which include ASEAN countries. Like Philippine's, Singapore, Malaysia, Cambodia, Vietnam. Japan, Australia, New Zealand, Madagascar, and Reunion (France).

## Maritime Security Concerns in India's Maritime Neighbourhood

Maritime security concerns primarily originate from the threats having bearing on the maritime interests of all the stakeholders in the region. The region is a vast and stretches from African continent and West Asia in the West to East Asia and Australia in the East. It includes the Persian Gulf, Arabian Sea, Bay of Bengal in the North and Southern Indian Ocean in the South. Indian Ocean forms the most critical part of the maritime highway of the World as it connects, the Middle East to South East Asia and East Asia, as well as countries of Africa, Europe and American continents. Some of the threats envisaged are discussed in succeeding paragraphs.

Indian Ocean region has several key choke points of the world for shipping transportation, namely Strait of Hormuz in the Persian Gulf, Bab-el-Mandeb, Mozambique channel, Malacca Strait, Sunda Strait and Lombok Strait. These are bottlenecks that connects two important waterways. Guarding of these choke points is critical for safeguarding maritime of interests of India and its neighbourhood. India being the largest nation, and its central location in the Indian Ocean has prominent role to play in ensuring free flow of shipping traffic in the region. Any threat to these choke points would result in devastating effect on regional as well as global economy.

Safety and security of choke points and SLOCs are dependent on peace and stability in the region. This region faces numerous security challenges which are both - traditional and non-traditional in nature. Such challenges include piracy, terrorism, armed robberies, human trafficking, drug trafficking, illegal trafficking of arms and ammunition, smuggling, illegal fishing, etc. There are numerous reasons for such challenges but primary reasons appear to be political instability, inadequate maritime security capability, economic backwardness, lesser importance accorded to maritime security among the countries in the region. Growing piracy in the region has been classical example of the same.

## India's Neighbourhood Foreign Policy

In the contemporary times, India accords utmost priority to its neighbourhood in its foreign policy. Accordingly, India has initially adopted the Neighbourhood First Policy, followed by Act East policy, Extended Neighbourhood policy for Central Asia and Think West policy for the Gulf and Arab Countries. 'Vasudhaiva Kutumbakam' which has been commonly used India's slogan forms central theme of India's contemporary foreign policy. In the recent times there is another important policy initiative called 'Security and Growth for All in the Region (SAGAR)' initiative which has been articulated in 2015. It is a maritime initiative. It envisages strengthening of economic and security cooperation with the maritime neighbours. It also visualises providing assistance in developing maritime security capabilities of maritime neighbours.

## India's Maritime Policy

As the largest maritime nation in the region, India has important role to play in safeguarding the maritime domain in the neighbourhood. India's maritime policy directives and naval linkages did start in 90s but is only in the last decade that it has picked up momentum. Soon after independence and the occurrence of incidents at that time led to continental approach. However, even then significance of maritime sector was acknowledged. This necessitated acquiring of sea defence capability for enhancing overall defence capability and for protection of shipping trade. However, India lacked both economic and industrial resources to build its maritime capability. 1962 China war further eclipsed maritime strengthening. 1965 conflict with Pakistan saw limited involvement of Navy but decisive role played in 1971 war made all the difference among the policy makers and brought significant change in their maritime outlook. Since then, there has been emphasis on building maritime power with enhanced budgetary allocation to build maritime infrastructure as well as enhancing maritime power. Economic liberalisation in 90s has been one of the most significant factors for development of maritime sector. As the economy opened up, India became a trading nation. Trading has been largely seaborne and therefore country's maritime interests grew exponentially. This also necessitated India to build its maritime infrastructure by developing its economic and industrial resources. One of the most critical requirements was to have sea power capable of providing protection to SLOCs, shipping trade and maritime assets in its maritime zones. It led to building up of maritime infrastructure not only in civil sector but even building certain sea defence capability to enhance overall defence capability and also to ensure free flow of seaborne trade. Besides economic considerations, there has also been numerous developments in India's neighbourhood where India's maritime forces had a critical role to play as security provider.

## Role of a Security Provider in Maritime Neighbourhood

India had begun to undertake the role of maritime security provider in the Indian Ocean Region (IOR) from the beginning of 80s. There have been numerous instances where India had actively come in support to assist its maritime neighbours in political crisis as well as in dealing with maritime security challenges.

| Year | Operation | Brief Description |
|---|---|---|
| | | Political Crisis |
| 1983 | Operation Lal Dora | There was a likelihood of coup in Manutius against Mauritian Prime Minister Anerood Jugnauth in 1983. Mr Jugnauth had sought assistance from India. India had ordered Army and Navy for intervention against possible coup. |
| 1986 | Operation Flowers are Blooming | INS Vindhyagiri was deployed in the Seychelles as part of the operation codenamed "Operation Flowers are Blooming" to help abort coup against then Seychelles President Rene. |
| 1987 | Operation Pawan | In 1987, India intervened in Sri Lanka's civil war under the operation codenamed 'Operation Pawan' at their request. Navy played crucial role in providing logistics support, transport troops, ensure safe passage of supplies and equipment to Indian Peace Keeping Force. |
| 1988 | Operation Cactus | Operation Cactus was launched on 04 Nov 1988 to help Maldives against a coup launched by the mercenaries. Operation was successfully conducted; all hostages taken by mercenaries were freed, mercenaries were captured and handed over to Maldives. |
| | | Maritime Security |
| 2002 | Escort Mission in Malacca Straits | Indian Naval ships provided escort mission to US and other coalition ships carrying 'High Value' cargo for operations for the military operations in Afghanistan and other areas across Malacca Straits to provide security against piracy. |
| Oct 2008 onwards | Anti-piracy Patrol | Indian Navy has been undertaking anti-piracy patrol and escorting ships transiting through Internationally Recommended Transit Corridor from Oct 2008 onwards in the Gulf of Aden. |
| Jun 2019 | Operation Sankalp | Indian Naval Ships were deployed in Persian Gulf to ensure safety of Indian Flag Merchant vessels carrying high import and export cargo |
| 2022-23 | Anti-Piracy Missions in the Gulf of Guinea | Indian Naval Ships Tarkash and Sumedha were deployed in the Gulf of Guinea aimed at suppression of piracy activities. Such deployment also demonstrated its proactive role in global maritime security. |

## Role in Humanitarian Assistance and Disaster Relief (HADR)

Besides political crisis, natural disasters are another area of concern for number of countries in the region. Natural Disasters have been a common phenomenon in Indian Ocean Region and has always posed severe challenges. Maritime nations face difficulties in dealing with numerous natural disasters originating from sea like Tsunami, cyclone, tropical storms, etc. Such disasters cause immense loss of life, property, infrastructure, and disrupts normal functioning for a prolonged duration. India being one of the largest nations in the region has always been coming forward to render assistance to its maritime neighbours in such difficult times.

| Year | Country | Brief Description |
|---|---|---|
| 2021 | Madagascar | Madagascar was hit by cyclone in Jan 2021. INS Airavat was dispatched to render assistance. Airavat carried clothing, food items, medicines, diving equipment, communication sets and undertook evacuation of personnel. |
| 2020 | Operation Samudra Setu | Indian Navy carried out several deployments to Gulf nations during Covid period for evacuation. |
| 2020 | Mission Sagar | Mission Sagar commenced in May 2020 as part of India's initiative to assist countries in the region during the Covid-19 pandemic. Indian Naval Ships were deployed to number of countries in the region which included Sri Lanka, Maldives, Bangladesh, Indonesia, Thailand, Vietnam, Comoros, Madagascar, Mozambique, Cambodia, Djibouti, Eritrea, Sudan, Mauritius, and Seychelles. Ships provide relief materials which included medicines, medical stores and food items. |
| 2019 | Mozambique | Mozambique was ravaged by Clone Idai in Mar 2019. Indian Navy ships Sujata, Sarathi and Shardul were diverted on receiving request from Government of Mozambique to render HADR and India became the first international responder to Cyclone Idai in Mozambique |
| 2017 | Bangladesh | Cyclone Mora had hit Bangladesh in 2017. India deployed INS Sumitra, INS Gharial and P-81 aircrafts for HADR. |
| 2014 | Maldives | In Dec 2014, desalination plant of Maldives for providing drinking water caught fire and became dysfunctional affecting more than 10000 people. Besides airlifting fresh water bottle, INS Deepak and Sukanya were dispatched to render assistance in meeting fresh water requirements. |
| 2008 | Myanmar | Cyclone Nargis had hit Myanmar in May 2008. INS Rana and INS Kirpan rendered HADR as part of Operation Sahayata. |
| 2004 - 2005 | Sri Lanka, Maldives, Indonesia | Tsunami in 2004 caused severe destruction in number of Indian Ocean Rim countries. India despite facing brunt of Tsunami itself undertook massive relief operations for its neighbouring countries Sri Lanka (Operation Rainbow), Maldives (Operation Casta) and Indonesia (Operation Gambhir). Around 40 ships were deployed for rendering HADR. |

Such missions have not been restricted to South Asia alone. India has been undertaking HADR missions even for the countries in its Extended Neighbourhood. Some of the such crisis situation in extended neighbourhood where India has actively participated are enumerated below.

| Year | Country | Brief Description |
|---|---|---|
| 2006 | Lebanon | India launched **Operation Sukoon** in 2006. Three warships (INS Mumbai, Brahmaputra and Betwa and a naval tanker INS Shakti) formed task force and evacuated 2280 people which included Sri Lankans, Nepalese and even Lebanese nationals besides Indians. |
| 2011 | Libya | Indian Government ordered **Operation Blossom** in Feb 2011 to evacuate its citizen from the Libya during its civil war. INS Mysore, INS Aditya and INS Jalashwa formed part of **Operation Safe Homecoming.** |

## Enhancement of Maritime Prowess – A Necessity

India's geo-strategic location in the Indian Ocean makes imperative on building maritime power to facilitate safe and secure maritime environment in the region. Though India has been very reluctant in the past view numerous reasons but the changed security scenario demands its active participation in its maritime domain and even beyond. A modest beginning was made in 80s, when India rendered assistance to its maritime neighbours (immediate as well as extended) in political crisis. India embarked on a major naval expansion programme in 90s to develop a 'blue water' capability. Accordingly, there has been gradual and significant rise in budgetary allocation for the same. This has led to significant build up in its naval capabilities. Rising incidents of maritime terrorism since the beginning of twenty-first century has further added to government increasing its budgetary allocation not only for the Indian Navy but also other maritime security forces like Indian Coast Guard, Marine Police, etc. Enhancement in capabilities of the Indian Coast Guard only complements Navy in taking on maritime security challenges in the coastal environment of the Indian sub-continent by enhanced policing functions and creating deterrence against non-traditional security threats.

Since the beginning of twenty-first century, India has been the first responder in the region in HADR as well as in maritime security related problems has seen significant rise and same has been evident from the response of the Indian Navy in political crisis, maritime security or in HADR. Undertaking role of first responder obviously demand enhanced maritime prowess to quickly respond in various kinds of crisis over such a large maritime domain.

In the last two decades there has been significant attention given by the government to strengthen maritime forces. Though enhancement in maritime capability is largely taken positively by most of the nations in the immediate as well as extended neighbourhood. However, it is important to see that our acts in responding to various crisis in the region which has been well appreciated in the past should only work towards further building of such trust in the future. Such roles played by the maritime forces has been catalyst in promoting India's foreign policy and especially so in the maritime arena.

## Conclusion

India, being a largest nation among the Indian Ocean Rim countries, is looked upon by most of the countries in the region for assistance during various types of crises. Maritime aspects have a very important role to play as sea acts as highways connecting all the nations in the IOR and beyond. Dependence on sea for trade is only going to increase in the future and any threat to maritime trade would be catastrophic. India has critical role in ensuring security in the region. However, India as a fifth largest economy and fourth largest military power has to be seen as friend and not as an aggressor. India through its acts is seen as a friend. It has been clearly evident that India has never shied away from responding to various crisis in the region. On most of the crisis India has been the first responder. Growth of region is largely linked to sea and therefore it is essential to see that maritime environment in the region is peaceful and secure against all kinds of threat. Presence of adequate maritime force is must to maintain safe and secure maritime environment. As a maritime power India has played significant role in maintaining security at sea in the past and has been accordingly enhancing its maritime prowess to meet future challenges. Significant enhancement of maritime prowess remains the key factor in enabling India to undertake such responsibility. Adequate maritime assets are necessity not only for the India's development but for the region as whole as it would enhance safety and security in the maritime domain. Enhancing maritime prowess in order to ensuring security of the maritime domain and becoming first responder in any sort of crisis would certainly act as catalyst for the maritime neighbourhood policy.

## References

1. Knapp Stephen. India's Ancient Maritime History - Part 1 (2017), Retrieved from https://pragyata.com/indias-ancient-maritime-history-part-1/
2. Knapp Stephen. India's Ancient Maritime History - Part 2 (2017), Retrieved from https://pragyata.com/indias-ancient-maritime-history-part-2/

3. Gupta, Ananya (2023). Vasudhaiva Kutumbakam G 20 Meaning, History, Significance and Importance, Retrieved from https://pwonlyias.com/vasudhaiva-kutumbakam-g20/#what-is-vasudhaiva-kutumbakam
4. Prakash, Anupama (2023). Friday Focus: Vasudhaiva Kutumbakam, Retrieved from https://www.uaf.edu/news/friday-focus-vasudhaiva-kutumbakam.php
5. India's Foreign Policy (2022). Retrieved from https://www.drishtiias.com/daily-updates/daily-news-editorials/india-s-foreign-policy-1
6. Malhptra, Achal (2019). India's Foreign Policy: 2014-19: Landmarks, Achievementsand Challenges Ahead, Retrieved from https://www.mea.gov.in/distinguished-lectures-detail.htm?833
7. Principles of India's Foreign Policy. Retrieved from https://byjus.com/free-ias-prep/principles-of-indias-foreign-policy/#:~:text=Non%2Dalignment%20is%20the%20most, after%20the%20Second%20World%20War.
8. Singh, Abhijit (2023). India's maritime Power is growing, but challenges loom, Retrieved from http://20.244.136.131/expert-speak/indias-maritime-power-is-growing-but-challenges-loom#:~:text=To%20counter%20China%2C%20India%20has,the%20 dependence%20on%20foreign%20suppliers
9. Rao, Nirupama (2011). Speech at the National Maritime Foundation, Maritime Dimensions of India's Foreign Policy, Retrieved from https://www.mea.gov.in/Speeches-Statements. htm?dtl/53/Address+by+FS+on+Maritime+Dimensions+of+Indias+Foreign+Policy
10. Indian Council of World Affairs (2023). Celebrating 75 Years of India's Foreign Policy, Retrieved from https://icwa.in/pdfs/INdia75%20Web.pdf
11. Ensuring Secure Seas: Indian Maritime Security Strategy (2015). Retrieved from https://www.indiannavy.nic.in/sites/default/files/Indian_Maritime_Security_Strategy_Document_25Jan16.pdf
12. Bisen, Anurag (2022). India's Maritime Security: Five Concerns, Retrieved from https://idsa.in/issuebrief/indias-maritime-security-five-concerns-abisen-180522
13. Roy-Chaudhury, R. (1998). India's maritime security. India International Centre Quarterly, 25/26, 129–139. http://www.jstor.org/stable/23005537
14. Panda, Ankit (2015). When India Almost Intervened in Mauritius, Retrieved from https://thediplomat.com/2015/08/when-india-almost-intervened-in-mauritius/
15. Operation Lal Dora. Retrieved from https://en.wikipedia.org/wiki/Operation_Lal_Dora
16. Brewster, D. & Rae, R. (2011). Flowers Are Blooming: the story of the India Navy's secret operation in the Seychelles. Retrieved from https://openresearch-repository. anu.edu.au/bitstream/1885/13331/2/Brewster%20Flowers%20are%20Blooming %20Naval%20Review%202011.pdf
17. Transition to Eminence: The Indian Navy 1976-1090, Operations, Retrieved from https://www.indiannavy.nic.in/te/operation.htm
18. Basu, Pratnashree (2012). Maritime India: The Quest for Steadfast Identity, Retrieved from https://www.orfonline.org/research/maritime-india-the-quest-for-a-steadfast-identity/
19. Brewster, D. (2010). An Indian Sphere of Influence in the Indian Ocean? Security Challenges, Retrieved from http://www.jstor.org/stable/26459796

20. Gurjar, Sankalp (2021). Locating Indian Ocean Island States in India's Foreign Policy, Indian Foreign Affairs Journal, Vol. 16, no. 1, 2021, pp. 36–53. JSTOR, https://www.jstor.org/stable/48720474. Accessed 16 Dec. 2023.
21. Hall, I. (2019). India's clever alliances with island states. Retrieved from https://www.lowyinstitute.org/the-interpreter/india-s-clever-alliances-island-states
22. Kulshrestha, S. (2014). Humanitarian and Disaster Relief by Indian Navy, Retrieved from https://www.spsnavalforces.com/story/?id=322
23. Ministry of External Affairs. (2019). India-Seychelles Relations. Retrieved from https://mea.gov.in/Portal/ForeignRelation/Ind_Seycelles_2019.pdf23.
24. Ministry of External Affairs. (2020). MISSION SAGAR: A major Milestone in India's Engagement with IOR Countries. Retrieved from https://www.mea.gov.in/press-releases.htm?dtl/32803/
25. Ministry of External Affairs (2021). India-Madagascar Brief, Retrieved from https://mea.gov.in/Portal/ForeignRelation/ madagascar2 1nw.pdf
26. Ministry of External Affairs. (2021, June 9). India-Comoros Brief. Retrieved from https://mea.gov.in/Portal/ForeignRelation/Comros21nw.pdf
27. Muralidharan, MP (2020). Maritime Dimensions of India's Foreign Policy, Retrieved from https://www.indiandefencereview.com/spotlights/maritime-dimensions-of-indias-foreign-policy/#:~:text=Maritime%20security%20and%20linked% 20issues,in%20the%20IOR%20and%20beyond.
28. Canyon Deon, India Leading International HADR Cooperation in South Asia, Retrieved from https://dkiapcss.edu/nexus_articles/india-leading-international-hadr-cooperation-in-south-asia/

# 6

# India and Arab Gulf - Extended Neighbourhood

**Prof Pradeep V. Kamat**

## Introduction

Neighbours are not only those with whom one shares geographical boundaries but also those with whom hearts meet, Prime Minister Narendra Modi said on India's $74^{th}$ Independence Day, asserting that India has deepened its relations with all countries in extended neighbourhood. Modi said India's ties with West Asian and ASEAN countries have grown manifold in key sectors. "India is constantly trying to deepen its age-old cultural, social and economic ties with its neighbouring countries. South Asia is home to one-fourth of the world's population and we can create infinite possibilities of development and prosperity of such a large number of people through cooperation," Modi said in his address to the nation from the Red Fort on India's $74^{th}$ Independence Day. Asserting that all leaders of the region have big responsibility for development and prosperity of their people, the Prime Minister said more peace and harmony there will be in the region better it will be for humanity". "Today, neighbours are not only those with whom we share geographical boundaries but also those with whom our hearts meet... In recent times, India has strengthened its relations with all countries in the extended neighbourhood," Modi said. Rapid progress has been made in India's political, economic and human relations with West Asian countries and trust with them has also grown, he said. "With these countries, our economic relations, especially in the energy sector, are very important. A large number of our brothers and sisters are working in these countries. The way these countries helped Indians in the times of coronavirus and honoured the Indian government's requests, India is thankful to them," he added.

## India's multifaceted relations with West Asia

The term 'civilisational link' is perhaps most sacred expression in Indian foreign policy lexicon invoked very often to describe India's relationship with individual as well as collective nations of West Asia. India's relationship with Arab – Islamic world is rooted in history and has been enriched over centuries by an intense and prolonged phase of exchange of ideas and people across both sides. The old cultural link assigns a unique status to Indian relationship with West Asia (Siddiqui, 2022). This closeness and proximity in cultural and civilisational terms between two regions are well reflected at present when one witnesses the level of trade between the two and presence of large number of Indians working in different countries of West Asia. India through its cultural and geo-strategic prism locates the Arab world in three parts, namely, Gulf, Maghreb and West Asia (Abyhankar, 2013).

The cultural connection between India and West Asia points towards some of the stark similarities between them because no other civilisation on the Asian continent has had long and sustained historical engagement with the West Asia region as that of India, and that emphasizes the significance of present-day connection between their mutual relations which make their historic meeting unique and extraordinary. Over the centuries, customs, goods, languages and people have crisscrossed the continent largely as a result of conquest and commerce (Siddiqui, 2022):

**Socio-economic Relations:** India's connection with West Asia goes back to ancient times. These ties between the two cultural zones consolidated constantly with fast-spreading cultural, economic and social interactions between the two civilisations. The cultural crisscross between India and West Asia is quite manifest in many perspectives that one can see here how the Islamic world has been enriched as a result of these interplays. West Asians translated numerous Indian works spread over a diversity of subjects and went on to work out original creations based on treatises they translated. The fields of Indian knowledge they studied included books on ethics, logic, politics, veterinary art, philosophy and science of war.

**Customs and traditions:** Many social rituals of both civilisations manifest common features as regards social intercourse like common assembly for considerations on social and political issues, marriage proceedings, usage of household utensils, birth and death ceremonies and rituals towards dead ancestors.

**Religion:** Many religious rituals including religious symbols of both civilisations reflect commonalities between them. The Aryan deity *'agni'* occupies second important position among Vedic *dev-mandal* (a group of gods), and that also figures prominently in Zoroastrianism as revealed in Zend-Avesta. The Boguz qui inscriptions from this region have close similarities with Indian Vedic deities viz. *Varuna, Indra, Mitra,* and *Nasatya.*

**Architecture:** One of most well-known features between two cultures lies in common architectural designs of both civilisations manifested in making of domes, decorations on house walls, roof arches and doors. They manifest themselves today in different ways as regards similar architecture and sculptures.

**Medicines and Science and Technology:** Arab sources dating back to tenth and thirteenth centuries reveal about several Indian works on medicines and therapeutics that were transliterated into Arabic at direction of Caliph-Harun-al-Rashid, ruler of Baghdad from AD 286 to AD 809. Indian scholars were also invited in these translation works. *Sushruta Samhita* was translated into Arabic by Indian scholar – Mankh. In realm of Astronomy, two famous works viz. *Brahama-Sphuta-Siddhant* known to Arab world as *Sindluin* and *Khandakhadyak* (known as *Arkand*) were brought to Baghdad from Sindh with the help of Indian Scholars. They were transliterated into Arabic by Alfarari. The Arabs acknowledged their debts to India by calling mathematics "*Hindisa*" (about India). India imbibed a prominent exchange from West Asian cultures which has become an inextricable element of Indian cultural ethos (Siddiqui, 2022).

In modern times, India's connection with West Asia acquired a new geo-strategic dimension to this civilisational link. Besides historical linkages and economic interactions, in past two decades, West Asia has occupied an important place in India's relations, figuring prominently not only in India's economic growth but also in its great power aspirations (Siddiqui, 2022). Prime Minister Narendra Modi has been signaling greater importance of West Asia for India. Without any declaratory statement, Modi has delineated the parameters and components of the relations, through intense political engagements to transform the transactional nature of the bilateral ties and add economic and strategic substance (Kumarswamy, 2018).

## The Gulf Cooperation Council (GCC) Countries

In wake of ravages of Second World War, regional groupings were established in various parts of the world including Middle East, where seven former Arab possessions of Ottoman empire came together to form the Arab League in 1945. Today the organisation has twenty-two states and territories as members. Despite its growth and impressive achievements in some areas, the Arab League had poor track record in promoting cooperation at regional level. Due to lack of cohesion, persistent rivalries among members, and influence of external powers on inter-Arab politics, Arab unity has been an elusive goal for the Arab League (Miller, 2016). In 1981, Arab Gulf States, all members of the Arab League came together at sub-regional level to form Gulf Cooperation Council (GCC). Gulf Cooperation Council is a consortium of following six oil-exporting countries:

1. The Kingdom of Bahrain – Its 1.2 million people enjoy GDP per-capita of $50,700.
2. Kuwait – Its 2.8 million residents enjoy 11th highest standard of living in the world ($71,900 per person). The country holds 6 percent of world's oil reserves.
3. The Sultanate of Oman – It has 3.4 million residents and its GDP per capita is $46,100.
4. Qatar – The second richest country in the world, with GDP per-capita of $125,100 for each of its 2.3 million residents. It has 25 billion barrels of proven oil reserves and 13 percent of world's natural gas reserves.
5. The Kingdom of Saudi Arabia – The largest of GCC countries (28.5 million people) has 16 percent of world's proven oil reserves. Its GDP per capita is $55,300.
6. The United Arab Emirates (UAE) – Its 6 million people enjoy per capita GDP of $68,100 (Amadeo, 2017).

GCC was established in 1981 as a response to Iranian Revolution and outbreak of Iran– Iraq War in 1980 (Goldman & Rapp-Hooper, 2013). The initial hope for formation of GCC was that this would provide security in wake of revolution in Iran. One thing that has bound GCC together is shared belief among Gulf states that they are vulnerable to external actors who view them as rich and militarily weak states. This has engendered a deeply held belief among Gulf rulers that safety of their kingdoms is more likely to be achieved by working together than by acting apart. When their sovereignty has been threatened, GCC states have put their grievances on hold and have given out united response in political, economic and military realms. Despite sharing same security challenges, Arab Gulf States do not share same national interests. They have engaged in stand-offs over oil, borders, Iran, Israel etc. Though there have been intra-Gulf disputes over territorial rights, hampering development of bonds needed for GCC member states to trust each other fully with their own strategic security, they have never militarised their differences with each other beyond localised clashes. The belief in benefits of collective security is very strong in GCC (Miller, 2016). The quest for regional security in midst of political upheavals prompted these countries to consider different options for security cooperation. The fall of Arab regional system, wider instabilities in Afghanistan compounded threat perceptions. Similar political systems, shared values and common bonds between Gulf nations have contributed to emergence of GCC (Ramazani, 1988).

Though the policies of Gulf Cooperation Council (GCC) states are not coordinated centrally by the Council's secretariat and no treaty binds the external conduct of its member-states, the GCC has been recognised as a regional bloc and empowered to act on behalf of its members in a number of arenas, including negotiating economic agreements with other states and regional blocs and forming common diplomatic platforms over a range of regional security matters. The GCC has emerged as West Asia's most important regional organisation and the role it and some of its six members now play in Middle East and North Africa (MENA) region has credited the parties as a whole with new status in the region and internationally. Due to their considerable wealth and purchasing power, several GCC states – Saudi Arabia and Kuwait, Qatar and the United Arab Emirates (UAE) have gained international footprint. The GCC as a bloc is a financial force to be reckoned with (Ehteshami, 2015).

It should be noted that the GCC was forged in raging fires of Iran–Iraq War and it is conflict which shaped the conditions for emergence of this first sub-regional organisation in MENA regional system. The GCC is above all a security organisation, bringing like-minded states under single protective umbrella (Al – Hamad, 2002). In spite of its loosely framed common security structure, over time the GCC's external security blanket has been extended to provide cover for internal security of its ruling elites as well. Thus, while its Peninsula Shield Force may be still be more of a shell than a defensive blanket, its existence enables the GCC states to act in defence of each other and, if need be, against external threats. Despite its many structural weaknesses, then – small native populations, presence of large expatriate communities, weak security and military structures, varied size of its member-states, geographical domination of one over other five parties, and collective exposure to hydrocarbons price fluctuations, – the GCC has survived and prospered. Its survival and development are arguably due to the inherent strengths of its member-states and their intuitive responses to regional and sub-regional crises. Their similar regime types, the assuredness of their ruling families, the durability of their 'ruling bargain', and the elites' abilities to globalise without social dislocation have all helped the GCC to develop into an influential regional bloc since its birth in 1981. Also, the GCC states' ability to negotiate close and durable security partnerships with the West, has acted as a backstop for them, thus enabling them to take foreign policy initiatives more comfortably when pressed (Ehteshami, 2015). To understand the GCC states' foreign policy conduct, we need to understand not only the nature of decision-making in these states but also the conditions under which decisions are being crafted -The drivers of foreign policy; and secondly, the context for foreign policy, the arena in which foreign policy takes effect (Wright, 2011).

The GCC states' globalisation, resulting from their hydrocarbons wealth has been further fueled by these countries' strong financial muscle and augmented by their extraordinary information and communications technology (ICT) penetration. The KOF Index of Globalisation ranks four of the GCC states (Bahrain, Kuwait, Qatar, UAE) in the top 50 most globalised countries in the world, and in terms of social globalisation the UAE and Kuwait lead the region. The GCC's complex globalisation has set the Council members apart from the rest of the region, has encouraged deeper cross-border relations, and has given these societies and their elites the ability to seize opportunities presented outside of the region (Ehteshami, 2013).

There are number of contextual forces which should be considered as factors shaping the GCC states' foreign policies. The first is manifold pressures on Arab region arising from dynamic changes following Iranian revolution in 1979 and resultant war (1980–8), leading to a fragmenting Arab order in 1980s, which in 1990s resulted in polarisation and ultimate implosion of Arab order (Noble, 2008). Added to these structural tensions are demise of Iraq as a regional actor, new regional power dynamics arising from collapse of Ba'ath regime in Iraq, and subsequent rise of Iran (Kostiner, 2011).

The complex geopolitical conditions arising from Arab Awakening have brought their own tensions since 2011, causing rifts in GCC bloc as the Arab region has further fractured. Despite their many similarities, the GCC states are not alike; their different leaderships, social bases and geography have dictated their own conditions on these countries' foreign policies, and therefore, on many occasions, have pushed them in different directions. It could thus be argued that despite its organisational paraphernalia the GCC has never been a unified bloc representative of all its members, and despite its members having held surprisingly close positions on wide range of issues since its birth – threat of Iran, place of Iraq in Arab order, Shi'a rising, stability of Yemen, Arab–Israeli conflict, threat of al-Qaeda – their interests have also diverged quite spectacularly on numerous occasions (Ehteshami, 2015).

The GCC's multipolarity has been tested by the Arab revolts and the role that the Islamist forces have come to play in these uprisings. For some GCC states the rise of the *Ikhwan* is a direct threat and one bolstered by one of their own, leading them to take public action against Qatar (Policy Analysis Unit, 2014). Regional dynamism has entrenched change as a permanent structure in which the GCC now plays a leading if not *the* leading part (Korany, 2010).

Aware of problems of relying on finite resources such as oil, GCC countries embarked on massive diversification programmes to reduce their dependence on those resources for income (Sultan, 2012). During the last decade, GCC countries embarked on massive infrastructural programmes aimed at diversifying their economies and creating job opportunities for their citizens, spending hundreds of billions of petrodollars on building new cities; accumulating massive financial reserves known as Sovereign Wealth Funds and using them to invest internationally through buying commercial outlets and shareholdings in major foreign businesses (Sultan, 2012). UAE wants to become world's new tourist attraction. Qatar hopes to become destination for world events and conferences. Saudi Arabia is trying to become region's economic powerhouse. They have invested heavily in urban spaces to turn them into attractive destinations for the more refined traveler. This 'instant urbanisation' (Abu-Lughod, 1983), has taken place alongside with an aggressive campaign to attract major sporting and cultural events to their new cities. Qatar's success in being awarded world's most popular sporting event, the FIFA Football World Cup is an example of this (Miller, 2016). Some GCC countries like UAE have invested in renewable and potential future energy fuels such as solar and nuclear (Sultan, 2012). Kawach (2009) believes that GCC countries could spend about $ 200 billion on such projects in next two decades. In Dubai non-oil sector in mid 1990s were already contributing 82 percent of the emirates GDP and in 2006, the figure may have been 95 percent (Davidson, 2008). Projects in infrastructure and utilities are carefully selected and implemented according to predetermined framework and linked to macro indicators (Saif, 2009). The massive infusion of oil wealth and ambitious attempts to rapidly modernise societies with only small pools of citizen labour explain huge rise in number of foreign workers entering the Gulf from Arab and Non-Arab worlds. They provided cheap labour needed to build and staff airports, hotels, hospitals, schools, universities, communication networks (Sayigh, 1978). Major constraint on GCC countries is limited supply of local skilled manpower resulting in reliance on huge expatriate labour force (Ramady, 2012).

The 36th Annual GCC Summit took place in Riyadh on 9th December 2015 which saw broad consensus on political, social and economic issues such as combating extremism, security cooperation, economic integration, support for political solution to crises in Yemen and Syria, and firm support for Palestinian cause (*Gulf News,* 2015). The 37th annual GCC summit was held in Manama, Bahrain on 7th December 2016 (*Arab News,* 2016). The promotion of GCC unity and economic integration among GCC member states was important point of discussion (Khatana, 2018). GCC states control 29 percent of world's crude oil reserves, highlighting relative global importance of Gulf petroleum sector. GCC states also held 22.3 percent of world's natural gas reserves. Fueled by massive oil revenues, value of GCC real GDP was $ 1,479.3 billion in 2017 enjoying one of world's highest GDP per capita. State Revenues are largely driven by exports of hydrocarbons that stood at $ 345 billion in 2018 (U-Capital, 2018). GCC states' financial surpluses and sovereign wealth funds are among highest in the world. Total GCC funds are close to $ 2.9 trillion in total assets, which is 40 percent of global sovereign wealth funds (Rachman, 2017).

## Gulf Cooperation Council (GCC) and India

India adopted Look West policy in 2005 for deepening engagement with West Asian countries who have been considered as 'extended' neighbours. India's former Minister of External Affairs, Sushma Swaraj, attending 9th ministerial meeting of Gulf Cooperation Council (GCC) in 2015, pushing for GCC – India Free Trade Agreement (FTA) said that Gulf was "extended part of India's neighbourhood" (Taneja, 2020). As Sushma Swaraj explained in August 2016, "In our diplomatic engagements in the last two years, you will therefore find that major focus now is using international partnerships to advance domestic flagship programmes" This tight meshing of domestic and diplomatic goals is one of the hallmarks of Modi Doctrine" (MEA, 2016). The then Indian Foreign Secretary S. Jaishankar laid out India's foreign policy agenda in a speech in March 2015 (MEA, 2015). He noted that India's West Asia policy in past had been "an evolutionary happening that was relatively autonomous of strategic calculations."

## Reorientation of India – GCC region Foreign Policy

A reorientation of Indian foreign policy in Gulf region is seen since

Mr Narendra Modi became Prime Minister, as the region has been receiving considerable political, diplomatic, strategic, economic attention and new focus towards the Gulf region was brought about by Mr Modi's active role and engagement with overseas Indian community in the Gulf (Kumarswamy, 2018). Prime Minister Modi galvanised it by creating an exceptional personalised style at highest level of leadership, with results in form of investment commitments, extradition of wanted criminals, counter-terrorism cooperation, *security* cooperation, energy security, diaspora welfare and business expansion having multiplier effect on bilateral relationship (Trigunayat, 2020).

Broad parameters of India's West Asia policy were largely in place when Narendra Modi was elected Prime Minister of India in 2014. The new government followed same course, intensifying what was known as "Look West" policy, by focusing on three main axes: Arab Gulf countries, Israel and Iran (Burton, 2019). During this tenure, he visited UAE twice, Saudi Arabia, Iran, Qatar, Jordan and Palestine. These visits cemented a renewed and revitalised outreach for India towards West Asia. The joint statement concluded during these visits had recognised India as 'strategic partner' of these competing countries. History is littered with strong ties between India and West Asia, capitalised efficiently and effectively, by Narendra Modi. Modi's visits to Gulf countries can be seen as an effort to consolidate economic ties. The interest has been reciprocal as Saudi Arabia, UAE and other GCC countries increasingly see India as an important emerging market for their energy exports, foreign investments and joint venture opportunities. Upon his victory, the crown prince of Abu Dhabi, Mohammed bin Zayed, was one of the first world leaders to congratulate Modi over a telephone call. UAE conferred Modi with their state's highest state honour, the Zayed Medal for bringing ties between two regions to an all new level. In 2016, Saudis also conferred Modi with their highest civilian honour, the King Abdulaziz Sash during his visit to Riyadh. The answer to success lies more within interests of Gulf nations than Modi government's outreach. These cash rich states looked towards Indian economy to secure their own future financial interests. As US becomes mostly self-sufficient on oil, Asian economies led by India and China, are expected to lead purchases of crude. This market capacity makes for ideal destination for Gulf's rich wealth funds (Taneja, 2020).

When manifestation of Qatar crisis occurred in mid-2017, India was under pressure to take sides. Instead it resisted and adopted neutrality as a way of maintaining economic relations with both sides (Al-Tamimi, 2017; Siyech, 2019). India's present approach has been helped by wider structural context in which the region finds itself (Burton, 2019). The Middle East has become more multipolar, with power diffused among regional and extra-regional actors (Cavatorta, 2014; Kamrava, 2018). India's approach balances different parties (Burton, 2019).

## Challenging Gulf Scenario

The changing dynamics of domestic and regional politics in West Asia ensured continued turbulence during 2015 and 2016. GCC monarchies remained embroiled in firefighting issues, ranging from economic troubles due to lower oil prices, Saudi-led military intervention in Yemen, ISIS threat, and growing Iranian regional influence (Khatana, 2018). The 2011 'Arab Spring' had been fundamental change for many Arab countries, but with exception of Bahrain and Oman, GCC countries seem to have been an oasis of relative calm compared to rest of Middle East (Ramady, 2012). The Qatari support for Egyptian Islamists angered al-Saud and contributed to temporary breach of diplomatic relations in 2014 when Saudi Arabia, Bahrain and U.A.E. withdrew their Ambassadors from Qatar (Kirkpatrick, 2014). While Oman did not join hands with this Saudi-led move, Kuwait sought to mediate. Even though three ambassadors returned to Qatar in December 2014, tensions continued. Saudi-led military offensive against Yemen, *Operation Decisive Storm* (March–April 2014) and *Operation Restoring Hope* (April 2015– present) highlighted differences within GCC. Saudi Arabia blamed Iran for Yemeni crisis. Oman maintained its neutrality, partly due to its traditional policy of regional autonomy and partly due to closer ties with Iran. Other GCC countries joined Saudi-led military offensive. The Gulf monarchs settled for popular co-option through financial largesse to blunt demands for political reforms (Kumarswamy, 2018). The oil prices—which had reached $ 60 per barrel in December 2014—continued to fall, and dropped to $ 50 per barrel in December 2016 due to slow growth of global economy and energy alternatives. Falling oil prices affected oil-rich Gulf Arab countries. GCC countries were forced to introduce small portion of taxes to meet budgetary deficits. Saudi Arabia imposed limits on overseas remittances by expatriate workers (Flanagan, 2011). Bahrain reduced subsidies on key issues such as water, electricity and fuel (Naar, 2016). Saudi Arabia and Kuwait were forced to dip into sovereign wealth to bridge current account deficits (Townsend, 2016). According to Al-Rasheed (2017) economic prosperity, the back bone of Gulf political ambitions, is stumbling under pressure of drastic decline in oil prices. Many GCC countries already adopted economic and social visions for reform. Saudi Arabia was the last country to join visionary trail of economic transformation in April 2016 when it announced implementation of Vision 2030. The visions are bound to impact traditional domestic Gulf politics and ability of governments to continue to convince domestic and global audiences of merits of stability and security at expense of political dynamism. The visions are confined to moving state centric oil-based capitalist economies into open liberal finance, privatisation, diversification, without any visible political transformations (Al-Rasheed, 2017). The 2017–18 Qatar diplomatic crisis began when Saudi Arabia, United Arab Emirates, Bahrain and Egypt abruptly cut off diplomatic relations with Qatar in June 2017 withdrawing ambassadors and imposing trade and travel bans. The crisis is escalation of Qatar-Saudi Arabia proxy conflict. The Saudi-led coalition cited Qatar's alleged support for terrorism as main reason for their actions. Saudi Arabia and other countries criticised Qatar's relation with Iran (Wikipedia, 2018). Regional tensions, sectarian divide, Arab-Persian rivalry, falling oil prices marked 2015 and 2016 (Kumarswamy, 2018).

## India and GCC Economic Engagement and Interdependence Relations

Importance of GCC for India lies in its energy security, volume of trade, and large presence of Indian expatriates. Due to lower oil prices and international slowdown, trade figures witnessed more than 30 percent decline between 2013 and 2016 (Khatana, 2018). India's trade deficit with GCC has fallen from $ 46 billion to $ 14 billion in last three years (*The Hindu,* 2016). The drop in oil prices impacted remittances from the region, leading to 2.2 percent fall. In 2014–15, remittances to India from GCC amounted to $ 36.7 billion, and dropped to $ 35.9 billion in 2015–16 (*The Hindu,* 2016). According to World Bank, if oil prices stay low for prolonged period, or undergo unforeseen drops, remittances from GCC to India could fall further in future (Bundhun, 2016). GCC countries are biggest source, contributing 60 percent of total remittances received by India in 2015–16 which contributed nearly 3.3 percent to its GDP. Remittances help develop organic link between India and GCC countries (*The World Bank*, 2016). In 2015–16, India's exports to GCC stood at $ 41.71 billion (Embassy of India Riyadh, 2016). India's economic engagements with GCC countries during 2015 and 2016 were dominated by two challenges: continuing global economic slowdown and falling oil prices. While latter meant lesser hydrocarbon imports, former meant considerable drop in foreign trade. Since 2011–12, India's total trade has been declining: from being close to $ 800 billion, it dropped to $ 758 billion in 2014–15 and reached $ 642 billion in 2015–16—that is, slightly more than in 2010–11 when its foreign trade stood at just over $ 620 billion. The fall in trade as well as in oil prices were reflected in India's economic engagement with GCC countries. Indian export sector has gained 2.6 percent in the Gulf region during FY 2017-18 (Ministry of Commerce and Industry, Government of India, 2018). Indian political and business leaders realised that countries like Saudi Arabia and Qatar could supply more oil and gas, respectively (Siyech, 2017) and wealth accumulated made Gulf countries potential sources of foreign investment (Choudhury, 2017).

UAE, which for short period remained India's largest trading partner, has been losing its position since 2012–13 and became third largest partner after China and US, followed closely by Saudi Arabia. Gap between India's trade with UAE and China has been widening and, during 2015–16, it was more than $ 20 billion. With about US$ 49.7 billion in trade, UAE accounts for 7.5 percent of India's total foreign trade. Because of domination of energy trade, GCC countries continue to be among India's leading trade partners and in 2015–16, three countries were among India's top 25 trade partners; Saudi Arabia was in fourth slot; Qatar in 19th (Kumarswamy & Singh Roy, 2018). The Persian Gulf countries account for substantial portion of known oil and natural gas reserves in the world. Because of low cost of production and logistical considerations, the region will continue to be of vital importance to India. India's growth story will remain intrinsically linked to Persian Gulf region (Kumarswamy & Singh Roy, 2018). GCC as a bloc is India's largest trading partner. In period from March 2018 to April 2019, bilateral trade touched $ 121.25 billion. India's imports from Gulf countries reached US 79.70 billion compared to $ 41.55 billion worth of exports from India to Gulf region. GCC countries account for 15 percent of India's total imports and 12 percent of the country's total exports in value terms. UAE accounted for major chunk of India's exports and imports with $ 30.08 billion and $ 29.77 billion respectively for fiscal year 2019.

India and GCC states have strong economic ties which increased to $ 84.96 billion in 2017-18, from $ 7.8 billion in 2003-04. The Gulf region accounts for 12.98 percent of India's total exports, while it has 13.76 percent share of its total imports. Trade was mainly restricted to oil, spices and labour until 2000 (Pant, 1999). In past 20 years, its scope has expanded to fertilisers, petrochemicals, services, IT, gold and textiles. India and GCC states are signatories of Framework Agreement of Economic Cooperation (FAEC) which was signed in New Delhi on August 25, 2004. India-GCC industrial forum was established in February 2004, which enhanced trade and technology transfer activities (Pradhan, 2010). India granted Most Favoured Nation (MFN) status to GCC states hoping to help secure a FTA (Ahmed & Bhatnagar, 2012). According to Dubai Chambers of Commerce

(DCC), Indian companies are eager to invest in Dubai. In 2008, 12,359 Indian companies were registered with DCC. This figure tripled in a decade. Currently, 38,238 Indian companies are registered, while DCC has opened its international office in India to facilitate business community (Dubai Chamber of Commerce, 2018). More than 800 leading Indian companies have opened their businesses in Jebel Ali Free Zone and many Indian business houses have strong presence in Dubai and Abu Dhabi. Hundreds of Indian companies actively engaged in business activities in UAE Free Economic Zones. India is one of largest trading partners of UAE (Augustine, 2016). Further opportunities are opening up as UAE is looking to diversify its economy, strengthen its financial and service sectors and establish Emirates as global tourism and sports hub. UAE is creating a knowledge-based economy to adjust to changing market needs (Quamar, 2018). From 2001 to 2016, FDI from UAE to India increased manifolds. UAE invested more than $ 5 billion in India in 2017 which makes it third largest investment partner after China and US (John, 2018). MoU for investment in India's National Investment and Infrastructure Fund (NIIF) was signed with Qatar Investment Authority in 2016 (*Times of India,* 2016). Qatar's Sovereign Wealth Fund held by Qatar Investment Authority (QIA), other State-owned entities and private investors in Qatar are attractive investment propositions for India's growing market (Hussain & Ghosh, 2015). Qatar has several large-scale investments in India, including more than $ 1 billion stake in telecommunications company Bharti Airtel (*BQ Magazine*, 2015). India's corporate sector has many operations in Qatar. These include Larsen & Toubro, Punj Lloyd, Shapoorji Pallonji, Voltas, TCS, Wipro, Mahindra Tech, HCL etc. SBI, ICICI and other Indian banks have limited operations under Qatar Financial Centre or private exchange houses (*BQ Magazine*, 2015). On 7th June 2016, Supreme Committee for Delivery & Legacy (SCDL) announced that Qatari company, Al Balagh Trading & Contracting and L&T had been appointed as main contractors to build 40,000 seat capacity Al Rayyan Stadium for football for World Cup matches 2022 (Supreme Committee for Delivery and Legacy, 2016). In November 2015, Indian Engineering, Procurement and Construction companies secured contracts worth $ 5 billion for development projects in housing, hospitals, oil and gas, power transmissions in Kuwait (*The Economic Times,* 2015). On 26th January 2015, Shapoorji Pallonji and Co. Ltd. signed $ 150 million contract with Kuwait University for construction, operation and maintenance of buildings of colleges in Sabah Al-Salem University City (*The Times,* 2015). Kuwait National Petroleum Corporation awarded contract worth $ 77 million to Larsen and Toubro in May 2015 to replace power substation at Al-Ahmadi refinery (*DNA,* 2015).

The economic and commercial relations between India and Oman has been strengthened by the presence of Indian private sector companies like Wipro, Larsen & Toubro, Shapoorji Pallonji, Jindal, Aditya Birla Group, Nagarjuna Construction Company, Simplex and KEC who are engaged in various projects in Oman. An Indian-Omani joint venture—Sebacic Oman will be constructing Sebacic Duqm Acid refinery which is worth $ 1,200 million. Oman is among top five sources of fertilisers for India accounting for 5.26 percent of India's fertiliser imports. India imports 8 Metric Tons (MT) of urea, 25 percent of which is supplied by Oman India Fertiliser Company (OMIFCO) (Ahmed & Soni, 2017). According to Saudi Arabia General Investment Authority (SAGIA), there were 426 Indian companies registered for business in Saudi Arabia by 2017, compared to 190 in 2007, which shows 150 percent growth (Embassy of India, Riyadh, 2018). During 2020-21, India's exports to GCC were $ 28.06 billion. The bilateral two-way trade during the period was $ 87.36 billion, registering a decline of about 27 percent over the previous year.

India's strong linkages with GCC are analysed by Kulkarni and Bandekar (2019). According to them, inter linkages of Indian Economy with trade blocs and financial markets has significantly increased. They explored economic tie-up with GCC considering today's dynamic socio-political scenario. Such collaboration is significant as India is aiming at tag of $ 5 Trillion economy in forthcoming years. The important factors that give cutting edge to India's relationship with GCC are Oil, Remittances and Indian Diaspora in GCC. It is most vital that India needs to nurture its tie-up with GCC in forthcoming years (Kulkarni & Bandekar, 2019). GCC investments in India, China and Africa are occurring on an unprecedented scale. These Investments are more comfortable due to diasporic links and cultural ties (Abdelal *et.al,* 2008).

India –GCC bilateral export is positively determined by size of economies, trade openness and diaspora and is negatively determined by distance between India-GCC and import tariffs (Alam & Ahmed, 2018). According to Kulkarni and Bandekar (2019), perennial deficit of current account is more to do with merchandise, in particular oil imports, which are dependent on global crude prices. The demand supply, geopolitical situation affects the international crude prices. India is more vulnerable to price fluctuation as approximately 64 percent of India's oil need is imported from volatile Middle East region. The volatility of oil price affects GCC as well as India. Whenever oil price goes up, India's import bill soars. If oil price goes down it effects economy and investment scenario of GCC, which results in less exports from India to GCC and shortfall in remittance to India from GCC region. Thus, India is vulnerable to oil price volatility. In light of this, India needs safety net to manage impact of oil price volatility in better way. The INR priced oil imports and special lines of credit to GCC countries in terms of bilateral trade with India may help in better management of international trade and finance (Kulkarni & Bandekar, 2019).

India has a high economic and commercial stakes in the Region as it receives a huge amount of remittance from the GCC Countries. Trade, remittance, investments, and expenditure by Gulf citizens visiting India etc. would total up to $ 200 billion or more in 2011 -2012 (Gupta, 2013). This total volume in terms of value is much more than the values of India's financial ties with any other groupings in the world including the European Union (EU), Association of Southeast Asian Nations (ASEAN) or North America (Ahmad, 2013). A new level of socio-cultural exchanges between India and Saudi Arabia takes place due to a large number of Indian Hajj pilgrims to the holy shrine and these pilgrims also add a new dimension to this relationship. Saudi Arabia had reached out to India to upgrade and expand the confines of its economic activities and as a result a low profile relation was transformed into a strategic relationship with Riyadh Declaration signed in 2011. The Riyadh Declaration commits both sides to significant expansion of its defence, security, economic and cultural ties (Ahmad, 2013). This extensive economic engagement and interdependence has been reciprocated with political warmth for India by Gulf countries. Trade and investment are vital factors in evolving Indo-GCC relationship.

## Energy Security – India and Arab Gulf

In 2014-15, India imported 109.88 million tons of oil from the world, out of which 58 percent came from Gulf region. Due to India's rapid economic growth, it is among world's top four oil consuming countries (*Economic Times. 2016).* Saudi Arabia, Iran and Qatar have all been vital suppliers of hydrocarbons (*Economic Times*, 2019). Saudi Arabia, Kuwait and UAE are supplying 26,882 tons, 14,611 tons, and 10,433 tons oil to India, respectively. Qatar and Oman are its largest natural gas suppliers. Qatar is supplying 8.25 billion cubic meters' natural gas, while Oman and UAE are exporting 0.35 billion cubic meters and 0.17 billion cubic meters, respectively (BP Statistical Review of World Energy, 2010). Qatar is largest supplier of LNG to India, accounting for 65 percent of its global imports and 15 percent of Qatar's export of LNG. India is establishing Strategic Petroleum Reserve with help of UAE (*Times of India,* 2017). Energy security has provided stimulus for India's security cooperation with GCC States.

## China Factor and GCC

It is not only India has substantial interest in GCC but China is also interested in GCC due to its oil richness. (Nader, 2011). According to Qian and Fulton (2017), China-GCC economic relations can be expected to intensify due to FTA. The FTA will also enhance cooperation opportunities for China and GCC under the "Belt and Road" Initiative, which will play an important role in expanding China's regional presence. According to Chinese Ministry of Commerce, trade between China and GCC countries exceeded $ 171 billion in 2017 (Ministry of Commerce, People's Republic of China, 2017). China is aggressively pursuing Gulf region for signing FTAs for which nine rounds of talks have been completed (Ministry of Commerce, People's Republic of China, 2016). If China secures FTA from GCC, it is likely that Indian economic interests will be negatively affected since each is competing for cheaper oil agreements and export of non-oil goods such as textile, iron, steel, rice, wheat, kitchen items, household articles and electronics, in which India is currently lagging behind China. GCC-China Business Forum and GCC-China Strategic Dialogue are strategic forums for institutionalisation of bilateral trade and investment (Pradhan, 2011). China has also been promoting cooperation with GCC countries under Belt and Road Initiative (Qian, 2017). India considers growing Chinese influence in Gulf region a challenge to its economic and strategic interests. India also considers China a challenge to their energy and maritime security. This is apparent from Indian Maritime Doctrine of 2004 and India's Maritime Strategy of 2015, which point to China as major security threat to its maritime security. India wants to secure four major entry points — Strait of Hormuz, Suez Canal, Strait of Bab-el-Mandab and Cape of Good Hope (*Indian Navy*, 2015). Therefore, Indian Navy has been extensively engaged with naval forces of GCC countries through regular exercises to ensure its active presence in the region. China has emerged as another factor behind India's evolving relationship with GCC.

## Security Cooperation between India and GCC

From the strategic point of view, India and GCC share the desire for political stability and security in the region. The common political and security concerns of India and GCC translate into efforts for peace, security and stability in the Gulf region and South Asia. The emerging common security perceptions create further opportunities for GCC-India cooperation in the future. The GCC States are going through important changes and transformation; the process of understanding and integration is coming of age. Along with it areas for cooperation are also widening beyond investments, trade & commerce and sharing & development of human resources to security. If one looks at emerging relations between India and some GCC countries, their engagements are no longer restricted to traditional oil-energy related cooperation or remittance related financial activities, but are gradually entering security domain as well. The rising importance of security and defence cooperation is evidenced by Memorandum of Understandings (MoUs) that have been signed by India with its GCC partners recently. India has bilateral defence cooperation with Saudi Arabia, UAE, Oman and Qatar for military training, intelligence sharing, combating terrorism and money laundering. This is a paradigm shift in their relations which have been dominated by oil and energy trade while security ties remained dormant. Such engagements with GCC countries, such as Saudi Arabia, UAE, Bahrain, Oman and Qatar are on the rise. Among all GCC states, Oman holds special attention as it signed a military protocol in 1972; Air Force-to-Air Force staff talks in 2009 (Kemp, 2010) and signed MoU on military cooperation which provides Indian Navy access to Duqm Port in 2018 (Roy, 2018). The two have signed several defence agreements such as MoU on Crime and Combating Terrorism 1996; Defence Cooperation MoU 2005 and formed Military Cooperation Committee in 2006. According to Grare (2016), such agreements are part of India's strategy to keep an eye on and act as balancer to China. India and UAE signed Strategic Dialogue in 2003 which allows import and export of arms (Kemp, 2010). Both regularly hold meetings under India-UAE Defence Cooperation Committee which was established in 2003. UAE has extradited number of terrorists to India (Kemp, 2010). The extradition of around twenty alleged Indian terrorists from Saudi and UAE in recent years suggests deep routed nature of growing security cooperation and concern in both the countries (MEA, 2020). Saudi Arabia's decision to train its cadets at National Defence Academy of India is a strategic change (Hassan, 2018). Defence and security cooperation in addition to the commercial ties have added another boosting dimension to core feature of India's relation with the GCC. Security cooperation has emerged as vital component of India's deepening ties with Arab world. Issues like counter-terrorism, terror financing, money laundering and sea lane of communication figure prominently in talks between India, UAE and Saudi Arabia (Siddiqui, 2022). The growing importance given by India as well as some GCC countries towards strengthening security cooperation is due to evolving geopolitical dynamics and security challenges in South Asia and Gulf region.

## Indian Diaspora in the Gulf - India's unique soft power advantage

The presence of Indian diasporic communities' abroad act as source of influence through spread of culture, faith, languages, skills which they transcend to host countries along with reinforcing positive image of India. India is developing close cooperation with hosting Gulf countries for security and well-being of its Diaspora and has signed various protocols and agreements with hosting GCC nations for protection and better treatment of its citizens. According to Organisation of Economic Cooperation and Development (OECD) report, India-UAE is world's second largest migration corridor, with 2.8 million Indians migrating to UAE between 1995 and 2015 (Deulgaonkar, 2017). Since oil boom of mid-1970s, number of Indians living and working in GCC countries has grown rapidly. In GCC countries, number of Indians was estimated at around 5.7 million in 2012, rising to 8.5 million by 2018 (Irudaya Rajan, Varghese and Jayakumar, 2015; MEA, 2018; Abraham, 2012). India as world's highest recipient of remittances (World Bank, 2017) receives 50 percent of its total remittances from GCC countries; and among GCC, nearly 38 percent comes from UAE (Bundhun, 2015).

The World Bank estimates that non-resident Indians remitted around $ 79 billion to India during 2018 – 2019 and significant proportion of this came from the Diasporas in the Gulf countries (*Economic Times*, 2019). GCC countries account for more than 54 percent of annual $ 83 billion foreign remittances to India in 2019. Saudi Arabia continues to be most favoured destination for Indian workers, followed by UAE, Kuwait and Qatar. There are no accurate figures on actual number of Indian workers in GCC countries. Current estimates suggest that there are around 9 million Indians in GCC countries, who are the backbone of the remittance part of the Indian economy, with over 3 million in Saudi Arabia. followed by about 2.8 million in UAE. There are about 923,000 in Kuwait, 316,000 in Bahrain, 600,000 in Qatar, and 796,000 in Oman (MEA GOI, 2016).

In West Asia, one of India's most distinct soft power assets is the diaspora and its role in shaping a positive image of the country. Indian workers are known for being tolerant and willing to work hard under harsh conditions. The diaspora builds upon, cements and acts as present-day reminder to public in West Asian countries of historical and cultural links between two regions (Pethiyagoda, 2017b). Indians continue to be preferred migrant community due to their high quality of expertise, discipline, capacity to easily adjust to social lifestyle in Gulf and their reputation for being peaceful and accommodative individuals (Panda, 2009). For India, Gulf states are viable source of remittances migrants send to India and for

Gulf region, India provides favourable environment for development of its economies with presence of skilled Indians.

## Cultural Diplomacy

India's overall positive image has been strengthened due to India's cultural diplomacy. Here Indian film industry has played a significant role. In October 2007, Abu Dhabi organised an International Film Festival where Bollywood dominated the show. Indian government started 'Project Mausam' to highlight India's historic maritime trade and civilisational links with Gulf countries (Ayres, 2018). Through this project, Indian Ministry of Culture is organising cultural events in GCC states on regular basis. It is because of such cultural initiatives and positive image that UAE allowed establishment of Hindu temple in Abu Dhabi (Sankar & Ashwani Kumar, 2018). Despite being non-Arab state India enjoys its observer status in the Arab League. India was invited by Foreign Minister of UAE Sheikh Abdullah bin Zayed Al Nahyan to attend meeting of Organisation of Islamic Cooperation (OIC) as 'guest of honor' (*Times of India,* 2019). These developments indicate that India enjoys positive image, which helps it further expand its economic and political interests in GCC region.

## Strategic Realignments in Gulf

The Gulf region is a volatile place because of prevalent threats to internal and external security to nations found in the area (Ulrichsen, 2009). Gulf region has been going through massive strategic realignments in aftermath of Arab Spring in 2011. The fall of dictatorial regimes, war in Yemen, rise and fall of Islamic State of Iraq and Syria (ISIS), intra-Arab conflicts such as Qatar diplomatic crisis, Iran's nuclear deal and subsequent US exit, have shaped strategic thinking of Arab ruling elite. The sharp fall in global oil prices has intensified debate among Arab elite regarding need to rethink socioeconomic structures in order to address challenges to social and political sustainability (Ulrichsen, 2009). These countries are diversifying their economies as well as expanding diplomatic relations with Asian countries in general and India in particular, to seek international support for their regimes, reduce their overwhelming reliance on US-led Western countries in terms of economic, political support and arms sales. India has voted thrice against Iran's nuclear programme in the UN, which is explicit support to Arab ruling elite against their perceived threat from Iran (Bhatnagar, 2018). India has adopted policy of neutrality in intra-Arab conflicts. GCC states realise India's significance as an emerging political and economic power in Asia and beyond. India is aspirant for important positions in various international foras, like UNSC which is likely to be seen positively by GCC states. Modi's effort is to "transform transactional nature of bilateral ties and add economic and strategic substance" (Kumarswamy, 2018). India's expanding regional aspirations across the Indian Ocean are also a factor. India sees the Gulf and South Asia as strategically interactive and interrelated regions, and has increased its focus on the Gulf accordingly (Pethiyagoda, 2017a).

## Epilogue

Indian policymakers seem determined to raise India's profile internationally, shed old mindsets and to help India position itself in a positive role rather than just a balancing force, adding that India engages the world with greater confidence and assurance. The growth of India's power and standing and its active diplomacy can be seen in its renewed focus on GCC countries. Acknowledging that India's 'footprint' in the region has been relatively autonomous of strategic calculation, Indian policymakers recognize the need to develop a holistic engagement strategy, which seeks to strengthen economic ties and institutionalise long term security cooperation. PM Modi's visits to Gulf countries and engagement with their leaders have provided critical political content to bilateral relations. These developments indicate that India enjoys positive image, which helps it further expand its economic and political interests in GCC region.

## References

Abdelal, R., Khan, A. & Khanna, T. (2008). Where Oil Rich Nations are Placing Their Bets. *Harvard Business Review,* September, 119-128.

Abraham, R. (2012). "India and its Diaspora in the Arab Gulf Countries: Tapping into Effective 'Soft Power' and Related Public Diplomacy," *Diaspora Studies* 5, 2, 124-146.

Abu-Lughod, J. (1983). Urbanisation and Social Change in the Arab World. *Ekistics,* 50 (300), p. 227.

Ahmed, F. & Soni, A. (2017). Enhancing India-Oman Economic Engagement: Four Promising Initiatives. 28th March, *Middle East Institute*, http://www.mei.edu/content/map/enhancing-india-oman-economic-engagement-fourpromising-initiatives.

Ahmed, Z.A. & Bhatnagar, S. (2012), Gulf States and the Conflict between India and Pakistan, *Journal of Asia Pacific Studies,* 1 (2), 259-291. https://www.humanitarianlibrary.org/sites/default/files/2014/02/8.%20Zahid.pdf.

Alam, I. & Ahmed, S. (2018). A Panel Gravity Model Analysis of India's Export to Gulf Cooperation Council Countries. *Journal of International Economics*, 9 (2), January –June, 72-86.

Al-Hamad, Turki (2002). Imperfect Alliances: Will the Gulf Monarchies Work Together? In Barry Rubin (ed.), *Crises in the Contemporary Persian Gulf,* London: Frank Cass, , pp. 21-32.

Al Kitbi, E. (2013). GCC-India Relations: Need for Strategic Cooperation, In S. Devare and S. Singh, *India and the GCC Countries, Iran and Iraq* (New Delhi: Pentagon Press, 2013).

Al-Rasheed, M. (2017). The Gulf: Reshaping Regional & International Norms without "Political Dynamism". *Singapore Middle East Papers,* SMEP No. 26, 1 – 15. https://mei.nus.edu.sg/publication/volume-26-the-gulf-reshaping-regional-international-norms-without-political-dynamism/

Al-Tamimi, N. (2017). The Gulf Crisis: Why is India still neutral? *Arab News*, July 29, 2017, http://www.arabnews.com/node/1136101/columns.

Amadeo, K. (2017). Gulf Cooperation Council Countries: Six Rich Countries That Own the World's Oil. *The Balance*. https://www.thebalance.com/gulf-cooperation-council-3306357

*Arab News* (2016). 37th GCC Summit issues final communiqué, 8th December, http://www.arabnews.com/node/1021001/saudi-arabia

Augustine, B.D. (2016). India to Become UAE's Largest Trade Partner in 2030, *Gulf News*, December 15, 2016, https://gulfnews.com/business/sectors/tourism/india-to-become-the-uae-s-largest-trade-partner-by-2030-1.1947103

Ayres, A. (2018). *Our Time Has Come: How India is Making its Place in the World.* New York: Oxford University Press.

BP Statistical Review of World Energy (2010). *BP Statistical Review of World Energy June 2010*, report (London: BP p.l.c, June 2010), www.bp.com/statisticalreview

*BQ Magazine* (2015). Qatar-India trade at USD 133 bn. 6th December, http://www.bq-magazine.com/energy/oil-energy/2015/12/qatar-india-trade-at-usd-133-bn

Bhatnagar, S. (2018). The US Shadow over India's Iran Policy. *Interpreter*, July 23, 2018, https://www.lowyinstitute.org/the-interpreter/us-shadow-over-indias-iran-policy.

Bundhun, R. (2016). India Suffers Steep Decline in Remittances from GCC Nations. *The National*, 22nd May, http://www.thenational.ae/business/economy/india-suffers-steep-decline-in-remittances-from-gcc-nations

Burton, G. (2019). India's "Look West" Policy in the Middle East under Modi. 6th August 2019, Middle East Institute, https://www.mei.edu/publications/indias-look-west-policy-middle-east-under-modi

Cavatorta, F. (2014). International Politics of the Middle East. In Ellen Lust (ed.), *The Middle East* 13th ed. (pp. 341-370) Washington DC: CQ Press.

Choudhury, P.P. (2017). "Think West to Go West: Origins and Implications of India's West Asia Policy under Modi (Part 1)," Middle East Institute, September 26, 2017, https://www.mei.edu/publications/think-west-go-west-origins-and-implications-indias-west-asia-policy-under-modi-part-i.

Davidson, C.M. (2008). *Dubai: The Vulnerability of Success*. New York: Columbia University Press.

Deulgaonkar, P. (2017). India-UAE Ranked World's Second Largest Migration Corridor in 2015, Says OECD. *Arabianbusiness.com*, 17 January, http://www.arabianbusiness.com/india-uae-ranked-world-s-second-largest-migrationcorridor-in-2015-says-oecd—659681.html

*DNA* (2015). Indian EPC firms awarded projects worth over Rs 3,3185 crore in two years. 9th November, http://www.dnaindia.com/money/report-indianepc-firms-awarded-projects-worth-over-rs-33185-crore-in-two-years-2143727

Dubai Chamber of Commerce and Industry (2018). Dubai Chamber Strengthens Global Presence with Opening of India Office, http://www.dubaichamber.com/whats-happening/chamber_news/dubai-chamber-strengthens-global-presence-with-opening-of-india-office.

Embassy of India, Riyadh (2016). India-GCC Relations. 26th May, http://www.indianembassy.org.sa/Content. aspx?ID=890

Embassy of India, Riyadh (2018). India-Saudi Arabia Bilateral Relations.http://www.indianembassy.org.sa/india-saudi-arabia/india-saudi-bilateral-relations.

Ehteshami, A. (2013). *Dynamics of Change in the Persian Gulf: Political Economy, War and Revolution,* New York: Routledge.

Ehteshami, A. (2015). GCC Foreign Policy: From the Iran-Iraq War to the Arab Awakening. In *The New Politics of Intervention of Gulf Arab States*, Collected Papers, Vol. I, London: Middle East Centre, London School of Economics, pp. 13-22.

*Financial Express* (2017). "Despite PM Narendra Modi's Push, Mega UAE-India Infrastructure Fund Plan at Risk," *Financial Express*, January 27, 2017.

Flanagan, B. (2011). Saudi Cap on Remittances 'a deterrent' for Expats. *The National*, 20th November, http://www.thenational.ae/business/economy/saudi-capon-remittances-a-deterrent-for-expats

Goldman, Z. K., & Rapp-Hooper, M. (2013). Conceptualizing containment: The Iranian threat and the future of Gulf security. *Political Science Quarterly, 128*(4), 589

Grare, F. (2016). *India Turns East: International Engagement and US-China Rivalry.* London: Hurst Publishers.

*Gulf News* (2015). 36th GCC Summit Final Communiqué. 10th December, http://gulfnews.com/news/gulf/saudi-arabia/36th-gcc-summit-final-comminque-1.1635378

Hassan, R. (2018). Saudi Cadets to Undergo Training in India. *Arab News*, 19th March 2018, http://www.arabnews.com/node/1328011/saudi-arabia.

Hussain, S. & Ghosh, D. (2015). RMZ to raise Rs 1000 cr funding from Qatar Investment Authority. *Forbes India,* 2nd April, http://www.forbesindia.com/article/special/rmz-to-raise-rs-1000-cr-funding-fromqatar-investment-authority/39959/1

Irudaya Rajan, S., Varghese, V.J. and Jayakumar, M.S. (2011). *Dreaming Mobility and Buying Vulnerability: Overseas Recruitment Practices in India,* London: Routledge.

*Indian Navy* (2015). *Indian Maritime Security Doctrine 2015.* https://www.indiannavy.nic.in/content/indian-maritime-doctrine-2015-version.

John, I. (2018). UAE-India Trade likely to Cross $100 Billion by 2020. *Khaleej Times*, April 17, 2018, https://www.khaleejtimes.com/business/economy/uae-india-trade-likely-to-cross-100-billion-by-2020

John, S. (2017). "India's Balancing Act in the Gulf," MEI Middle East-Asia project (MAP), May 9, 2017, http://www.mei.edu/content/map/indias-balancing-act-gulf.

Kamrava, M. (2018). Multipolarity and instability in the Middle East, *Orbis* 62(4), 598-616.

Kawach, N. (2009). GCC likely to pump $ 200 bn. into renewable energy plans. *Emirates Business 24/7*, http://www.business24-7.ae/Articles/2009/7/Pages/06072009/07072009_fac9aea9 e6d7477aa68ffff8fa4f4354.aspx

Kemp, G. (2010). *The East Moves West: India, China and Asia's Growing Presence in the Middle East.* Washington, D.C.: Brookings Institution Press.

Khatana, P. (2018). GCC. In P.R. Kumarswamy and M. Singh Roy, (Eds.), *Persian Gulf 2016 - 17: India's Relation with the Region.* New Delhi: Pentagon Press and Institute for Defence Studies and Analyses. pp. 191-202.

Kirkpatrick, D. (2014). 3 Gulf Countries Pull Ambassadors from Qatar over its Support of Islamists, *The New York Times*, 5th March, https://www.nytimes.com/2014/03/06/world/middleeast/3-persian-gulf-states-pull-ambassadors-from-qatar.html

Korany, B. (2010). Looking at the Middle East Differently: An Alternative Conceptual Lens. In Bahgat Korany (ed.), *The Changing Middle East: A New Look at Regional Dynamics.* Cairo: American University in Cairo Press, pp. 7-42.

Kostiner, J. (2011). GCC Perceptions of Collective Security in the Post-Saddam Era. In Mehran Kamrava (ed.), *International Politics of the Persian Gulf,* New York: Syracuse University Press, pp. 94-119.

Kulkarni, N.S. & Bandekar, P. (2019). The Importance of GCC countries in India's Quest for Economic Power House: A Review. FINS Journal of Diplomacy & Strategy, 1st October 2019. https://finsindia.org/journal/the-importance-of-gcc-countries-in-indias-quest-for-economic-power-house-a-review/

Kumaraswamy, P. R. (2018). Modi Turns West: India and the Persian Gulf. *ISAS Working Paper,* No. 312, 23 November 2018, https://www.isas.nus.edu.sg/wp-content/uploads/2018/11/ISAS-Working-Paper-312-.pdf

Kumarswamy, P.R. & Singh Roy, M.(2018). *Persian Gulf 2016 - 17: India's Relation with the Region.* New Delhi: Pentagon Press and Institute for Defence Studies and Analyses.

Miller, R. (2016). *Desert Kingdoms to Global Powers – The Rise of the Arab Gulf.* New Haven: Yale University Press.

Ministry of Commerce, People's Republic of China (2016). The 9th Round of China-GCC FTA Negotiations Concluded. http://english.mofcom.gov.cn/article/newsrelease/significantnews/201612/20161202372433.shtml.

Ministry of Commerce, People's Republic of China (2017). *Achievements of Economic and Trade Cooperation between China and West Asia and Africa since the Holding of the Eighteenth National Congress of the Communist Party of China,* October 18, 2017.

Ministry of Commerce and Industry, Government of India (2018). *Annual Report 2017-18,* http://commerce.gov.in/writereaddata/uploadedfile/MOC_636626711232248483_Annual%20Report%20%202017-18%20English.pdf

Ministry of External Affairs, Government of India (2015). Joint Statement between the United Arab Emirates and the Republic of India. 17 August 2015. http://

mea.gov.in/bilateral-documents.htm?dtl/25733/ Joint_Statement_ between_the_United_Arab_Emirates_and_the_Republic_of_India

Joint Statement between the United Arab Emirates and the Republic of India (2015). August 17, 2015, http://www.narendramodi.in/joint-statement-between-the-united-arab-emirates-and-the-republic-of-india-253654

Ministry of External Affairs, Government of India, (2015). Joint Statement between the United Arab Emirates and the Republic of India, August 17, 2015.

Ministry of External Affairs, Government of India, (2015). "Joint Statement during the State Visit of the Emir of the State of Qatar to India," New Delhi, March, 16, 2015, http://mea.gov.in/bilateral-documents.htm?dtl/25012.

Ministry of External Affairs, Government of India (2015). "Speech by Foreign Secretary at Raisina Dialogue," New Delhi, March 2, 2015, http://mea.gov.in/Speeches-Statements.htm?dtl/26433/Speech_by_Foreign_Secretary_at_Raisina_Dialogue_in_New_Delhi_March_2_2015

Ministry of External Affairs, Government of India (2015). Text of speech by Shri Anil Wadhwa, "Address by Secretary (East) at the Inaugural Session of Second ORF-MEA West Asia Conference in New Delhi," April 27, 2015, Government of India, Ministry of Foreign Affairs.

Ministry of External Affairs, Government of India (2016). Joint Statement between India and Saudi Arabia during visit of Prime Minister to Saudi Arabia. April 3, 2016, http://www.mea.gov.in/bilateral-documents.htm?dtl/26595/IndiaSaudi_Arabia_Joint_Statement_during_the_visit_of_Prime_Minister_to_Saudi_Arabia_April_03_2016.

Ministry of External Affairs, Government of India (2016). "Speech at the First Gateway of India Dialogue," Mumbai, June 13, 2016, http://www.mea.gov.in/Speeches-Statements.htm?dtl/26902.

Ministry of External Affairs, Government of India (2016). Joint Statement between India and Saudi Arabia during visit of Prime Minister to Saudi Arabia. April 3, 2016, http://www.mea.gov.in/bilateral-documents.htm?dtl/26595/IndiaSaudi_Arabia_Joint_Statement_during_the_visit_of_Prime_Minister_to_Saudi_Arabia_April_03_2016.

Ministry of External Affairs, Government of India, (2016). Remarks by External Affairs Minister at the launch of the book 'The Modi Doctrine,'" New Delhi, August 13, 2016, http://www.mea.gov.in/Speeches-Statements.htm?dtl/27314/Remarks+by+Exte…; http://www.mea.gov.in/Speeches-Statements.htm?dtl/26910

Ministry of External Affairs, Government of India (2016). Joint Statement between India and Saudi Arabia during the visit of Prime Minister to Saudi Arabia April 3, 2016, http://www.mea.gov.in/bilateral-documents.htm?dtl/26595/IndiaSaudi_Arabia_Joint_Statement_during_the_visit_of_Prime_Minister_to_Saudi_Arabia_April_03_2016.

Ministry of External Affairs, Government of India (2016). Population of Overseas Indians. December, http://mea.gov.in/images/attach/NRIs-and-PIOs_1.pdf.

Ministry of External Affairs, Government of India (2018). "Population of Overseas Indians" (Compiled in December 2018), http://mea.gov.in/images/attach/NRIs-and-PIOs_1.pdf.

Ministry of External Affairs, Government of India (2020). https://mea.gov.in/press-releases.htm?dtl/33160/indiagcc+political+dialogue

Naar, I. (2016). Bahrain, Oman Cut Petrol Subsidies as Oil Hits 12-year Low. *Al-Arabiya*, 12 January, https://english.alarabiya.net/en/business/energy/2016/01/12/Bahrain-Oman-cut-petrol-subsidies-as-oil-hits-12-year-low.html

Nader, H. (2011). Growth in economics relations of China and India with GCC Countries. *Asian-Pacific Economic Literature*, 25 (2), 52-67.

Noble, P. (2008). From Arab System to Middle Eastern System? Regional Pressures and Constraints, in Bahgat Korany and Ali E. Hillal Dessouki (eds), *The Foreign Policies of Arab States: The Challenge of Globalisation,* Cairo: American University in Cairo Press, pp. 67-165.

Panda, R. (2009). Migration Remittances: The Emerging Scenario, *India Quarterly*, 65 (2), 167-183.

Pant, G. (1999). The Changing Gulf Market and India: Trends and Prospects. In *Perspectives on India and Gulf States,* A.K Pasha (Ed.), pp. 112-126, New Delhi: Détente Publishers.

Patrick, S. (2016). World Order: What, Exactly, are the Rules? *The Washington Quarterly*, 7-27.

Pethiyagoda, K. (2017a). India – GCC Relations: Delhi's Strategic Opportunity. February 2017.

https://www.brookings.edu/wp-content/uploads/2017/02/india_gcc_relations.pdf

Pethiyagoda, K. (2017b). How India's diaspora affects its role in a multipolar middle east. 15th June 2017. https://www.brookings.edu/blog/order-from-chaos/2017/06/15/how-indias-diaspora-affects-its-role-in-a-multipolar-middle-east/

Policy Analysis Unit (2014). *Recalling GCC Ambassadors from Doha: A Background and Future Predictions,* Doha: Arab Center for Research and Policy Studies, March.

Pradhan, B. (2004). "Changing Dynamics of India's West Asia Policy," *International Studies* 41, 1-88, https://journals.sagepub.com/doi/pdf/10.1177/002088170404100101?casa_token=ouh_yGIzLmcAAAAA:jZn3-gzZeVMEm1L8DXqD_rM79vTaTm1tL88-qACOKh9iP2pgweg8V35TFZUC1iYxW6GIuDWrdWJb6A

Pradhan, P.K. (2011). *Accelerating India's Look West Policy in the Gulf*, report. New Delhi: Institute of Defence Studies and Analyses.

Pradhan, P.K. (2011). GCC-Iran Rivalry and Strategic Challenges for India in the Gulf. *Indian Foreign Affairs Journal,* 6, (1), 45-57.

Pradhan, S. (2010). India and the Gulf Cooperation Council (GCC): An Economic and Political Perspective, *Strategic Analysis,* 34(1), 93-103, https://doi.org/10.1080/09700160903351340.

Qian, X. (2017). The Belt and Road Initiatives and China-GCC Relations. *International Relations and Diplomacy,* 5(1), 687-693.

Qian, X. & Fulton, J. (2017). China-Gulf Economic Relationship under the "Belt and Road" Initiative, *Asian Journal of Middle Eastern and Islamic Studies*, 11(3), 12-21.

Quamar, M.M. (2018). UAE. In P.R. Kumarswamy and M. Singh Roy, (Eds.), *Persian Gulf 2016 - 17: India's Relation with the Region.* New Delhi: Pentagon Press and Institute for Defence Studies and Analyses. pp. 153-169.

Rachman, G. (2017). 'The Qatar crisis has global implications', *The Irish Times*, 20 June. https://www.irishtimes.com/opinion/gideon-rachman-the-qatar-crisis-has-global-implications-1.3126419 .

Raja Mohan, C. (2006). India and the Balance of Power. *Foreign Affairs* (July/August 2006):

Ramady, M.A. (2012). Overview. In M.A. Ramady (Ed.) *The GCC Economies: Stepping Up To Future Challenges.* Springer: New York. p. xxi.

Ramazani, R. K. (1988). *The Gulf Cooperation Council: Record and Analysis.* Charlottesville: University of Virginia Press.

Roy, S. (2018). India Gets Access to Strategic Oman Port Duqm for Military Use, Chabahar-Gwadar in Sight. *Indian Express*, February 13, 2018, https://indianexpress.com/article/india/india-gets-access-to-strategic-oman-port-for-military-use-chabahar-gwadar-in-sight-5061573/

Saif, I. (2009). The Oil Boom in the GCC Countries, 2002 – 2008: Old Challenges, New Dynamics. *Carnerige Endowments for International Peace,* No. 15.

Sankar, A. & Ashwani Kumar (2018), First Hindu Temple in Abu Dhabi to be Completed by 2020, Khaleej *Times*, February 11, 2018, https://www.khaleejtimes.com/uae-india-ties//First-Abu-Dhabi-Hindu-temple-to-come-up-on-55,000-square-metres-of-land-.

Sayigh, Y.A. (1978). *The Economies of the Arab World: Development since 1945.* London: Taylor & Francis.

Siyech, M.S. (2019). India-Qatar Relations: Navigating Turbulent Seas. Middle East Institute, April 9, 2019, https://www.mei.edu/publications/india-qatar-relations-navigating-turbulent-seas

Sultan, N. (2012). Working on a Sustainable GCC Future: Relections on Policies and Practices. In M.A. Ramady (Ed.) *The GCC Economies: Stepping Up To Future Challenges.* Springer: New York. pp. 3-10.

Supreme Committee for Delivery and Legacy (2016). Main Contractor for Al-Rayyan Stadium announced as Qatari-Indian Joint Venture. 5 June, http://www.sc.qa/en/news/al-rayyan-stadium-qatari-indian-joint-venture

Taneja, K. (2020), How Modi turned the Gulf to his favour. https://www.orfonline.org/expert-speak/how-modi-turned-the-gulf-to-his-favor-52652/

*The Economic Times* (2015). Indian EPC firms awarded projects worth over $5 billion in Kuwait. 9th November http://economictimes.indiatimes.com/news/industry/indl-goods/svs/engineering/indian-epc-firms-awarded-projectsworth-over-5-billion-in-kuwait/articleshow/49722856.cms

*The Economic Times* (2016). Revised Qatar LNG deal cuts gas price to below $5 per mmBtu: Dharmendra Pradhan. May 3, https://economictimes.indiatimes.com/articleshow/52084660.cms?utm_source=contentofinterest&utm_medium=text&utm_campaign=cppst

*The Economic Times* (2016). India's Oil Imports from Middle East rises to 59%. *Economic Times*, 25th April https://economictimes.indiatimes.com/news/

economy/foreign-trade/indias-oil-import-from-middle-east-rises-to-59/articleshow/51979614.cms.

*The Economic Times* (2016). "Government plans 3 more sub-funds under NIIF," *Economic Times*, September 26, 2016, http://economictimes.indiatimes.com/news/economy/infrastructure/government-plans-3-more-sub-funds-under-niif/articleshow/54524031.cms

*The Economic Times (2018)*. Narendra Modi's call to Saudi King helped India's Operation Rahat in Yemen: Sushma Swaraj. https://economictimes.indiatimes.com/news/politics-and-nation/narendra-modis-call-to-saudi-king-helped-indias-operation-rahat-in-yemen-sushma-swaraj/articleshow/62405284.cms?from=mdr

*The Economic Times*, (2019). "Iraq continues to be India's top oil supplier, imports from US rises 4-fold," *Economic Times*, May 1, 2019,

*The Hindu* (2016). Indian merchandise exports to 6 GCC nations down 19% in 2015-16. *The Hindu*, 23[rd] May, http://www.thehindubusinessline.com/economy/indianmerchandise-exports-to-6-gcc-nations-down-19-in-201516/article8636579.ece

*The Times* (2015). Shapoorji Pallonji and Co. Ltd. finalized contract with Kuwait University. 29th January, http://www.timeskuwait.com/Times_Shapoorji-Pallonjiand-Co.-Ltd.-finalized-contract-with-Kuwait-University

*The Times of India* (2016). NIIF, Qatar Investment Authority sign MoU to boost infra investments. 9th June, http://timesofindia.indiatimes.com/city/delhi/NIIF-Qatar-Investment-Authority-sign-MoU-to-boost-infra-investments/articleshow/52673623.cms

*The Times of India* (2017). UAE Strategic Oil Reserves Deal: 10 Things to Know. *Times of India*, January 26, https://timesofindia.indiatimes.com/business/india-business/india-uae-strategic-oil-reserves-deal-10-things-to-know/listshow/56793334.cms

*The Times of India* (2018). Air India makes history by flying to Israel via Saudi airspace. 23[rd] March, https://timesofindia.indiatimes.com/india/air-indias-maiden-flight-to-israel-ends-decades-old-overfly-ban-by-saudi-arabia/articleshow/63423842.cms

*The World Bank* (2016). Personal Remittances, Received (% of GDP). http://data.worldbank.org/indicator/BX.TRF.PWKR.DT.GD.ZS?name_desc=false.

*The World Bank* (2016). United Arab Emirates Economic Outlook: Spring 2016. *MENA Economic Monitor Report: Spring,*http://pubdocs.worldbank.org/en/141211460471550773/UAE-MEM-eng.pdf.

*The World Bank* (2017). Migration and Development Brief 27. April, http://pubdocs.worldbank.org/en/ 992371492706371662/MigrationandDevelopmentBrief27.pdf

Townsend, S. (2016). The Gulf's Sovereign Dilemma. *arabianbusiness.com*, 9th April, http://www.arabianbusiness.com/the-gulf-s-sovereign-dilemma-627766.htm.

Trigunayat, A. (2020). GCC and the Indian diaspora in the context of covid 19. 20[th] April 2020. https://www.vifindia.org/2020/april/20/gcc-and-the-indian-diaspora-in-the-context-ofcovid-19

U-Capital (2018). *GCC Budgets – 2018*, February. http://www.u-capital.net/pdf/GCC%20Budgets%20-%202018.pdf

Ulrichsen, K.C. (2009). Internal and External Security in the Arab Gulf States, *Journal of Middle East Policy,* XVI,(2), https://doi.org/10.1111/j.1475-4967.2009.00390.x

*Wikipedia.org (2018)*. 2017–18 Qatar Diplomatic Crisis. https://en.wikipedia.org/wiki/2017–18_Qatar_diplomatic_ crisis

Wright, S. (2011). Foreign Policy in the GCC States. In Mehran Kamrava (ed.), *International Politics of the Persian Gulf,* New York: Syracuse University Press, pp. 72-93.

# 7

# India, 'France of Asia' – Convergence in or Influence on Foreign Policies?

**Dr B. Krishnamurthy**

It is said that a country can cherry-pick its friends, but, cannot choose its neighbours. Immediacy and propinquity between and among the countries are considered as prerequisite for being neighbours. However, being a neighbour is not only the choice of geography but also of history, and especially of international politics/relations. Though physically away from India, France happened to be the immediate neighbour, historically. Due to its possession of island territories in the Western Indian Ocean region, France continues to remain India's distant neighbour. The present paper argues that as a result of the convergence in foreign policy goals and commonality of purposes, distance between them has become immaterial, and the strategic partnership between India and France is rated as the best by leaders and analysts of both the countries as it serves mutual benefits and common interests.

On the eve of the Indian independence in 1947, France remained India's immediate neighbour *de facto* till 1954, when it handed over its settlements in India[1] and *de jure* till 1962, when the Indo-French Treaty of Cession of the French Establishments of Pondicherry, Karaikal, Mahe and Yanam of May 28, 1956 was ratified by the National Assembly of France on July 12, 1962. The instruments of ratification were exchanged subsequently in New Delhi on August 16, 1962. As such, August 16 is celebrated every year as Independence Day by the Government of the Union Territory (UT) of Pondicherry and the occasion is being celebrated with a cultural festival called *Fete de Pondicherry.* As of now, around 10,000 French nationals are present in the UT and around 7000 among them vote in the elections for the French President, National Assembly, referenda, Councilors of French citizens abroad of the Superior Council of Overseas French, a body that advises the French Government on behalf of the 1.5 million French expatriates and the European Parliament. Besides, French remains one among the five official languages of the UT. Again, there is considerable number of French citizens of Indian origin living in France, especially in Paris.

Further, France possesses seven *Departément et Territoire d' Outre Mer* (DOM-TOMs - Overseas Districts and Territories) including Mayotte and La Réunion islands in the Western Indian Ocean region with a population of about 1,173,748 in 2022. On the strength of its overseas Districts, France continues to engage in the regional organisations such as the Indian Ocean Commission, Indian Ocean Rim Association (IORA), Quadrilateral Defence Coordination Group, and the Indian Ocean Naval Symposium (IONS). As such, France remains one of the distant neighbours of India. Though France is physically a distant neighbour, for all practical purposes, it acts as an immediate neighbour due to the following factors:

## Peaceful Settlement of French India Problem

The French India problem, the issue of France handing over its territorial possessions in the Indian soil to the newly independent Indian Union, was sorted out through constitutional means, without leaving behind any bickering or bitterness between the parties. Nehru claimed that the Indo-French settlement of October 27, 1954 over the *de facto* transfer of the French Indian settlements to the Indian Union honours both the Governments of the Republic of India and of the French Republic "as all fine settlements always do".[2] This warmth continued to guide close, cordial and mutually beneficial relations between the two countries in the politico-diplomatic domain and also led to cooperation between them in the spheres of art and culture, economy, science and technology and defence and security.

## Non-Alignment and Un-Alignment

In the Indian perception, France seems to be the closest to their political views. India and France are deeply wedded to the notions of national sovereignty and strategic autonomy and are determined to take foreign policy decisions independently and to make their strategic choices without any external inference and interference. France's 'unalignment' policy under President Charles de Gaulle was quite well-perceived by the non-aligned India under Premier Nehru.[3] Since the aim of the non-aligned countries and the Gaullist government's desire to remain independent of the global Bloc politics converged at certain point and because of the policies and the personality of its president, France was perceived by India as a natural partner.

In 1965, Jean Daridan, the then French ambassador to India, referred about the keenness of the Indian leaders to find an interlocutor in Europe, which could be none other than France and to secure its support. In March 1966 there was a meeting between the Indian Prime Minister Indira Gandhi and the French President de Gaulle, who tried to impress on her that Pakistan was not capable of doing much harm to India and so it did not represent an excessively important factor for India. China, he maintained, too would not be a challenge to India in the near future as it needed at least three decades to attain its full strength, as was the case with India. Both the leaders seemed to agree on all important issues of international politics, including bi-polarism and the issue of Nuclear Disarmament. The French President drew certain similarities in the position of France and India in the bi-polar international politics and proposed: "... it would be in their interest to distance from the game played by the three world powers, viz., the United States, China and Russia".[4] This meeting had given forth to the emergence of a sort of convergence of opinion between the two countries on the most important international issues.

The French leaders deliberately practiced the role of the un-alignment rebel, in spite of the fact that France was constrained to be part of the Western, capitalist bloc. Again, they claimed that France was an ally of the Americans, but, not aligned with the US and maintained that they preferred to be the Europeanists than Atlanticists, if it means denial of sovereign equality. In early 1980s, Claude Cheysson, the then French Foreign Minister under President François Mitterrand, took pleasure in calling France as a 'genuinely non-aligned' country and maintained that the industrialised states should get a better understanding of the non-aligned concepts.[5] India's non-aligned and France's unaligned policies reflected well in their approaches to and activities in the international political arena, especially in their relations with the US and this factor had compelled Alyssa Ayres to term India as 'France of Asia'.[6]

## Strategic Partnership

The Indo-French Strategic Partnership of 1998, the first of its kind signed by India, has significantly enhanced cooperation between the partners in fields covering civilian nuclear and defence cooperation, space, counter-terrorism, education, research and development in science and technology, culture, urban development, climate change, economic relations and people-to-people contacts. India's strategic partnership with France proved to be successful, fruitful and mutually beneficial and the best among the partnerships signed with the member countries of the European Union (EU). The Foundation for National Security Research graded India's strategic partnerships on a 10-point scale for present performance, sustainability, and potential of these partnerships for India in three areas of cooperation: politico-diplomatic ties, defence ties and economic relations and methodically ranked them with a corresponding score out of 90 points. In the final ranking, Russia came out on top with 62 points, followed by the United States (58), while France came out with 51points, followed by the UK (41), and Germany (37).[7] Incidentally, India's strategic partnership with France was rated better than the one with the EU as well.[8] The Indo-French strategic partnership is considered by the partners as the best asset to shape the post-pandemic world, to defend common values, and to promote a multipolar world. It is believed that this strategic partnership is "grounded on enduring shared interests and an exceptional level of trust built over decades".[9]

## Issue of Nuclear Non-proliferation and Civilian Nuclear Cooperation

On the face of the Soviet nuclear threat and the US-UK nuclear cooperation, France had to opt for an independent nuclear programme and to barge into the Nuclear Club in early 1960s. The French were against the nuclear disarmament negotiations and treaties entered into by the Super Powers over their head, but, involving their nuclear arsenal as well. They rebelled against and refused to sign the Nuclear Non-Proliferation Treaty (NPT) for almost two decades. India was also against the discriminative NPT and was not ready to be a party to it. This factor brought India and France together over the issue of nuclear disarmament.

On several occasions, France displayed its resolve to support India's quest for nuclear energy to ensure its energy security and to achieve sustainable development. The French supported the Indian efforts to galvanise the nuclear energy for peaceful purposes by training the Indian nuclear scientists and technologists and by supplying nuclear reactors and fuel.[10] When India conducted nuclear tests in May 1974 and later in May 1998, the French leaders approached the issue sympathetically and opposed the imposition of economic and technological sanctions on India. Instead, they advocated civilian nuclear cooperation with India in order to help it in meeting out its ever-increasing energy requirement.[11]

Both India and France resolved to add a new impetus and thrust to their strategic partnership by engaging in developing nuclear energy for peaceful purposes and signed a treaty on the Development of Peaceful Uses of Nuclear Energy on September 30, 2008, which not only provided for establishing a 9,900 MW Nuclear Power Plant at Jaitapur but also relevant technology transfer.[12] The French firm Areva signed first commercial agreement with India on civilian nuclear cooperation in February 2009 to set up six nuclear power plants and on the supply of nuclear fuel, thereby bringing an end to the nuclear apartheid till then faced by India.[13]

## Defence and Security Cooperation

Since early 1950s, France supplied India fighter aircrafts, military helicopters, submarines and other arms and ammunitions. By the turn of the millennium, the French military sales to India have been averaging €300 millions to €2 billions a year, making their defence industries the third largest weapons and armament system suppliers to India after Russia and the US.[14] Between 2008 and 2017, France had sold defence equipment worth €13.411 billion to India.[15] Besides arms supply, France is also involved with India in the production of armaments by the latter under the French license, as well as under the framework of joint and collaborative Projects. It is interesting to note that France is involved in the up-gradation of fighter aircrafts, supplied earlier by the French companies as well as by the Russians, already in the Indian inventory.[16] France is committed to offering the best of its defence technology with a high "Make in India" component.

Raja Mohan claims that France has foregone the opportunity to sell major weapons systems to Pakistan and has focused on a strong defence partnership with India and wonders "whether France has become India's new Russia".[17] Roger, while analysing the Indo-French Defence Cooperation wonders whether both the countries are 'friends in need or friends indeed'.[18]

India and France act conjointly in the Indo-Pacific maritime realm, which has gained new geo-strategic importance due to its politico-economic potentials and especially as a result of the over-arching role played by China in the maritime space in general and in the South China Sea in particular. Sharing the same geographical definition of the Indo-Pacific makes it easy for New Delhi and Paris to come together and their shared maritime vision, which intends to uphold the Law of the Sea in the Indian Ocean region, secure the Sea Lines of Communication, respond to humanitarian disasters and to promote sustainable blue economy, smoothly synchronise their strategic thinking and follow up actions in the Indo-Pacific maritime domain.[19] As the only credible military power with undiminished political will and a historic presence in the Indo-Pacific, France can be a privileged partner for India in strengthening peace and security in this maritime realm.[20]

France and India have engaged in regular defence exercises of their three services through joint exercises and manoeuvres between their Navies (*Varuna*), Air forces (*Garuda*) and Land forces (*Shakti*). The *Varuna* exercises have become an integral part of the institutionalised interactions that is getting developed between the two navies and reflect a convergence of interest in achieving their goals.[21] It is significant to note that France is the only non-neighbouring country (in the conventional sense) with which India conducts coordinated patrols, an indication of its level of trust in and bonhomie with France.

## Support for Playing an International Role

While taking a stand on any national or international issues, the Indian leaders used to be concerned with what the international community – the US, Europe and China - would think or how they would react. The Indian foreign policy remained singularly Pakistan-centric, and India's relations with the third countries were invariably influenced by the Pakistan factor – nature of their bilateral relations with Pakistan. This prompted scholars like Raja Mohan, well-known Indian strategic analyst, to capture India's foreign policy stance by the image of the porcupine —'vegetarian, slow-footed and prickly' and to maintain that defensiveness usually remained "the hallmark of Indian approach to the world" and that as a reactive power, India puts up its "sharp quills to ward off the threats, when the world impinges on it".[22] Further building on this depiction of India, Mark Leonard, Director of the Foreign Policy Centre, London, maintained that this image perception hints at the perceived vulnerability of India's international agency, which 'uses its quills to deter aggressors and hides in a cave, especially when Pakistan is mentioned'.[23]

The French leaders were the first to take cognizance of this fundamental flaw in the Indian foreign policy establishment. Mention has already been made to De Gaulle's advice to Indira Gandhi against giving undue attention to China and Pakistan. In the post-Cold War era, Hubert Védrine, the then French Foreign Minister, identified India as a prospective pole in the ensuing Multipolar world order. Védrine defended his choice on the ground that India remains a popular democracy. At the same time, he suggested India to eschew its Pakistani orientation and to behave like a major power, expanding its horizon beyond South Asia.[24] His prescription for India was loud and clear: leave behind the Pakistani obsession; come out of the cocoon of South Asian region; and surge into international political arena by assuming international responsibilities of a global player. Induction of India as a prospective pole in the multipolar world by the French remains the clear cut proof of the fact that France is a more credible partner for India in constructing a more equitable world order through a new concert of major powers.[25]

The French not only suggested India to abandon Pakistan-centric foreign policy, but also extended a helping hand in achieving this. While other Western powers hyphenated[26] India with Pakistan, Jean-Pierre Raffarin, the then French Premier, during his visit to India in February 2003, discarded this practice and dared to put it in categorical terms.[27] The White Paper on Defence and National Security of 2013 brought out by the French administration assigned a high place for India in the French security strategy and referred about India in the same terms with the closest of France's allies. It perceived India as a factor of stability in the South Asian region, referred about the privileged strategic partnership between the two countries and highlighted India's emergence as a major developing economy.[28]

The French were the first among the western powers to identify the primacy of India in South Asia as well as to recognise India's quest to play an active and influential role in the contemporary international politics, commensurate with its size, population and economy. While India remained a 'good competitor' for the UN Security Council permanent seat, France remained an 'enthusiastic' supporter of the Indian claim.[29] The French leaders maintained that India should secure its 'rightful place' in the UNSC and the UN reform cannot wait forever.[30] Both the partners stressed on the need to make the Security Council more 'representative and responsible' institution corresponding with the present day realities.[31] In January 2015, the Permanent Mission of France to the United Nations in New York, pushed for the expansion of the Security Council with the inclusion of Germany, Brazil, India, Japan, as well as a greater representation for African countries.[32]

By way of recognising the developments achieved by India in the economic sphere, President Chirac took personal initiative in 2003 to have an 'enlarged dialogue' between the G-8 and twelve developing countries, India being one among them, on questions of globalisation and international governance. This factor may be taken as the French effort to rope India into the international economic and financial architecture. President Macron invited Premier Modi to participate in the G7 Summit held in Biarritz, France on August 26, 2019, as 'Partners of Goodwill - Biarritz Partner'.[33]

France called for ending India's nuclear isolation and advocated the reframing of the international rules of nuclear commerce to facilitate civilian atomic energy cooperation with India. Recognizing India's positive non-proliferation record as well as its willingness to further contribute to global non-proliferation efforts, France was prepared to jointly work with India towards its increased participation with international non-proliferation initiatives and full membership of multilateral export control regimes such as the Nuclear Suppliers Group, the Missile Technology Control Regime, the Australia Group, and the Wassenaar Arrangement. France actively toiled in building consensus among members of these regimes on this issue, by impressing on them that India's accession will add value to the aims and objectives of these regimes.[34] The French help to India in entering or in its efforts to enter the multilateral nuclear architecture is noteworthy.

The International Solar Alliance (ISA) remains a major Indo-French initiative in response to climate change, which intends to provide a common platform for cooperation among sun-rich nations to ramp up solar energy, with the intention to contain global greenhouse emissions as well as to generate and exploit clean and cheap energy. Around fifty six countries have signed the ISA Framework Agreement and twenty six nations have already ratified it. The ISA remains the first treaty-based international organisation to be based in New Delhi.[35] This has offered a new stature to India in international politics, and France's helping hand in this regard is worth remembering.

Though the French suggestion to deny unwarranted importance to Pakistan was not taken seriously by the earlier regimes, the present Modi regime has succeeded in approaching the India-Pakistan relations in the proper perspective. By abrogating Article 370 and erasing the special status till then enjoyed by Jammu-Kashmir, India had legally denied Pakistan any levarage in the Kashmir issue. The Home Minister had made it abundantly clear that if there will be any dialogue with Pakistan in this regard, it will revolve around the Pakistan-occupied Kashmir and its eventual merger with India. The surgical strikes, in response to the Pakistani-sponsored cross border terrorist attacks, unfolded a new, resounding retort to Pakistani mis-adventures. India is no more a porcupine and the US Intelligence Annual Threat Assessment Report released in February 2023 maintains that Modi Government's most-likely response to threat emanating from China and Pakistan would be through military retaliation.[36]

On the other hand, India's singular and swift response to the incidence of earth quake in Turkey displays the country's resolve in taking its international responsibilities of a global player seriously and sincerely. Humanitarian and development assistance to the South Asian neighbours including Taliban-infested Afghanistan and the African countries remains yet another case of India's upholding international obligations.

## International Terrorism

Similar experience makes France to be sympathetic towards India, the victim of cross border terrorism aided and abetted by Pakistan. France listed the Pakistani terrorist organisation - *Lashker-e-Taiba,* which continues to be very active in the Indian soil, on its terrorist list in October 2001. The Indo-French Extradition Treaty signed in January 2003 was a significant step towards bilateral cooperation in fighting terrorism.[37] The leaders of both the states resolved to boost their collaborative activities against international terrorist organisations through increased "operational interactions". Moreover, the French acted in favour of the long-standing Indian demand for getting the chief of the UN-proscribed *Jaish-e Muhammad* (JeM), Masood Azhar, designated as a global terrorist, for the nefarious activities of his network in India. Consequently on May 1, 2019, the UNSC 1267 Sanctions Committee designated Masood as a global terrorist. Besides, France led the initiative to implement the Christchurch Call for Action to Jettison Terrorist and Extremist Online Content, as resolved in Paris in May 2019. Along with India, France too called upon all the UN member countries to implement the UNSC Resolution 2462 on Fighting Terrorist Financing adopted on March 28, 2019; called upon them to root out terrorist safe havens and infrastructure, and to disrupt terrorist networks and their financing channels.[38] France also stresses on the need for the early adoption of the Comprehensive Convention on International Terrorism (proposed by India as early as 1996, which has been lying in limbo due to opposition of countries like the US and Pakistan over the definition of terrorism and terrorist), by the UN General Assembly.

## Mutual Appreciation of 'Good Neighbourliness'

As a tradition, India chooses to honour the Head of the State or Government of a third country by inviting him/her as Chief Guest at the annual Republic Day functions. The choice is predicated on India's politico-economic relations of the country concerned and its leadership at that particular juncture and intends to set the tone and tenor of the relationship for the years to come. The invitation also gives an opportunity for the guest to nurture and strengthen bonds of political, economic, cultural, defence and strategic cooperation with India. International geopolitics and strategic partnerships quite naturally play a critical role in the preference of Republic Day chief guest. It is noteworthy that this exceptional honour is extended to the French Heads of State or Government the highest number of times, five times to be precise, more than the leaders of any other country. President Jacques Chirac remains the only leader to have been the guest-of-honour at the Republic Day twice, first as Prime Minister in 1976 and then as President in 1998. Other French leaders who were chief guests at the Republic Day parade were Valéry Giscard d'Estaing (1980), Nicolas Sarkozy (2008) and François Hollande (2016).

Again, it is noteworthy that members of armed forces of India and France have participated in each other's national day parades. For instance, when Manmohan Singh attended the Bastille Day Parade in July 2009, a 400-strong Indian armed force contingent too participated in the programme. This was the first time that the Indian troops have taken part in the national day parade of another country. Likewise, the French military contingent and a military band participated in the 67$^{th}$ Republic Day Parade in 2016 along with President Hollande as Chief Guest. Incidentally, France had been the first country to receive such an honour.

## Conclusion

It is quite significant to note that the Indo-French relationship is firmly rooted in the political and popular support that goes beyond the bipartisan framework and cohabitation in both the countries. While the political leadership belonging to the United Front, Congress, and Barathiya Janata Party equally nurtured the Indo-French relationship, the Gaullist, Centrist and Left governments of France, displayed unflinching earnestness and enthusiasm in fostering partnership between the two countries. It is noteworthy that the French President and the Prime Minister, who belonged to diametrically opposed political orientation, were united in their decision to sign the strategic partnership with India in 1998 and successive Governments continued to nurture the relationship in the years to come. This factor has ensured 'continuity' as a rule rather than an exception.

The level of the convergence of foreign policies and political understanding between India and France remains quite remarkable and this dynamic has enthused France to act as an immediate neighbour of India in spite of the physical distance between the two countries. Chirac, during the course of his visit to New Delhi in January 1976, pronounced vividly: India "... a country dear to us ... whatever the distance between them". The foregoing account on the Indo-French strategic partnership proves him quite correct. Physical 'distance' between India and France has become immaterial and irrelevant. More than mutual 'influence', convergence and commonality of purpose in the foreign policies guide Indo-French relations and ensure its success and sustenance. Divergence remains low in comparison with other western powers, especially the US, and both the powers don't mind 'agree to disagree', if it calls for. Scholars like Raja Mohan describe the friendship between India and France as the 'most exceptional' and the strategic partnership between them is celebrated as the 'First', 'original' and 'effective'. For India, partnering with France has tangible benefits.

To be precise, France has clearly identified India as a privileged partner in the South Asian region and has decided to contribute to its rise. This factor has come out apparently in a significant statement made by Jean-Yves Le Drian, the then French Defence Minister, in 2013, when he declared that, "apart from our Allies and European partners, there are few countries across the world with which we are prepared to go as far as we do with India".[39] While Le Drian predicted that the "Indo-French strategic partnership would grow further in scope, maturity and strength", the Indian President Pranab Mukerjee responded with equal enthusiasm: "France has been one of India's oldest, closest and most reliable partners". It is hoped a day may come when Alyssa Ayres or some other western scholars will contemplate writing a paper titled, *"Is France emerging as India of Europe".*

## Notes

1. *Les etablisments français de l'Inde, Notes Documentaires et Etudes*, No.735, *serie France d'Outre-Mer* –XXVIII, Paris, September 30, 1947, p.3. By mid-twentieth century the French were holding in all five settlements - Pondicherry, Karaikal, Mahe, Yanam and Chandernagore - covering an area of 509 Sq. Kms. with a population of 323,295 souls. Besides, the French were holding on eleven *loges* or sites of their warehouses at Surat, Kasimbazar, Dacca, Patna, Jougdia, Calicut, Masulipatnam, Balasor and so on. In all, these *loges* were approximately covering an area of four Sq. Kms. with 2000 inhabitants.
2. *Jawaharlal Nehru's Speeches*, Vol. III, March, 1953 – August 1957, The Publication Division, Ministry of Information and Broadcasting, Government of India, New Delhi, 1958, p. 462.
3. B. Krishnamurthy, "Nehruvian Non-Alignment and Gaullian Unalignment: Contemporary Relevance", *International Journal of South Asian Studies,* Vol. 1, Issue 1, 2008, pp. 1-17.
4. Gilles Boquérat, "France's Political Interaction with India through the Quai d' Orsay" Archives (1947-1972), in Max-Jean Zins and Gilles Boquérat, *India in the Mirror of Foreign Diplomatic Archives,* Manohar, New Delhi, 2004, pp. 26-8.

5. *Time International,* June 21, 1981, p.11 (Interview with Claude Cheysson).
6. Alyssa Ayres, *Is India Emerging as France of Asia?,* Yale Global Online, 21 November 2006, accessed at yaleglobal.yale.edu/display.article?id=8452 on 10/04/2016. Ayres describe India as 'France of Asia', an 'ally of the United States which shares many values with Americans, but pursues its own course'.
7. Foundation for National Security Research, *India's Strategic Partners: A Comparative Assessment*, New Delhi, November 2011, pp. 5, 10, 12-3.
8. B. Krishnamurthy, "India's Strategic Partnerships with the EU and France: A comparative Assessment", in Mohanan Bhaskaran Pillai (ed.), *India's Strategic Vision and Foreign Policy: Options and Challenges*, How Academics, Delhi, 2023, pp. 253-282.
9. Rajat Pandit, 'India foremost strategic ally of France in Indo-Pacific region', December 17, 2021 (Excerpts from the interview with Florence Parly, French Minister of Armed Forces), accessed at https://timesofindia.indiatimes.com/india/india-foremost-strategic-ally-of-france-in-indo-pacific-region/articleshow/88329463.cms on 6/4/2022.
10. 50 *years – Scientific and Technological Cooperation between France and India, Service Culturel Scientific et de Cooperation de New Delhi, Centre de Documentation Universitaire, Scientifique et Technique, Ambassade de France en Inde,* New Delhi, 1998.
11. B. Krishnamurthy, *Indo-French Relations. Problems and Perspectives,* Shipra Publications, New Delhi, 2005. For a detailed account refer Chapter 9 on Indo-French Nuclear Cooperation.
12. Nayanima Basu, Macron backing India on J&K shouldn't be a surprise - the French have always stood by India, *The Print,* August 23, 2019, accessed at www.theprint.in/diplomacy/on 12/6/2020.
13. *The Hindu,*(Chennai), February 5, 2009.
14. Constance Roger, *Indo-French Defence Cooperation. Friends in Need or Friends Indeed.* Institute of Peace and Conflict Studies, pp. 1-32, New Delhi, 2007, accessed at files.ethz.ch/isn/55131/IPCS-ResearchPaper7-Constance.pdf on 14/06/2020.
15. Ministry of Defence, Government of the Republic of France, *France and Security in the Indo-Pacific 2019*, p. 17, accessed at https://www.defense.gouv.fr/content/download/532754/9176250/file/ France and Security in the Indo-Pacific – 2019.pdf on 24/8/2019.
16. Krishnamurthy, n. 11. Refer Chapter 6 on France and the Indian Defence Preparedness for further details.
17. C. Raja Mohan, 'France India's New Russia', *The Indian Express,* (New Delhi), March, 09, 2018, accessed at https://indianexpress.com/article/opinion/columns/france-indias-new-russia-emmanuel-macron-narendra-modi-5091279/ on 19/6/2020. Earlier, Russia had unambiguously chosen India as its partner in the South Asian region and used to supply arms to India only and desisted from the temptation of supplying them to Pakistan. Of late, it has started entertaining Pakistani demands and France has stepped into the Russian shoes.
18. Roger, n. 14.

19. B. Krishnamurthy, "India, Europe and the Indo-Pacific" in Rajendra K. Jain (ed.), *India, Europe and Asia. Convergence and Divergence*, Palgrave Macmillan, Singapore, 2021, pp. 161-85.
20. C. Raja Mohan, Raja-Mandala: A most exceptional friendship, January 26, 2016, accessed at

    https://indianexpress.com/article/opinion/columns/raja-mandala-a-most-exceptional-friendship/ on 18/9/2020.
21. Isabelle Saint-Mézard, *The French Strategy in the Indian Ocean and the Potential for Indo-French Cooperation*. S. Rajaratnam School of International Studies, Nanyang Technological University, Policy Report, March 2015, p. 7, accessed at www.rsis.edu.sg/wp-content/uploads/Strategy.pdf on 17/8/2019.
22. C. Raja Mohan, *Crossing the Rubicon: The Shaping of India's New Foreign Policy,* London, Palgrave, 2004, p. 260.
23. Mark Leonard, 'India Joins the West', *Prospect*, November 15, 2005, p. 10, accessed at http://www.cer.org.uk/articles/leonard_prospect_november05.html
24. Hubert Védrine, *Les cartes de la France à l'heure de la mondialisation*, Fayard, Paris, 2000, passim.
25. Raja Mohan, n. 20.
26. To the great discomfort and dismay of India, which rated itself at par with China, was treated at par with Pakistan by the Western powers under the framework of their two countries policy, which meant that any foreign dignitary visiting the South Asian Region would visit India and then go to Pakistan on the way back home or the other way round.
27. *The Hindu,* February 3, 2003. Premier Raffarin made it very clear that President Chirac insisted that he should make India as his first major destination and he was visiting India only and it was not part of a larger trip to the South Asian region as such.
28. Ministry for the Armed Forces, Government of the Republic of France, *French White Paper on Defence and National Security – 2013*, p. 56, accessed at https://www.defense.gouv.fr/english/dgris/defence-policy/white-paper-2013/white-paper-2013 on 10/10/2020.
29. Ayres, n. 6, pp. 1-2.
30. Ministry of External Affairs (MEA), Government of India, *Joint Statement Issued on the Occasion of the visit of the President Nicolos Sarkozy to India,* January 25-26, 2008, New Delhi, accessed at mea.gov.in/bilateral/multilateral-documents/ on 10/03/2015.
31. MEA, *Joint Statement issued by India and France on the occasion of the president Francois Hollande visit to country,* January 25, 2016, New Delhi, accessed at mea.gov.in/bilateral-documents/on 05/05/2016.
32. *Ministère de l'Europe et des affaires étrangèrs*, Government of the Republic of France, *The security council of the United Nations.* Permanent mission of France to the United Nations in New York, 2020, accessed at onu.delegfrance.org/ on 10/10/2020.
33. MEA, *Annual Report 2019-20*, p. 29, accessed at www.mea.gov.in on 27/5/2021.

34. MEA, *India-France: Partnership for the Future,* December 06, 2010, accessed at mea.gov.in/bilateral-documents on 13/05/2016.
35. Harsh, V. Pant, Macron and Modi: What France Can Do For India and What India Can Do For France, March 09, 2018, accessed at https://thediplomat.com/2018/03/macron-and-modi-what-france-can-do-for-india-and-what-india-can-do-for-france/ on 24/8/2019.
36. Shishir Gupta. India under Modi more likely to respond with military: US intel on Pak goading, March 09, 2023, accessed at https://www.hindustantimes.com/india-news/us-intel-fears-threats-to-india-from-china-and-pakistan-101678332957215.html on 14/3/2023.
37. *The Times of India,* (Bangalore), January 25, 2003.
38. Dipanjan Roy Chaudhury, Countries must dismantle terror hubs: India, France. *The Economic Times,* August 23, 2019, accessed at economictimes.indiatimes.com/news/on 11/10/2020.
39. Jean-Yves Le Drian's Lecture on "Indo-French Defence Partnership: the Choice of Strategic Autonomy" at New Delhi on July 26, 2013, accessed at https://idsa.in/keyspeeches/IndoFrenchDefencePartnership_Jean-Yves on 30/8/2019.

# 8

# Bootlegging in South Asia's Neighbourhood: The Eastern Himalayas and India's Northeast in focus

**Dr Anup Shekhar Chakraborty**

## I

### The Shifting Ideas of the Neighbourhood and Friendships

The inherited territorial geographies of South Asia are unclear and contested. In the 1980s and 1990s, Nepal anticipated that India would intervene when Bhutan's cultural nationalism resulted in the expulsion of Nepali-speaking Lhotsampas. Nepal accused India of not meddling in the affairs of its neighbour (Chakraborty, 2021a). Nepal has recently asserted sovereignty, visibility, and participation in neighbourhood politics, including the revival of the SAARC, a winding but uninterrupted route to the sea for landlocked BIMSTEC (Bay of Bengal Initiative for Multisectoral, Multilateral, and Multilateral Economic Cooperation) countries. Nepal desired geopolitical equidistance between South Asia and the Trans-Himalayas (Chakraborty, 2020).

India has prioritised pragmatic friendship to address the region's lack of trust. Democratic voices have demanded new geopolitical interpretations and a reevaluation of India's historical ties. Bhutan's "right to seek new friends" and protect its national interests, such as diversifying its foreign policy, is a topic of political debate. China is interested in Bhutan because some Bhutanese have been won over by China's soft power and future assurances. Friendship has been re-calibrated, customised, and made conditional, with or without reciprocal benefits. In South Asia, "neighbourhood ties" have always ranged from anxiety to hostility (Chakraborty, 2021b).

Bhutan engaged India while avoiding China's expansionism. Bhutan preferred economic talks with its southern neighbour over its northern neighbour. India's relations with its neighbours have changed as Bhutan, the "Norbu Dragon" (lit., peaceful jewelled dragon), changes and new democracies emerge. China wants to rebuild Himalayan trade and culture. China-Bhutan relations are strained. In 1988, the PLA occupied Bhutan and built roads. India supported the "Norbu Dragon" while the West ignored China's territorial expansion, which South Asia and the Indo-Pacific view as aggressive. In 2017, China invaded Doklam to undermine regional stability and India's trust. In Doklam, China exposed Bhutan's vulnerability. China seems interested in Bhutan. China's "debt diplomacy" and Sri Lanka, Pakistan, and a few African nations' experiences should concern proponents of the "right to look" for new allies. Before starting a new "dance," Bhutan should assess its "bromance" with its southern neighbour (Chakraborty, 2021a).

However, the region's friendships' recalibrations and customisations have little impact on material flow across borders and passes. Bootlegging is still common in the region. "Bootlegging" refers to smuggling, selling, and transporting illegal goods, but it originally meant smuggling and selling alcohol. Smugglers from Canada and the Bahamas brought alcohol into the US when it was illegal. In a specific historical context, a "bootleg" was an unlicensed audio or video recording distributed without the artist's permission. These recordings are usually made live. This kind of illegal activity creates a black market that defies legal norms. However, since the goods are cheaper and desired by a large portion of the population, the question of whether they should be legalised is being debated (as was alcohol at the end of the Prohibition era). "Bootlegging" today means bootleggers' illegal activity. Bootlegging is a common term for illegal activity that some people pursue as a career.

## II

## Disgruntled Geographies and Lung Dragon's Shadow's Flip Side

I call the Eastern Himalayan borderlands from North East India to Chin state and Sagaing region in Myanmar "disgruntled geographies" because of the interaction between the region's natural (heavily forested, mountainous, riverine, resource-rich) and human-made (linguistically and religiously diverse, split along sectarian lines, sparsely populated) features. Also, the region has seen a rise in the number of armed insurgent groups with unquenchable anger. This is because the region has limited or no connections, little industrial growth, and few job opportunities. The discussion tries to figure out how the multiple Patriarchies and their agencies create new maps of ethnic connections and cultural ties through 'regulated insularity' and 'control,' with the constantly changing geopolitical anchors of 'disgruntled geographies.' So, the discussion ties together assemblages of material cultures and social imaginations that operate covertly in the borderlands of North East India, and how they move from radical to analytical negotiations of their experience of colonialism, modernity, and the global market economy, and thus find their way into a slippery world of their own choosing (Chakraborty in Sengupta and Singh (ed.) 2022).

Ethnic insecurities have become institutionalised, and "rentier capitalism" and the enclosure of territories have become the new norm (Buchanan *in* Buchanan, Tollison & Tullock (eds.) 1980:3-15; Tullock *in* Buchanan, Tollison & Tullock (eds.) 1980:16-38). Alongside this, the region has witnessed an increase in the engagement of competing or contending patriarchies in the making of claims. In a paradoxical turn of events, the sizeable ethnic communities have been eagerly anticipating the opening of the borders and the erasure of 'Colonial lines' that have been crisscrossed around the region and have separated specific tribes in the area from cousins across the Chin Hills and South East Asia. Mizoram's Young Men's Association (YMA) just recently (in 2018) sent a letter to the governments at the centre and the federal units, requesting that they expedite the opening of the borders, increase the connectivities across the region through the Act East Policy, to bridge the people-to-people contact, and bring the *Zo hnahthlak* on the Indian side of the borders and those in the Chin Hills of Myanmar closer together.

The region of North Bengal, which serves as the gateway to the North-East via the "Siliguri-Coochbehar corridor," has not been incorporated into the region, despite the fact that it is geopolitically closer to the "North-East." However, the desire to be included within the region remains strong (as evident from the social imaginaries) among communities therein. This is an important point to note. For instance, in 2007, the West Delhi Police published a book with the title "*Security Tips for Northeast Students/Visitors in Delhi*" (Dholabahi, 2007; The Times of India, July 16, 2007). This book claimed "to help the people from the region to overcome the handicap of their 'foreign' features," which resulted in a great deal of anger among the students and the people of Darjeeling. It is in the light of this observation that I include Darjeeling and North Bengal as part of the "North-East" region even though they are not technically located there (Chakraborty and Chakraborty, 2016 *in* Banerjee *et. al.* (eds)).

## III

## A method for studying bootlegging: "Seeing like a Bootlegger"

How could the study of bootleggers be done? How could information be found out about bootleggers? How does the method or process work in detail? The intimidating nature of the study and the huge geographical scope of the research, which includes the differences found at multiple points of contact, such as differences in ethnicity, language, or the noise of bazaars and middlemen. All of this, along with how hard it is to travel through the different landscapes, led to the idea of a long-term study. The research grew and changed over the course of a decade. Changes in the subtle movement of materials and improvements in technology made it even more important to do a study that lasted a long time.

The research was carried out between the years of 2008 and 2022 using snowball sampling to contact individuals in multiple locations for in-depth, in-person interviews and longer conversations that were spaced out to accommodate the schedules of both the interviewer and the interviewee. The researcher could build rapport with the subjects over time and glean nuggets of information through casual conversation. This study was carried out as a multi-decade endeavour because of the breadth and depth of the problems that needed to be solved; and, as is customary in migration studies, it revealed trends in migration and movement of materialities within the country as well as to neighbouring countries and further afield, such as the South East Asian region.

This research has shed light on the intricate webbed nature of migrations, mobility, and the flow of materialities across the Eastern Himalayas. This research both challenges and confirms many commonly held beliefs about the reasons behind people's migrations from rural to urban and urban to metropolitan areas. By reexamining the social imaginaries of the region, the study adds another layer of complexity to the idea of mobility itself, which in this context refers to the movement of materialities across time and space. In addition to this, the study makes use of its ethnographic data in order to suggest potential future research directions and analytical implications pertaining to bootlegging and the flow of goods.

The respondents' intricate involvement in illegal activities necessitated the development of an additional significant strategy that I call "Seeing like a Bootlegger". In keeping with their activities, the strategy included concealing their identities as well as the geospatial operational sites from which they conducted their activities. As a result, the respondents' names and other identifying information have been changed, and the exact location where the survey was conducted has been obscured. In order to provide support for the assertions and observations made by the investigation, both primary and secondary sources, including articles from newspapers, were consulted.

Typical economic theories of regulation view government officials and regulators through the lens of intermediaries between competing interest groups (Kahn, 1988). The concept of "*Bootleggers and Baptists*" originates from the subfield of regulatory economics, which aims to foresee which interest groups will succeed in obtaining rules favourable to them (Smith and Yandle, 2014). The theory posits that competing groups are better off working together under a common rule than they are working separately.[1] Baptists play an active role in the administration of the laws they help to pass (a law against Sunday alcohol sales without significant public support would likely be ignored, or be evaded through bribery of enforcement officers). Therefore, bootleggers and Baptists is more than just a scholarly reiteration of the widespread political charge that undisclosed for-profit interests are using front organisations representing the public interest to advance their own agendas of deceit. Politicians and administrators are viewed as middlemen by the mainstream economic theory of regulation. Bootleggers and Baptists is a subfield of regulatory economics that attempts to predict which interest groups will be successful in obtaining rules favourable to them. It contends that coalitions of opposing interests that can reach an agreement on a common rule will outperform one-sided groups. Baptists do more than just advocate for legislation; they also help to monitor and enforce it. For instance, a law against Sunday alcohol sales without significant public support would likely be ignored, or be evaded through bribery of enforcement officers. Thus, bootleggers and Baptists is more than just an academic reiteration of the common political charge that shadow for-profit interests that hide behind public-interest groups to fund deceptive practices.

The neoliberal market and the freedom it affords are hidden from view in the "Throw-away culture" of convenience, 'Tragedy of the commons' propelling herd consumerism, and commodity fetishism. The market's primary motivation is making money, not protecting the environment (long or short term). In a post-global world, the neoliberal economy is solely motivated by profit, regardless of the impact on society or the environment. The term "Chinese Goods" refers to the finest example of "use and throw" products, also known as goods that have a short shelf life and are, for the most part, not repairable. At the very least, Chinese products have been around since the Song Dynasty, when the emperor mandated that his court wear be improvised and his hat and clothing system underwent rapid stylistic shifts after only a few years of use (*Hanfu Forum & Community*, 10 Oct. 2020). Chinese Goods are colloquially known by different names. In Nepal and parts of Darjeeling, Sikkim, and Kalimpong these Chinese products are known as "*Khasa ko maal*" (lit., product from Khasa). Khasa is a Chinese-controlled transit hub in Tibet. The commodity is portrayed in popular culture as something of low quality, possibly fake, quickly outdated, and sold at a low price. In Mizoram and adjoining areas these foreign items from China and the far-east are categorised as '*Khawchhak chuak', 'Khawthlang chuak'*. Terms based on cardinal directions reveal a boundary-aware subculture among Zo/Mizo peoples. Products from the near east, the south, and the far-east are referred to as '*Khawchhak chuak*,' '*Chhim lam chuak*,' and '*Khawthlang chuak*,' respectively. The terms '*Khawchhak chuak*' refers to Myanmar; '*Chhim lam chuak*,' to Thailand, Malaysia; and '*Khawthlang chuak*' to Bangladesh, Japan, Korea. In Manipur these items are called '*Moreh gi pot*' (lit., Moreh product) named after the transit town of 'Moreh' through which these materials enter the region.

## IV

## Bootlegging in the Himalayan Neighbourhood and around: '*Khasa ko maal*' in circulation

The '*trans-Himalayan trade and trade routes*' (von Furer-Haimendorf, (1975) 1988; Saxer, 2013) between Nepal and China that go through Tibet have come under increased Chinese control (*Kathmandu Post*, 24 Oct. 2022). The flow of transportation and materials coming from Lasha and Khasa has slowed down in Hilsa, Nagcha, Ko Rala, Gorkha Larka, Rasuwagadhi, Zhangmu-Kodari (Tatopani)[2], Lamabagar, Kimathanka, and Olangchung Gola. In the aftermath of the Tibetan uprising in 2008, all of these commercial hubs were eventually shut down, with the exception of Tatopani and Lamabagar. Post 2015 earthquake in Nepal, transit towns have come under China's control (MOFA Nepal).

According to Murton (2021), 'China trade includes the cross-border transportation of goods from Mainland China as well as the clandestine export of Chinese products to third countries.' This is in addition to the illegal movement of materials from China to Nepal known colloquially as *'Khasa ko maal'* (lit., goods from Khasa). The '*Khasa ko maal*' flows through the open borders in multi-directions and through a multiverse of interconnected highways through the region. The popular plains route connecting India and Nepal via Kakarvitta, Bihar-more to Siliguri, and the Duars. The other route is from Ilam (Nepal) to Darjeeling, Kalimpong, and Sikkim via the Pashupati-Mirik channel.[3] Though these China products are sourced from many other cities in China, they are labeled as '*Khasa ko maal*'.[4] Tibetan, Nepali, Bihari, Marwari, and Bengali traders and small businessmen are among the traders and bootleggers involved in North Bengal corridor. The reverse goods that flow from eastern Himalayas includes forest products, wildlife, banned pharmaceuticals from India, and the consignments channeled through the Northeast of India. The reverse flow experiences demonstrate deep imbalances as seen in the case of forest products such as the *Rudraksha* seeds to China (*Hindu Press International*, 28 May 2022).

Residents of the Chinese border town of Khasa, which was devastated by an earthquake, have been relocated to Xigatse, which is about 200 kilometres northwest of Khasa. The April 25, 2015 earthquake in Nepal had an impact on Khasa as well, and residents were forced to relocate as soon as possible after the quake. The earthquake struck Nepal's central and eastern regions. Few Nepali families who resided in the border region were relocated to Xigatse, while the remainder returned to Nepal. Recent reports indicate that the Chinese government is eager to rebuild Khasa and relocate mainland residents there. China intends to redevelop Nepal through investments in logistics that will enhance trade, transportation, and connectivity. This is a component of China's overall strategy in Nepal (MOFA Nepal).

The reverse goods that flow from Nepal and eastern Himalayas includes forest products, wildlife, banned pharmaceuticals from India, and the consignments channeled through the Northeast of India. The reverse flow experiences demonstrate deep imbalances in trade between Nepal and China caused by the absence of support from the Nepali government and the dominance of the Chinese market (*Hindu Press International*, 28 May 2022). The trade of *rudraksha* (dried seeds of the Elaeocarpus ganitrus tree) from the Himalayan foothills to China demonstrates this. Hindus revere these seeds known as *rudraksha* (lit., Lord Shiva's tears) in Sanskrit. *Rudraksha* beads have a special significance for Buddhists. This is because they are frequently depicted on the Buddha and other sacred figures in the area wearing them. In the past, Nepalese merchants sold the vast majority of the seeds to Hindus in India; however, this practice has recently begun to shift. Since 2014, Nepalese farmers and merchants have benefited financially from China's demand for seeds known as *bodhichitta rudraksha* (Buddhists' prayer beads). These seeds are sold in China's markets are a microcosm of the dynamics of the overall trade that takes place between the two countries, where Nepal is an exporter. Overall, China has a significant advantage over India in terms of the trade balance vis-à-vis Nepal. Between the middle of July 2021 and the middle of April 2022, Nepal imported a total of NPR (Nepali Rupee) 211 billion (1.7 billion USD) from China, as reported by the country's Department of Customs. In contrast, the total value of Nepal's exports to China during this time period was 622 million Nepali rupees (USD 5 million) (*The Third Pole*, 26 May 2022). The majority of Nepal's goods that are exported to China include hand-drawn paintings, carpets, medicinal plants, and sculptures. In the fiscal year 2020-21, Nepal exported a total of 280,874 kg of rudraksha seeds, which placed the country in tenth place among export categories (*The Third Pole*, 26 May 2022). China still makes money off the unofficial side of international trade. Nearly every respondent contacted for this study admitted to being involved in bootlegging activity in Nepal mentioned that they purchased items in large quantities from industrial and SEZ towns in China. China is a major manufacturer for international brands; the defective or flawed products that are produced there and packaged as "factory seconds" are then dumped to South Asia, where they are purchased in bulk by traders and middlemen who continue the cycle of bootlegging in the Eastern Himalayas.[5] They mentioned that their local Chinese contacts in China are located in cities such as Dongguan, Guangzhou, and Shijiazhuang.

Darjeeling, Kalimpong, Mirik (West Bengal), and Gangtok (Sikkim) in India are flooded with Chinese goods, including counterfeit. The availability of low-cost products that can be easily discounted by small shopkeepers makes it difficult for products manufactured in India or branded items with high prices to compete for customer loyalty.[6] Respondents who were contacted in the border trade zone of Pashupati (Indo-Nepal) en route to Mirik mentioned that drugs, gems, and gold were brought across the border in inventive ways. Consignments would be concealed in tin containers that were carrying *ghee* (clarified butter) or *gundruk* (indigenous nonsalted dry fermented vegetables; popular among the Nepali people) before being wrapped in polythene packets, which would then be sealed in plastic. Along the India–Nepal border, herdsmen transport water buffalo, goats, and other livestock while occasionally partaking in bootlegging and hiding shipments among the herds.[7] Because there was no border control, the movement of goods was unobstructed and uncomplicated.[8] Ecstasy (MDMA - Methylene DioxyMethyl Amphetamine), Amphetamine-Type Stimulants (ATS), banned pharmaceuticals - Phensedyl, and forest-based products are all transported throughout Bhutan using similar bootlegging strategies.[9] Many contraband items entering Bhutan are concealed in the tyres, spare tyres, toolboxes, or luggages of travellers.[10] Siliguri, Bagdogra, and the Kakarvitta-India-Nepal borders serve as hubs for drivers, handymen, and bootleggers to coordinate their activities and communicate with one another. While both sexes partake in bootlegging, women tend to have more success at it.[11]

## V

## Bootlegging in Disgruntled Geographies: Traces of the Lung Dragon

This section provides a microanalysis of the complex bootlegging activities that occur as a result of China's innocuous soft presence in South Asia's neighbourhood. This analysis is presented from the perspectives of several academic disciplines. The term "Asian transnational organised crime" refers to a variety of criminal groups and organisations, including "secret societies, tongs, triads, gangs, drug cartels, criminal networks, and so on," as well as "multiple goods and services that constitute criminal markets," such as "drug production and trafficking," "human smuggling and trafficking," "money laundering and debt collection," "vehicle crime and smuggling," and triad monopolies. The latter category consists of "multiple nations and national components," as well as "the control by various societies of private bus routes, fish markets, street markets, wholesale markets, second-hand clothes markets, entertainment centres, parking services, sales of counterfeit VCDs, prostitution, illegal gambling, and extortion and the violence that is associated with these crimes;" and "multiple markets and wholesale markets" (Finckenauer and Chin, 2007). Chinese authorities are concerned about drug bootlegging in the region, and they suspect that local and foreign-based drug syndicates are importing heroin from the neighbouring Golden Triangle and distributing it throughout China (Mu, Sun, and Amon, 2022). As criminal organisations become well-armed and violent, Chinese authorities are concerned about violent acts committed by mobsters against rival gang members, ordinary citizens, business owners, and government officials (Mu, Sun, and Amon, 2022). The region's criminal nexus spans the meandering international borders. According to bootleggers contacted from Chin (Myanmar) and Mizoram (India) for this study, the majority of these crime groups are Chinese and operate from Tahan (Myanmar). The nexus serves as a protective umbrella known locally as *baohusan*.[12] The nexus controls wholesale trade, labour recruitments and human trafficking/smuggling, parallel tax regimes in and out of the regions stretching from the South China Sea to Tibet and Nepal via northeast India.[13] The flow of materialities and trafficked persons flow in the opposite direction as well in the Asian Mediterranean routes to continental Europe and thereon to the USA.

Chinese officials take a muddled stance on human smuggling/trafficking in the region, despite the fact that tens of thousands of Chinese men and women are smuggled out of China every year and the arrival of large numbers of undocumented Chinese labourers or sex workers is a major concern in region (Smith, 1997; Kwong, 1997; Emerton, 2001; Brazil, 2004).Either brushing the problem under the rug as something normal or a regular issue in organised crime, or denying it entirely as not a Chinese problem because the majority of *snakeheads* (human smugglers) are Chinese-Americans (Chin, 1999). Both of these approaches are problematic for a number of reasons. One explanation is that it leads to willful ignorance of the problem and a stubborn refusal to acknowledge that one's own actions contribute to or even cause the region's problems.

### (a) Recreational drugs and Prescription drugs

People often use the term "Golden Triangle" to talk about drug smuggling in north-east India. It is known as one of the oldest and most dangerous ways that drugs get to Europe and other parts of the world. The region also produces the bulk of Southeast Asia's opium. Heroin is made in the Golden Triangle area of Burma, and it is then sent to the rest of the world through either Thailand or China. There is a market for heroin in China, which is growing quickly, and there are also markets in Australia and most of the countries in Southeast Asia. Methamphetamine is also made in the part of the Golden Triangle that is in Burma, but it is mostly sold in Thailand, which is its main market. Methamphetamine is brought into Thailand illegally through the border between Burma and Thailand, Laos, Cambodia, or both. Most of the amphetamine that is made is in China, but it is illegally brought into other Asian countries like Taiwan, Japan, the Philippines, and others.

The states of Nagaland, Mizoram, Manipur, and Arunachal Pradesh all have borders with Myanmar. The Indo-Myanmar border, which is approximately 1,643 kilometres long, acts as a point of transit for contraband goods travelling into the north-eastern part of the country. As a result of the trafficking of drugs into India from Myanmar, various agents in Dimapur, Imphal, Moreh, Churachandpur, Champhai, Vairegnte, Tlabung, Khawzawl, Silchar, Sonai, Shillong, Guwahati, and Siliguri are given consignments worth crores of rupees to distribute throughout their webbed network of active and sleeper suppliers. These are then subdivided further and distributed to various dealers throughout the states of Northeast India and North Bengal via the Silliguri corridor, after which they are taken to the metropolitan areas. When it comes to micro-operations, the difficulties that law enforcement agencies face in their mission to bring down drug cartels are significant. In addition, in order to deceive those who are responsible for law enforcement and security, bootleggers use unconventional methods of transportation. These methods include, among other things, motor vehicle engines, bumpers, and tyres. When communicating with their counterparts located in the disgruntled geographies, these suppliers hide behind aliases and various other fictitious names as an additional layer of protection. These people try to avoid being caught by using a number of different SIM cards, each of which is only used once before being thrown away. They do not use smartphones or GPS because they want to avoid detection and stay away from the radar of security and surveillance.[14]

Yaba tablets, a brightly coloured stimulant made of methamphetamine and caffeine, are bootlegged in the region. Myanmar's yaba production labs are mostly in Shandong, China (The Business Standard, 20 July 2022). Thailand imports most methamphetamine from Myanmar/Burma. Since the 1962 military junta, Myanmar has been a major methamphetamine producer (Dhaka Tribune, 25 Aug. 2022). Truckers and factory workers buy yaba pills. In 1989, Myanmar's military (Tatmadaw) and the rebel United Wa State Army (UWSA) signed a cease-fire. The UWSA and Myanmar's ruling junta stopped supplying drugs in 1989 in exchange for Myanmar's help fighting ethnic armies (The Business Standard, 20 July 2022). In the 1990s, mushroom labs across Myanmar continued to produce drugs (The Daily Star, 11 May 2018). The troubled state of Rakhine and the Sagaing Division, which produces a product called "World Is Yours," may have laboratories (The Daily Star, 11 May 2018).

The synthetic drug is shipped from Myanmar to Bangladesh via two Northeast Indian routes, according to past seizures. Yaba is one of many northeast Indian goods smuggled to Bangladesh. Mizoram's Champhai-to-India-Bangladesh border route is most popular. Tiddim, Mandalay, and Champhai SEZ are well connected. Narcotics are shipped from Bangladesh to North 24 Paraganas, Kolkata, and South 24 Paraganas in West Bengal by river.

Manipur, next to Myanmar's Sagaing Division, is the alternative route, respondents said. The political economy of the borderland ecology includes the Myanmar corridor for Chinese-invested drugs and commodities. The "Yaba Godfathers," also known as Jao pho, are Chinese-born drug dealers and agents in Myanmar and its neighbouring countries. They operate legally and illegally. They also have networks of associates and followers, close relationships with influential bureaucrats, police officers, and military figures, authority in the local administration, and a major role in democratic and institutional processes like elections.

Despite efforts, Myanmar's major arteries are still open. In Bangladesh's Cox's Bazar coastal district, tens of thousands of Rohingya refugees have several routes. Rohingyas bootleg Yaba (Pulitzer Center, 2018). Few Assam Rifles border post personnel reported that drug consignments like the Yaba are transported along illegal goods routes. The same gangs have smuggled many different goods multiple times. Myanmar's gold and heroin networks import Yaba and World Is Yours. The supply chain pattern suggests that many gangs are involved in illegal bootlegging. Trafficking groups near the India-Myanmar border collect the shipments. A chain of agents delivers these shipments to remote locations without knowing their origin. Bootlegging routes are immediately sought after older ones are made illegal. Illegal trade is common along the India-Bangladesh border due to low incomes and poor living conditions (Pulitzer Center, 2018).

Northeastern labs make phensedyl cough syrup illegally. Sting operations have identified the main perpetrators of these lab closures. This study found these labs still make illegal drugs for regional and international distribution. Respondents said the line between legal and illegal pharmaceuticals in Mizoram has blurred because the same person who works as a Medical Representative for a pharmaceutical company in a major Indian city also runs a local medicine manufacturing unit that makes counterfeit versions of legal medicines and occasionally banned pharmaceuticals. Drugs are smuggled from everywhere. Medical Representatives and Pharmacists in Mizoram profit from drug trafficking. Phensedyl overdose kills several people annually. Phensedyl traffickers sell to Bangladeshi addicts. Phensedyl enlarges the brain, blinds, and kills. After 2010, clandestine laboratories in north Bengal and the northeast began producing Ecstasy (MDMA - Methylene DioxyMethyl Amphetamine), ATS, dextropropoxyphene, injectable buprenorphine, diazepam, and nitrazepam, as well as licit opiate pharmaceuticals. Drugs from Myanmar, China, and Southeast Asia circulated in the northeast and major Indian cities until 2000. Authorities near Indian border SEZs and economic contact zones seized trucks carrying large amounts of the item several times. Before 2000, Chinese/Burmese women and men sold and bootlegged these substances through agents and suppliers, according to ex-servicemen. Traditional bamboo baskets used to transport piglets from Myanmar to Mizoram carried these substances during Christmas. Chinese drugmakers used the smuggled chemicals and raw materials in Myanmar. Distributing the finished product in India would follow the same route.

## (b) Wildlife and the Exotic

Bootlegging in disgruntled regions is aided by Southeast Asian wet market contacts and smugglers. Bootlegging is successful because of this. These people use India's northeast to smuggle endangered animals into the region (Sentinel Assam, 17 Oct. 2022). Multiple times, the forest departments of the region's states have saved endangered species. Each time, forest animals were saved from extinction. This suggests a risk to the species and ecosystem. The area's geography and forests make smuggling possible. Wildlife trafficking, the fourth greatest worldwide crime after drug, human, and counterfeit commodities, threatens endangered species' survival (IJCAR; Shankar 2022). From South America to Australia and Southeast Asia, gibbons, kangaroos, and exotic birds have been found in these habitats (The Diplomat. 22 June 2022; The Times of India; Down to Earth). Smugglers of endangered species remove animals from their natural habitats in Asia and sell them as pets or livestock at a profit of several million dollars annually (*North East India Broadcast,* 22 Aug. 2022). When the smugglers are caught by the authorities, they bribe their way to freedom and then immediately return to poaching. The illegal trade in wild animals, also known as "wildlife smuggling," places entire animal species in danger of extinction while simultaneously providing cover for the poachers who commit the crime.

According to Sawma, a former driver who was involved in bootlegging activity, "these consignments were for the pet trade, as well as private zoos and farms in India's blossoming metropoles."[15] Southeast Asian wet market contacts and smugglers smuggle wildlife into/through the region (*Sentinel Assam*, 17 Oct. 2022). Illegal wildlife trade ranks fourth after drug, human, and counterfeit goods trafficking (IJCAR; Shankar 2022). Gibbons, kangaroos, and exotic birds are smuggled through Eastern Himalayan borderlands (*The Diplomat*, 22 June 2022; *Down to Earth*, 14 April, 2022; *North East India Broadcast,* 22 Aug. 2022). When caught, smugglers bribe their way out and return to poaching. The illegal trade in wild animals, known as "wildlife smuggling," threatens animal species and provides cover for poachers. Most exotic animals enter Mizoram from Myanmar (*Northeast Now News*, 15 Apr. 2022).

As Chin Burmese merchants in Champhai (Mizoram) put it, "wildlife was smuggled out of India through Burma's forests from the 1970s to the 1990s." Ethnic insurgent groups poached and smuggled one-horned rhinoceros, golden langurs, tigers, elephants, and other forest-based products to supply China's pharmaceutical industry. "Today, the same routes and territorial passages have been rerouted and relabeled as multimodal highways in accordance with the Act East Policy." The same routes and jungle passages that once smuggled wildlife and forest produce from India to China and Southeast Asia now bring in exotic species for India's growing exotic pet market.[16]

### (c) Gold, Semiprecious gems, Betelnut/ Arecanut and Human Hair

A Talbung (Mizoram) resident Tlani mentioned the bootlegging method that was common in the 1980s in the region. 'Ethnic Chakma and Bru women would collect gold from intermediaries (*dalals*), which they would then break down into nuggets. Women bootleggers would ingest gold nuggets and cross guarded and unguarded borders to get to Chittagong (Bangladesh) or Tripura to Akhaura via Bairabi and Phuldungsei in Western Mizoram, where the gold consignments needed to be delivered. They would spend a few days there, consuming bananas and other laxatives to facilitate their expulsion through faeces.'[17] Recent trends in gold smuggling in the region reflect technological innovations, ranging from the use of condoms[18] to bootleg gold in paste form to the use of drones to air-drop consignments.[19]

In addition to seeking safety in Mizoram, Chin people from Tahan (Chin hill), Myanmar frequently cross the state's border to do business and commerce. They return to their homes on the Myanmar side of the border after trading their goods. Mizo people trade with Myanmar in a similar way. Betelnut/ Arecanut, cotton yarns, milk powder, sugar, malt-based health drinks, tinned condensed milk, and butter are just some of the many products that are smuggled into Myanmar.[20] There are both legal and illegal versions of these items floating around. Despite numerous opportunities, very few people were apprehended in Mizoram for possessing illegal goods. It was also discovered that families from Myanmar who cross the border to trade smuggled goods - contraband items - rely on Mizoram families. Bootlegged goods are those that have been imported or exported illegally from one country to another. They were also able to avoid being checked by border patrol agents on numerous occasions due to the porous and unfenced border. [21]

### *Some Concluding Observations*

Due to post-global connection and rapid technological progress, "illegal" transnational criminal networks have realigned, recalibrated, and restored their global presence by veering between legal and illegal, formal and informal. Non-state actors have always threatened states (Edwards and Gill, 2006). Authorities initially had no transnational crime plan. Military forces, border patrol, and intelligence deter non-state actors (Srikanth, 2016). States now "see and act like the non-state" and "see like a bootlegger" due to the post-global experience. Between 1960 and 1990, gold and semiprecious stones were the Indo-Myanmar route's main commodities. Gold and semiprecious stones like jade, rubies, emeralds, and sapphires were smuggled from Myanmar to Kolkata, Delhi, and Mumbai through the northeast. The junta in Burma/Myanmar forced ethnic communities and trafficked people to extract "blood gold and gems." The Indo-Burmese route exported blood gold and gems from Burma/Myanmar in the 1960s to 1990s. Myanmar produced 20–30 percent of the world's gold and 50 percent of its rubies by 1991. (Esterman, 2022). Observing regional bootlegging changes is fascinating. In the 1970s and 1980s, Chakma and Bru women bought gold from *dalals* and smelted it into nuggets. Bootlegging has changed with condoms for gold paste and drones for airdrops. Technology has shaped the neighbourhood's material movement patterns.

The Mizo and Chin of Tahan (Chin hill), Myanmar, bootleg betelnut/arecanut, cotton yarns, milk powder, sugar, malt-based health beverages, canned condensed milk, and butter. They're legal or illegal. Mizoram had few drug arrests despite many chances. Myanmar and Mizoram families trade illegally. Bootleggers bring in illegal goods through porous borders despite border patrols. This discussion highlights China's complex presence in the Eastern Himalayas and northeast India. China softly controls these unhappy communities. China has left an indelible mark, either as the driving force behind these new cultural idoms or as agents/intermediaries arranging the flow of alien cultural materialities, as shown by material movement and emergent culture manufacturing among ethnic or non-ethnic communities. The debate illuminates the neighbourhood's bootlegging web, including the flow of people and goods across borders and changing transit lines.

## References

'Border Security Force in Meghalaya Seizes 100 Kg Human Hair.' *Sentinel Assam*, 14 Apr. 2022, www.sentinelassam.com/north-east-india-news/meghalaya-news/border-security-force-in-meghalaya-seizes-100-kg-human-hair-587524.

'Composition of Song Dynasty Emperor's Clothing - Hanfu Culture.' *Hanfu Forum & Community*, 10 Oct. 2020, www.newhanfu.com/6147.html

'Dangerous Drug Yaba Invasion -1: Hostage to Myanmar.' *The Daily Star*, 11 May 2018, www.thedailystar.net/frontpage/hostage-myanmar-1575205.

'Do's and Don'ts irk N-E Students: IPS officer's Booklet Reinforces Stereotypes.' *The Times of India,* 16 July 2007.

'ED Busts Money Laundering Ring Linked to Human Hairs Smuggling to China.' *EastMojo*, 15 Feb. 2022, www.eastmojo.com/news/2022/02/15/ed-busts-money-laundering-ring-linked-to-human-hairs-smuggling-to-china.

'Exotic Wildlife Smuggling Through NE Into India on Rise.' *The Times of India*. www.timesofindia.indiatimes.com/india/exotic-wildlife-smuggling-through-ne-into-india-on-rise/articleshow/91157103.cms. Accessed 24 Oct. 2022.

'Expect More Surprises in Drugs Case.' *Deccan Herald*, 8 Sept. 2020, www.deccanherald.com/metrolife/metrolife-your-bond-with-bengaluru/expect-more-surprises-in-drugs-case-884557.html.

'Hair Smuggling Accused Holed up in Myanmar: Ed.' *Hyderabad News - The Times of India*, www.timesofindia.indiatimes.com/city/hyderabad/hair-smuggling-accused-holed-up-in-myanmar-ed/articleshow/89909729.cms. Accessed 24 Oct. 2022.

'Hair Worth Rs 2 Crore Smuggled Seized From India-Myanmar Border.' *India Today*, 30 Mar. 2021, www.indiatoday.in/crime/story/hair-seizure-tirumala-temple-india-myanmar-border-1785288-2021-03-30.

'How The Rudraksha Seed Captures Nepal's Trade Imbalance With China – Hindu Press International.' *Hindu Press International*, 28 May 2022, www.hinduismtoday.com/hpi/2022/05/28/how-the-rudraksha-seed-captures-nepals-trade-imbalance-with-china.

'Human Hair Smuggling From Hyderabad to China, ED Finds Trail.' *The Hindu*, 14 Feb. 2022, www.thehindu.com/news/national/telangana/human-hair-smuggling-from-hyderabad-to-china-ed-finds-trail/article65050003.ece.

'Illegal Human Hair Smuggling Racket Busted; Searches Held Across India.' *The Siasat Daily*, 14 Feb. 2022, www.siasat.com/illegal-human-hair-smuggling-racket-busted-searches-held-across-india-2275857.

'Kangaroos in Dooars! Is Jalpaiguri the New Wildlife Trafficking Hub.' *Down to Earth*, 14 Apr. 2022, www.downtoearth.org.in/news/wildlife-biodiversity/kangaroos-in-dooars-is-jalpaiguri-the-new-wildlife-trafficking-hub-82392.

'Liquid Cocaine From Brazil Being Smuggled in Delhi via Condoms.' *India Today*, 19 Apr. 2018, www.indiatoday.in/mail-today/story/liquid-cocaine-from-brazil-being-smuggled-in-delhi-via-condoms-1215342-2018-04-18

'Minister: Myanmar Junta Patronizing Smuggling of Yaba Into Bangladesh.' *Dhaka Tribune*, 25 Aug. 2022, www.dhakatribune.com/bangladesh/2022/08/25/minister-myanmar-junta-patronizing-smuggling-of-yaba-into-bangladesh.

'Mizoram: What Makes Champhai India's Wildlife Trafficking Hotspot?' *EastMojo*, 16 Sept. 2022, www.eastmojo.com/mizoram/2022/09/16/mizoram-what-makes-champhai-indias-wildlife-trafficking-hotspot.

'Myanmar Army Directly Involved in Trafficking Yaba to Bangladesh: Prof Imtiaz.' *The Business Standard*, 20 July 2022, www.tbsnews.net/bangladesh/myanmar-army-directly-involved-trafficking-yaba-bangladesh-prof-imtiaz-461982.

'Nepal's Trade With China Going Through Rough Patch.' *Kathmandu Post*, 24 Oct. 2022, www.kathmandupost.com/money/2022/02/05/nepal-s-trade-with-china-going-through-rough-patch.

'Nepal-China Relations.' *Ministry of Foreign Affairs Nepal (MOFAN)*, www.mofa.gov.np/nepal-china-relations. Accessed 24 Oct. 2022.

'Nepal-China Trade Imbalance Encapsulated by Rudraksha.' *The Third Pole*, 26 May 2022, www.thethirdpole.net/en/regional-cooperation/how-a-seed-encapsulates-nepal-china-trade-imbalance.

'No Exit: China's State Surveillance Over People Who Use Drugs.' *Health and Human Rights Journal*, 9 June 2022, www.hhrjournal.org/2022/06/no-exit-chinas-state-surveillance-over-people-who-use-drugs.

'Northeast Serving as Transit Route for Animal Trafficking, Says Assam Forest Official.' *Northeast Now News*, 15 Apr. 2022, www.nenow.in/north-east-news/northeast-transit-route-animal-trafficking-assam-forest.html.

'Northeast Serving as Transit Route for Animal Trafficking, Says Assam Forest Official.' *Northeast Now News*, 15 Apr. 2022, www.nenow.in/north-east-news/northeast-transit-route-animal-trafficking-assam-forest.html.

'Porous Borders Making Northeast Hub of Wildlife Trade.' *Sentinel Assam*, 17 Oct. 2022, www.sentinelassam.com/topheadlines/porous-borders-making-northeast-hub-of-wildlife-trade-618517.

'Smuggling of Exotic and Endangered Species From Myanmar Increasing.' *The Diplomat*, 22 June 2022, www.thediplomat.com/2022/06/smuggling-of-exotic-and-endangered-species-from-myanmar-increasing.

'Wildlife Trade in Northeast India With Special Reference to Herpetofauna and Some Measures of Control to Check the Trade.' *NE India Broadcast*, 22 Aug. 2022, www.neindiabroadcast.com/2022/08/22/wildlife-trade-in-northeast-india-with-special-reference-to-herpetofauna-and-some-measures-of-control-to-check-the-trade.

'Wildlife Trafficking for Trade in North East India: A Case Study.' *International Journal of Current Advanced Research (IJCAR).* www.journalijcar.org/issues/wildlife-trafficking-trade-north-east-india-case-study. Accessed 24 Oct. 2022.

'Yaba: The Red Pills and the Rohingya.' *Pulitzer Center*, 5 July 2018, www.pulitzercenter.org/stories/yaba-red-pills-and-rohingya.

Buchanan, James M. 1980. '*Rent seeking and profit seeking*' (pp. 3-15) in James M. Buchanan, Robert D. Tollison, & Gordon Tullock. (eds.). (1980). *Toward a theory of the rent-seeking society*, College Station: Texas A & M University.

Chakraborty, Anup Shekhar and Subhas Ranjan Chakraborty. 2016. *'Ambiguous Identities: Statelessness of Gorkhas in North-East India'.* (pp. 207-45) in Paula Banerjee, Anasua Basu Ray Chaudhury & Atig Ghosh, (ed.). (2016).*The State of Being Stateless: An Account of South Asia.* New Delhi: Orient Black Swan Pvt. Ltd.

Chakraborty, Anup Shekhar. 2020. 'Nepal-India Virtual Neighbourhood 'Halla Gulla'' *Multidimensions Magazine.* 19 July 2020. https://multidimensionmagazine.com/2020/07/19/nepal-india-virtual-neighbourhood-halla-gulla/ accessed on 15.05.2021.

Chakraborty, Anup Shekhar. 2021a. 'Dance of the Dragons and the Bromance: Friendships in the Neighbourhood.' *Multidimensions Magazine*. 04 January 2021. https://multidimensionmagazine.com/dance-of-the-dragons-and-the-bromance-friendships-in-the-neighbourhood/ accessed on 15.05.2021.

Chakraborty, Anup Shekhar. 2021b. 'Olipath, Centrality and Trust Issues: India-Nepal Muddled Neighbourhood Friendship.' *Multidimensions Magazine*. 26 September, 2021. https://multidimensionmagazine.com/olipath-centrality-and-trust-issues-india-nepal-muddled-neighbourhood-friendship/ accessed on 15.05.2021.

Chakraborty, Anup Shekhar. 2022. '*Muddled Friendships and Disgruntled Geographies: Lung Dragon in the Neighbourhood*' (pp. 139-153) in Anita Sengupta and Priya Singh (eds.) (2022). *Asia Matters 2: China in India's Neighbourhood.* Kolkata: Asia in Global Affairs. https://www.asiainglobalaffairs.in/wp-content/uploads/2022/08/Asia-Matters-2-final.pdf

Dholabahi, Nishit. 2007. 'Police Booklet for the Northeast students betrays prejudices: Delhi 'profiles' to protect', *The Telegraph*, 10 July 2007.

Edwards, Adam, and Peter Gill. 2006. 'Transnational Organised Crime.' *Perspectives on Global Security*, 2006, https://doi.org/10.1604/9780415403399.

Esterman, Isabel. 2022. 'Analysis: Myanmar's Gemstone Riches Bring Poverty and Environmental Destruction.' *Mongabay Environmental News*, 25 April. https://news.mongabay.com/2022/04/analysis-myanmars-gemstone-riches-bring-poverty-and-environmental-destruction/.

Finckenauer, James O., and Ko-Lin Chin. 2007. *Asian Transnational Organised Crime*. https://doi.org/10.1604/9781600214608.

Gelbard, Robert. 1998. '*Burma: The booming drug trade.*' in Robert Rotberg (ed.). (1998). *Burma: Prospects for a Democratic Future*. Washington, D.C.: Brookings Institution Press.

Kahn, Alfred E. 1988. *The Economics of Regulation: Principles and Institutions*. Cambridge, Massachusetts: MIT Press.

Lin, Mu, Nina Sun, and Joseph, J. Amon. 2022. 'No Exit: China's State Surveillance over People Who Use Drugs.' *Health and Human Rights Journal* 24/1 (June 2022). https://www.hhrjournal.org/2022/06/no-exit-chinas-state-surveillance-over-people-who-use-drugs/.

Lintner, Bertil. 2003. *Blood Brothers: The Criminal Underworld of Asia*. New York: Palgrave McMillan.

Murton, Galen. 2021. 'A Himalayan Border Trilogy: The Political Economies of Transport Infrastructure and Disaster Relief Between China and Nepal.' 3 June 2021, escholarship.org/uc/item/01t8w749.

Shankar, Priyanka. 2022. 'Why Is India a Major Hub for Wildlife Trafficking?' *Mongabay-India*, 8 June www.india.mongabay.com/2022/06/explainer-why-is-india-a-major-hub-for-wildlife-trafficking.

Smith, Adam, and Bruce Yandle. 2014. *Bootleggers and Baptists: How Economic Forces and Moral Persuasion Interact to Shape Regulatory Politics*. Washington, D.C.: Cato Institute.

Srikanth, H. 2016. 'Combating Transnational Crimes in the Era of Globalisation: Strategies for India and the ASEAN.' *International Studies, 53(2), 91–104. https://doi.org/10.1177/0020881717728157*. accessed 24 Oct. 2022.

Tullock, Gordon. 1980. '*Rent seeking as a negative sum game.*' (pp.16-38) in James M. Buchanan, Robert D. Tollison, & Gordon Tullock. (eds.). (1980). *Toward a theory of the rent-seeking society*. College Station: Texas A & M University.

## Notes

1. The regulatory economist Bruce Yandle proposed the term "Bootleggers and Baptists" to describe the two types of people who tend to support regulations: those who want the regulation's stated purpose, and those who stand to gain financially by undermining it.
2. The Zhangmu-Kodari border (also known colloquially as Tatopani in Nepal and Kasa or Dram in Tibet) was the first and, up until the 2015 earthquakes, largest border crossing between China and Nepal. Opened in the1960s with the construction of the Arniko Highway and the China–Nepal Friendship Bridge, this post has traditionally handled more than 80 percent of direct transnational trade between China and Nepal (however, a greater overall quantity of goods continues to come from China to Nepal via sea routes to Kolkata).Transferring an array of household, commercial, and industrial goods destined for Kathmandu, on a normal day dozens of Chinese trucks off load cargo in Zhangmu a critical step in an international exchange that is 90 percent import and only10 percent export for Nepal.
3. *Personal Interviews*: Krishna; Ram; Balram; Khansahab; Pyare. (Businessman selling Chinese goods). Bagdogra/Siliguri/Darjeeling/Kurseong/Gangtok. 15 March 2014.
4. *Personal Interviews*: Krishna; Ram; Balram; Khansahab; Pyare. *Ibid.*
5. *Personal Interviews*: Krishna; Ram; Balram; Khansahab; Pyare. *Op.cit.*
6. *Personal Interviews*: Krishna; Ram; Balram; Khansahab; Pyare. *Op.cit.*
7. Rupen Tamang. *Personal Interview*. Thamel, Kathmandu, Nepal. 26 July 2019; Bhim Thatel. *Personal Interview*. Thamel, Kathmandu: Nepal. 29 July 2019; Tenzing Bhutia. *Personal Interview*. Kalimpong: West Bengal. 11 November 2012; Rajen Biswakarma. *Personal Interview*. Lalitpur: Nepal. 27 July 2019.
8. Dhondup Bhutia. *Personal Interview.* West Bengal Police. Darjeeling: West Bengal. 05 March 2021; ShedupTamang. *Personal Interview.* West Bengal Police. Darjeeling: West Bengal. 05 March 2021; Rajiv Khambu. *Personal Interview*. Mirik: West Bengal. 08 November 2013.
9. Zigmi. *Personal Interview*. Royal Bhutan Police, Thimpu: Bhutan. 28 March 2018.
10. Sherub. *Personal Interview*. Royal Bhutan Police, Punakha: Bhutan. 30 March 2018.
11. Diki. *Personal Interview*. Businesswoman, Thimpu: Bhutan. 29 March 2018; Chimi. *Personal Interview*. Businesswoman, Thimpu: Bhutan. 29 March 2018; Chomu. *Personal Interview*. Businesswoman, Punakha: Bhutan. 30 March 2018; Tenzin. *Personal Interview*. Businessman, Punakha: Bhutan. 30 March 2018.
12. Pakunga. *Personal Interview*. Aizawl: Mizoram. 10 January 2008; Ruata. *Personal Interview*. Aizawl: Mizoram. 10 January 2008.
13. Kawla. *Personal Interview*. Shillong, Meghalaya. 24 February 2020; Roberta. *Personal Interview*. Shillong, Meghalaya. 24 February 2020; Thari. *Personal Interview*. Shillong: Meghalaya. 20 February 2020; Sawma. *Personal Interview*. Shillong: Meghalaya. 14 February 2020.

14. Tahair Alam. *Personal Interview*. Guwahati: Assam. 11 February 2020; Deka. *Personal Interview*. Guwahati: Assam. 11 February 2020.
15. Sawma. *Personal Interview. Op.cit.*
16. Pari. *Personal Interview*. Champhai: Mizoram. 24 January 2008; Zela. *Personal Interview*. Champhai: Mizoram. 24 January 2008; Ngura. *Personal Interview*. Champhai: Mizoram. 24 January 2008.
17. Tlani. *Personal Interview*. Tlabung: Mizoram. 11 January 2010.
18. Rema. *Telephone Interview*. Aizawl: Mizoram. 03 March 2022.
19. Nguri. *Telephone Interview*. Aizawl: Mizoram. 03 March 2022.
20. Zela. *Personal Interview*. Champhai, Mizoram. 26 January 2008; Ngura. *Personal Interview*. Champhai, Mizoram. 25 January 2008.
21. *Personal Interviews*: Zela; Ngura. *Op.cit.*

# 9

# Rise of Modi and Nepal–India Relations

**Prof Dhan Prasad Pandit**

Nepal and India share close and friendly relations characterised by age-old historical and cultural linkages, open border, and deep-rooted people-to-people contacts. The multifaceted relations between the two countries have renewed momentum in the last few years through intensified high-level political exchanges; regular meetings of bilateral mechanisms across diverse sectors of cooperation. The two countries are expanding their economic and development partnership, boosting connectivity, cooperative initiatives in water resources and hydropower sectors, defence, and security. No two countries of the world are as closely interdependent as India and Nepal. This is so because the relations between the two countries are fundamentally based on people-to-people relations rather than government-to-government relations. Because of this factor, even the occasional ruptures that arise in their relations at the government-to-government level get resolved soon. Nevertheless, there is no point in complacency amidst a situation in which different vested interest groups are trying to spoil such amicable relations.

## Historical connection of Nepal-India Relations

Historically, the Treaty of Sugauli governed the foreign relations of Nepal with India, during the British rule. Later after India's independence, the Indo-Nepal Treaty of Peace and Friendship established formal relations. The India-Nepal Treaty of Peace and Friendship is the most important pillar of the bilateral relations between India and Nepal. The last Rana Prime Minister of Nepal and the Indian Ambassador to Nepal signed the Treaty consisting of 10 articles in 1950. The treaty stands on the premise that both countries will maintain everlasting peace and friendship and recognizes each other's sovereignty, territoriality, and independence. According to Articles 6 and 7 of the Treaty, it was agreed that the nationals of the countries would be treated with the same privilege that they offer their citizens. This enabled the Indian and Nepalese to move freely across the open borders without any passport or visa. They can live, work and own property in either country.

During the 1950s India's influence on Nepal continued to grow. However, the royal family of Nepal was wary of India's growing influence, and after 1962 Sino-Indian war the relations between India and Nepal got severely affected (Savada,1991). During the 1960s, the situation became more stressful with Nepal questioning the security arrangement and asking India to withdraw the security check posts. India did withdraw its military check posts and liaison group in the 1970s (Singh, 2009). The tensions were much visible in the mid-1970s when Nepal condemned the annexation of Sikkim by India (Singh, 2009). After this, Nepal under the leadership of King Birendra Bir Bikram Shah Dev proposed that Nepal should be recognised as a "Zone of Peace" where military competition would be forbidden. This proposal was immediately supported by Pakistan and China. However, India remained silent on this as this was a sign of distrust for the treaty, which was signed in 1950. Despite such views, the proposal got the support of 112 countries in the 1990s. Some of the sources of dissatisfaction among the Royal family of Nepal were that India was sponsoring the opposing parties of Nepal and allowing them to launch campaigns against Nepal from its soil.

There was a major dispute between Nepal and India regarding the trade and transit treaty. Nepal refused to accommodate a single treaty for trade and transit resulting in hardline positions taken by both countries. With time, India put forth economic sanctions on Nepal (Savada,1991). During the late 1980s, Nepal decoupled its rupee with the Indian Rupee as well as India denied the port facilities in Calcutta. According to some sources, the GDP growth of Nepal was reduced to 1.5 percent which was 9.5 percent earlier (Blanchard and Norrin, 2013). Another reason for this political squeeze on the part of India was its dissatisfaction with Nepal imposing a permit rule for Indian citizens entering to work in Nepal. During 1988; it also attempted to get close with China by acquiring weaponry from it (*The New York Times*, 11 April 1989).

This situation prompted India to reconsider its economic relations with Nepal, which were at their worst phase. This could even have security implications for it. Nepal also realised the huge economic loss that it was bearing due to its strenuous relationship with India. A transformation in

Nepal's political system was also seen during this period. The King was forced to transition to parliamentary democracy. This phase saw a revival of friendly relations with India as the parties were pro-India. During the 1990s, Nepalese Prime Minister Girija Prasad Koirala visited India and treaties of separate trade and transit were signed along with other economic agreements, which benefitted Nepal. During the 2000s, the relations soured a bit during the rule of King Gyanendra, however relations were normalised with the visit of Prachanda in 2008.

During the 2010s the relations became amicable. India and Nepal pushed for a three-tier- mechanism i.e. ministerial, secretary, and technical levels, with regard to water resources. There have been perceptions in India regarding the increased Maoism and the influence of China which it alleges has separated Nepal from India.

## Nepal-India Relations Changes and Challenges Post the Rise of Modi

After the overwhelming votes gathered by the Bhartiya Janata Party in 2014, Mr Narendra Modi was appointed as the Prime Minister of India. Modi visited Nepal in August 2014 as a part of its "Neighbourhood First Policy". The visit was highly successful and Modi became the first foreign leader to address the constituent assembly of Nepal. Under Narendra Modi, India demanded some amendments in the constitution of Nepal. However, with the election of K P Oli as the Prime Minister there was evidence of a growing rift in Nepal-India relations. Therefore, in 2015 India and Nepal relations saw another downfall. India talked about its concerns over the new constitution and carried out an unofficial blockade preventing crucial supplies from entering the country. Oli clearly criticised the move and in response to the blockade signed a trade and transit agreement with China. Thus, playing the "China card", Oli swiftly tried to end India's monopoly on essential goods (Rae, 9 October 2021).

Nevertheless, we also witnessed India's quick response during the destructive earthquake that struck Nepal. It provided Nepal with relief assistance worth US$ 67 million (Jaiswal, 16 August 2017). In reality, India and Nepal relations are much higher than the treaties and agreements. Both countries have frequently organised visits and interactions which has reflected the importance that both accord to each other. However, there have been changes in the relations between India and Nepal after the rise of Modi. In fact, the relations have witnessed a crisis as Modi raised concerns on Nepal's constitution and the economic blockade came into the picture creating widespread anger among the Nepalese. This act was seen as interference in its sovereignty and resulted in a failed policy of keeping the neighbourhood first. In order to facilitate connectivity and strategic influence, India had to revise its relations with its neighbours.

In 2018, India and Nepal signed three new agreements on agriculture, connectivity, and railways. Both countries termed these three agreements as "path-breaking". The inauguration of a petroleum pipeline between Nepal and India was also carried out. However, both sides kept away from some key bilateral issues. After the second visit of Prime Minister Oli, a joint 12-point statement was issued. Before the visit, there were speculations that Oli would consider a revision of the 1950 Treaty of Peace and Friendship as this agenda formed a big part of what Oli promised during the election campaigns. He demanded the "resetting and redesigning" of relations with India. There were some clear messages sent to India during this visit:

- It upheld the sovereignty of Nepal and indicated that mutual respect is the key to friendly relations. Interfering in the internal politics of each other can have a drastic impact on bilateral relations.
- Oli represented the need for greater economic diplomacy in order to enhance the growth and prosperity of Nepal. Both countries should focus on economic and cultural issues rather than more hardline political issues (Bhattarai, 5 November 2021).

Since Sher Bahadur Deuba came to power there have been no top-level visits between India and Nepal. The ruling party also invited Bhartiya Janata Party's Foreign Affairs Department Chief Vijay Chauthaiwale where he met other top leaders of Nepal (Bhattarai, 5 November 2021).

The current ruling party of India has clearly indicated that it is willing to support Nepalese parties that are pro-Hindu. Some Nepali congress leaders also visited India and met External Affairs Minister S. Jaishankar as well as Uttar Pradesh Chief Minister Mr Yogi Aditya Nath. This visit was important as it helped the ruling party of Nepal to build party-to-party relations and also learn from BJP's organisation building. This meeting also provided Nepal an opportunity to raise certain key concerns. Deuba also met Modi on the sidelines of COP26 in Glasgow, where he invited Modi to Nepal.

In January 2021, the sixth meeting of Nepal-India Joint Commission (JC) was organised to discuss various bilateral issues such as COVID-19 vaccines, boundary and border management, connectivity, trade, culture, and education. After the meeting, India provided one million doses of Covid shield vaccine to Nepal.

## Recent High-level Exchanges

Indian Prime Minister Shri Narendra Modi has visited Nepal four times since 2014 and similarly, Nepalese Prime Ministers have paid their visits to India. There were two phone calls between the prime ministers of India and Nepal in 2021, including one to congratulate Mr Sher Bahadur Deuba on becoming prime minister on July 19, 2021. Both leaders also met in Glasgow, UK on 02 November 2021, on the sidelines of the COP26 Climate Summit and discussed ways to further strengthen the multiple aspects of the bilateral cooperation, including in the context of ongoing efforts against the Covid-19 pandemic. In fact, PM Deuba had visited India once during each of his four previous terms as the Prime Minister of Nepal and this was his fifth visit to India, in his fifth term as the PM of Nepal.

The engagement between Nepal and India was further strengthened with high-level visits and virtual meetings of various bilateral mechanisms. Indian External Affairs Minister Dr S. Jaishankar and the Foreign Minister of Nepal Dr Narayan Khadka had a bilateral meeting on the sidelines of UNGA in New York on 25 September 2021 and both held a telephonic conversation on 07 January 2022 to exchange New Year 2022 greetings and discuss bilateral cooperation between the two countries. Indian External Affairs Minister his remarks at the International Conference on Reconstruction of Nepal (ICRN) on 07 December 2021, as the largest partner of Nepal's recovery in the aftermath of devastating Earthquake in 2015. Earlier in 2021, the sixth meeting of the Nepal-Indian External Affairs Minister Joint Commission was co-chaired by the External Affairs Minister of India and the Minister of Foreign Affairs of Nepal in New Delhi on 15 January 2021.

Indian Foreign Secretary Shri Harsh Vardhan Shringla visited Nepal from 26 - 27 November 2020 and the Indian Chief of Army Staff General MM Naravane visited Nepal from 04-06 November 2020. In turn, the Chief of Army Staff of Nepal, Gen. Prabhu Ram Sharma visited India from 09-12 November 2021 on the invitation of his counterpart and was conferred with the rank of Honorary General of the Indian Army by the President of India, in continuation of age-old unique tradition between the two countries.

Some recent bilateral engagements include Project Monitoring Committee (JPMC) meeting on Earthquake reconstruction (September 2021, Talks between the Border Guarding Forces of the two countries (October 2021), India-Nepal Working Groups on Defense and Security issues (October 2021). Likewise, Railway Cooperation (October 2021), Joint Working Group (JWG) and Joint Steering Committee (JSC) on Power Cooperation (23-24 February 2022), Joint Steering Committee meeting on

Fertilizers (15 March 2022), JPMC on Hetauda Polytechnic (March 2022), Joint Commission on Inundation and Flood management (09-13 March 2022), JWG on Petroleum and Natural Gas (07 March 2022) also hold between two countries. The 15th edition of India-Nepal Joint Military Training, Exercise Surya Kiran between Indian Army and Nepali Army was conducted in Uttarakhand during September-October 2021.

## Collaborative Concerns

India remains Nepal's largest trade partner, with bilateral trade crossing US$ 7 billion in FY 2019-20. India provides transit for almost the entire third-country trade of Nepal. India's export to Nepal has grown over eight times in the past 10 years while exports from Nepal have almost doubled. Despite the difficulties due to the pandemic, India ensured an uninterrupted flow of trade and supplies to Nepal.

Nepal is India's 11th largest export destination, up from 28th position in 2014. In FY 2021-22, it constituted 2.34 percent of India's exports. In fact, exports from India constitute almost 22 percent of Nepal's GDP. Nepal's main imports from India are petroleum products, Iron & Steel, Cereals, Vehicles, and Parts, Machinery parts. Nepal's major items of exports include Soyabean oil, Spices, Jute fiber & products, synthetic yarn, and tea. India and Nepal concluded a Memorandum of Understanding (MoU) for long-term supply of Urea and DAP fertilizers from India to Nepal under a G2G arrangement on 28 February 2022.

Indian firms are among the largest investors in Nepal, accounting for more than 33 percent of the total FDI stock in Nepal, worth nearly USD 500 million. There are about 150 Indian ventures operating in Nepal engaged in manufacturing, services (banking, insurance, dry port, education, and telecom), and power sector and tourism industries. India and Nepal also signed the Double Taxation Avoidance Agreement, DTAA) in November 2011. The bilateral remittance flow is estimated at approximately $ 3 billion (Nepal to India) and $ 1 billion (India to Nepal).

From an economic standpoint, the pandemic has highlighted two crucial and contentious aspects of bilateral relations. It is the widening of Nepal's trade deficit with India and the country's porous borders. As the territorial dispute widens, these issues are gaining new prominence. Despite the border issue, the visit of Nepal's foreign minister to India successfully directed the sixth meeting of the India-Nepal Joint Commission.

Significantly, there has also been an improvement in the front of commerce, trade, and economic affairs between Nepal and India in the post-COVID-19 period. Because of the liberal attitude exhibited by the Indian government, Nepal for the first time started to export surplus electricity to India. Earlier, Nepal used to import power from India. Now, since quite a few other hydropower projects are likely to start their production, the chances of further exports of hydropower to India are high. Exports of hydropower to India have opened a new prospect of earning revenue from India, which could, to a certain extent, bridge the gap in the balance of trade with India. So far, the balance of trade between the two countries remained in favour of India.

Over and above, there has also been a substantial increase in Nepal's exports to India. India accounted for a 64.6 percent share in Nepal's total exports in 2018–19, which shot up to 71.75 percent in 2019-20 and further to 75.75 percent in 2020–21. During the first four months of 2021–22, the volume of Nepal's exportable items to India further increased to 81.5 percent. During the same period, Nepal's imports from India reduced to 59 percent in the first four months of the current fiscal year, which in 2018–19, 2019–20, and 2020–21 was nearly 66 percent. Nepal could have exported more to India, but because of its limitations to producing goods on a large scale, it was limited to 81.5 percent. Nepal performed well on the export trade front because India allowed the imports of goods from Nepal even at a time when several countries had imposed restrictions on the exports and imports of goods from this country due to COVID-19-related cases. Goods exported by Nepal are mostly produced by medium and small enterprises.

Significantly, many of those Nepalese who could not return to India due to the closure of the Nepal-India border during the COVID-19 period were allowed to enter India thereafter. Estimates are that six to eight million Nepalese, especially from the hill region of the country, get employment opportunities in India. Nepal receives a huge amount of remittance from these people. Because of the lack of data, it is not known how much remittance Nepal receives from India, but it is well known that the inflow of remittance has contributed substantially to poverty reduction in the country. Just within that last seven years, Nepal was able to reduce its poverty to half.

Foreign Direct Investment has been important for the economic development of Nepal. Investors have invested in sectors like tourism, hydropower, construction, etc. Nepal's location and ecology have always been a point of attraction for countries like India and China. This has been due to the availability of young and very affordable supply of labour and the diverse climatic conditions, which are favourable for investments in different sectors. It is also a great tourist attraction for both Indian and Chinese travelers.

Recently, there has been a large Chinese investment in Nepal. It has even surpassed Indian investment by three times. There was no FDI from India during the period of 1996-2006. So, India's investments in Nepal haven't been very significant. Indian investments are also behind the race accounting for 30 percent of the total FDI in Nepal. Some of the major Indian investments in Nepal include Surya Nepal, Dabur, Hindustan Unilever, State Bank of India, LIC, etc. It has also made investments in the hydropower sector. Many Hydropower projects are under work.

FDI in Nepal has been lower as compared to other countries having access to the sea due to the low investment cost. Since Nepal has been sandwiched between India and China, which are among the fastest-growing economy in the world, it is beneficial for Nepal to attract investors who are capable to export goods to these two Asian giants.

## Nepal-India Border and Borderland Communities During COVID-19

Nepal shares a border (1880 km) with India on the south, east, and west and with China (1439 km) on the north. While the border with India is open, the mighty Himalayas constitute the frontier with China. Nepal is 23 and 68 times smaller than India and China respectively. Nepal's population of 29 million is almost 46 times smaller than India's and 49 times smaller than China's. Nepal is among the landlocked and least developed countries. The nearest seaport is 1,127 and 2,700 kilometers away in India and China respectively. Kathmandu, the capital city of Nepal is 3,000 km away from Beijing and 900 km away from New Delhi. Nepal's location is of extreme strategic and economic importance to both of them. Nepal's land mass ranges from 57.3 meters at Musarniya in the south to 8848.86 meters' elevation of Sagarmatha (Mount Everest) in the north (Bhattarai, 2022).

In a speech at election rally at Uttarakhand last year, Modi stated that India has built a road and is planning to expand it via Lipulekh to Manas Khand which is a gateway to reach Man Sarovar, a Hindu pilgrimage in Tibet. Although the sole aim of Modi to claim the disputed region as a part of his initiative was to attract Hindu vote, it created widespread anger in Nepal (Poudel, February 2022).

India had also laid down claims of the territory of Lipulekh previously. After the up rise and concerns rose in Nepal, India released a press statement that they would only communicate via the established channels and the "most appropriate" venue for dialogue. In response to this, Nepal's foreign ministry also released its statement and reaffirmed its claim of three territories- Limpiyadhura, Lipulekh, and Kalapani. It demanded that India stop its construction activities in these territories.

This border dispute dates back to 2015, during the trade and transit agreement made between China and India (Poudel, February 2022). Nepal protested this by stating that it was a clear violation of its territorial integrity. The dispute revived again when India released a new political map in 2019 (Poudel, February 2022). In 2020, Nepal too issued a new map including the territories. The government led by Oli termed it a "historic moment" for Nepal and even circulated the new map to be published in school books (Bhattacharjee, 20 May 2020).

The territorial dispute is a major issue of concern in India-Nepal relations. Although the current Prime Minister of Nepal Sher Bahadur Deuba has remained silent on this dispute and is often pressured by the opposition parties led by Oli to speak up and make this a priority issue. Both countries should make efforts to solve the border dispute diplomatically. This is a political issue and cannot be solved merely through secretary-level discussions. Mr Modi clearly refused to accept the final report of the Eminent Persons Group (EPG), which consists of experts from both countries. In long term, such irritants in India-Nepal relations can cause anti-Indian nationalism in Nepal, which can harm the age-old friendship to a significant extent.

There is an open border regime along 1880-kilometer-long Nepal-India boundary. It has twenty major border crossing points to cross the international border. Nepalese and Indian borderlands community inhabitants could cross the porous border from anywhere many times a day without any obstruction and interrogation before the COVID-19 pandemic. During the coronavirus epidemic transitional period, the border was more or less restricted. Now, the border crossing points have been vigilant, i.e., neither fully opened nor strictly regulated, after pandemic cases have gone down.

There are more than six million Nepali people working in India in various capacities such as security guards, domestic workers, hotel restaurant waiters, industrial guards, porters, agriculture helpers, etc. In the same way, near about four million Indians are working in various parts of Nepal as school teachers, carpenters, masonry workers, plumbers, electricians, furniture makers, etc. They could come and go to their home for their livelihood without any obstruction. If the border police would suspect someone, he/she should produce his/her identity proof.

It was not necessary to show any identity proof by Nepali and Indian citizens, nor keep records of the movement of people while crossing the international border before Covid-19 pandemic. But the border had been closed since 24 March 2020 from both sides, when the Covid-19 pandemic started to spread. The border was still formally restricted, even though the lockdown is released officially on 21 July 2020. Nevertheless, the local frontier inhabitants could cross the border on foot. The border police do not care about them. Cargo trucks with foodstuff, fruits, vegetables, and merchandise were permitted to enter from either side. However, passenger vehicles had been still interrogated and they were asked to go to the border health desk. The number of armed police personnel patrolling had been increased to supervise and check-up the movement of borderland inhabitants with fear of transmission of the pandemic. Now, Covid-19 cases have decreased by a considerable number and the border between Nepal and India is more or less relaxed.

During the COVID-19 pandemic period, the situation of the border management system changed dramatically. The open and porous border was changed into a completely closed border system on both sides due to coronavirus pandemic. Formerly, Nepal had deployed 5,000 Armed Police Force (APF) along the border, establishing 120 BoPs, 6 to 10 kilometers apart in the plain area and 8 to 15 km apart in the hilly region. It had deputed 40 APF personnel in each BoP on average. Whereas, India had deployed 45,000 special security bureaus (SSB) with 530 BoPs, 2 to 4 km apart having 85 personnel in each and every BoP. There had been deputed immigration and customs officers, intelligentsia, and security personnel at the border crossing checkpoints.

During the effect of coronavirus spread beyond the border, the open and porous border system was changed into a completely closed border regime from both sides. Following the lockdown, which was announced on March 24, 2020, simultaneously in both countries, there was a restriction on cross-border travel. However, the cargo vehicles had been relaxed to and from one country to the other. In course of time, there were nearly 500 Nepalese stranded at the Indian frontier, as the border was restricted. However, after undergoing a general health examination-using thermal imaging devices, RDT, and PCR, those who were qualified were allowed to cross the Nepali border.

During the Covid-19 pandemic period, Nepal border security force was expanded to 22,000 personnel from 8,000. It had been added 320 temporary BoPs to make 500 numbers during the pandemic to vigil and obstruct the movement of people from India. However, special passes were provided by the local body and district administration to borderland community inhabitants to go to the funeral and ritual purposes on the other side of the border.

The Lockdown ended on 21 July 2020 in Nepal, with some restrictions in coronavirus much-affected areas, and continued to suspend public transport vehicles. However, Nepal-India border crossing gates were closed and somehow restricted the movement of people on surface routes as well as air routes. Nepal's government decided to continue the ban on people's movement across Nepal's border with India and China till 15 December 2020. (*Himalayan Times Daily*, 2020). Now, COVID-19 cases have more or less subsided and the number of BoP has gone down to 175 numbers with 10,000 armed police personnel. Nepalese workers started to travel to Indian cities for jobs, as they were out of work in their hometowns and other cities of Nepal. More than 140 Nepalese entered India at the Gaddha Chowki border point on November 17, 2020, according to border area security authorities. They were traveling to their Indian workplace.

The borderland communities were unhappy, as the border was closed for eight months during the coronavirus pandemic. Border closure had affected also the wedding programme of the borderland inhabitants. For example, twenty-year-old Nepalganj Municipality inhabitant Ali Shaiyad's marriage had been stalled for months and months. Scheduled to tie the knot with a boy across the border in April, the wedding was postponed indefinitely as the border was closed due to the coronavirus pandemic. The postponed wedding ceremony was held after the border crossing movement was relaxed to some extent.

Indian frontier community people were aggressive during Covid-19 spread period. They were not allowed to cross the border for their daily livelihood, or take their domestic animals on the other frontier for grazing and grass cutting. A group of 40 Indian community inhabitants tried to infiltrate the Nepali frontier from the Malangawa Municipality Bhediyari crossing point. Armed police BoP personnel stopped them towards the Indian frontier not letting them to enter into the Nepali territory. But they were furious and they hurled stones and logs on Nepali armed policemen. Indian national Mohan Yadav attacked Nepal Armed Police Force constable who was patrolling the border on 22 April 2020. The policeman was wounded on his head. In the meantime, the miscreants were driven away with the help of Indian SSB personnel.

On April 23, eight Nepali nationals returning from India forcefully tried to enter Belahiya, Nepal side. Nepal Police took them into control and they were sent back from where they had entered and ultimately handed them over to Indian Police. They were taken to Subash Chandra Junior

High School quarantine center at Sunauli No-man's land. Indian nationals 43-year-old Kodai Mullah, and 35 years of age Din Dayal fled away from the Nepal Siddhanagar Municipality-3 quarantine camp on 23 April 2020.

On 24 April, 152 Indians, who were staying in Bhairahawa (Belahiya Nepal side) quarantine were permitted to enter into Sunauli Indian side. Similarly, 296 Nepalese staying in Nautanuwa quarantine (Indian side) were brought to the Nepal side. They were examined by rapid diagnostic test (RDT), polymerase chain reaction (PCR) and Thermal Guns.

During the pandemic, however, the two nations became entangled in a border dispute, which began in November 2019 when India issued a new political map, which included the Kalapani, LipuLekh, and Limpiyadhura as part of Indian territory and was passed by its parliament. Nepal objected, claiming that Kalapani, LipuLekh, and Limpiyadhura belonged to Nepal by the Sagauli Treaty and that India should not use unilateral actions to hurt the sentiments of Nepali citizens. The newly constructed 80-kilometer route from Dharchula in Uttarakhand to Lipulekh increased tensions between the two countries. In return, Nepal revised its constitution in 2020 and published a new political map that claimed Kalapani, LipuLekh, and Limpiyadhura as Nepali territories, as well as three Indian villages as part of Nepal.

## China and Nepal-India Relations

While both India and China have their interests in Nepal, it is important for Nepal to continue balancing its policies in such a manner that it serves the twin interests of stability and development for its own country. For Nepal, mutual trust is the key to good bilateral relations with both India and Nepal. It seeks to bring investment in the country from both its neighbours for rapid economic development. Apart from investment and economic cooperation from both countries, one of the greatest concerns is COVID-19, which has certainly resulted in Nepal seeking vaccines from India. China which is rapidly increasing its footprint in South Asia also agreed on delivering the Sino pharm vaccine to Nepal (WION, 8 June 2021).

Thus, interdependence between India and Nepal is the key to improved bilateral relations. More than India, Nepal is dependent on it. There is an urgent need to revitalise cultural relations with India. This would not only attract Indian investments in Nepal but also increase the economic activities between them. This is a great way to engage India and create a conducive environment for interdependence. This aspect provides a great leeway to India as compared to China when it comes to developing cordial relations with Nepal.

## Conclusion

India-Nepal Relations after the rise of Modi have witnessed several ups and downs. The onus of improving the relations between countries lies on the leaders of political parties. The leaders must act wisely and objectively to improve bilateral relations. Although every relationship is bound and analyzed by historical ties, but when most of the baggage is negative the leaders need to free themselves of the old mindset. Nepal has always been an ally of India since British times, but it has its own foreign policy which is based on sovereignty. Nepal demands a more refined bilateral relationship with India. The inability to fulfill the aspirations of Nepal has certainly pushed it to enhance its relations with China, which certainly considers Nepal as an important ally for its own strategic objectives. This indicates that though people-to-people ties have mainly governed India-Nepal relations but there is also a need to boost the government-to-government ties. In order to achieve a high level of cordiality, both countries should sensitively understand each other's concerns. Both countries should adopt an approach where they should not resort to extreme means of manifesting dissatisfaction, for example, the economic blockade on part of India and the disputed map revealed by Nepal which claimed some territories of India. There is a need for both countries to understand the importance of each other's support not only to maintain regional stability but also to promote each other's interest globally.

## References

Bhattacherjee, Kallol (20 May, 2020). Nepal's new political map claims India's territories, The Hindu.

Bhattarai, Dinesh (2022). Understanding the primacy of geography in the conduct of foreign policy, Journal of Foreign Affairs, Vol. 2, Issue-1, March 2022, Institute of Foreign Affairs, Kathmandu, pp. 10.

Bhattarai, Kamal Dev, 5 November 2021. Nepal's New PM Deuba Seeks Better Ties with India, The Diplomat.

Blanchard, Jean-Marc F, Norrin M. (18 July 2013). Economic Statecraft and Foreign Policy. ISBN 978-1136225819.

Coronatracker (2022). Nepal Overview. Retrieved from: https://www.coronatracker.com/country/nepal/

Himalayan Times Daily, 20 November 2020.

Himalayan Times Daily, 24 November 2020.

Jaiswal, Pramod (16 August 2017). India-Nepal Relations: Mixed Fortunes, Institute of Peace and Conflict Studies.

JBR, Madhukar Shumsher (2014). FPRC Journal, 2014 Vol. 3 Retrieved from: https://www.fprc.in

Kantipur Daily, 18 November 2020.

Kantipur Daily, 22 March 2020.

Kantipur Daily, 26 April 2020.

Kantipur Daily, 26 April 2020.

Kathmandu Post Daily, 2 April 2022. Retrieved from: https://tkpo.st/3wZAsKy

Khanal, Giriraj & Thapa, Bir Bahadur (2017). Immigration Officer and Area Police Inspector respectively, Belahiya Border Check-post.

Nagarik Daily, 19 April 2022.

Nagarik Daily, 4 August 2014.

Nepal Government Health Bulletin, 24 November 2020.

Poudel, Santosh Sharma (9 February 2022). India-Nepal Territorial Dispute Flares up Again, The Diplomat.

Rae, Ranjit (9 October 2021). Resetting Nepal-India ties, The Kathmandu Post.

Savada, Andrea Matles, ed. (1991). "Foreign Policy: India", Nepal: A country study, GPO for the Library Congress.

Shrestha, Buddhi Narayan (2003). Border Management of Nepal, Bhumichitra Mapping Co. Ltd, Kathmandu, pp. 107.

Singh, Raj Kumar (2009). Global Dimensions of Indo-Nepal Political Relations: Post Independence. ISBN 9788121210256

The New York times. 11 April 1989. "Nepal's Economy is Gasping as India, a Huge Neighbour, Squeezes it Hard".

WIONm (8 June 2021). "Nepal resumes vaccination campaign with China's Sinopharm.

# 10

# Geopolitical Risk pertaining to India's Immediate & Distant Neighbours: A Review of Geopolitical Risk Management Practices of Selected Indian Listed Companies

**Dr. Nitin S. Kulkarni and Ms. Dharmishta Gala**

## Introduction

India has made significant progress since Independence (World Bank)[1]. The present status of the Indian Economy is elevated to lower middle-income from initially low-income nations. The current economic size of India is around 3 trillion United States Dollar (USD) and home to 1.4 billion people. Indian Per Capita GDP (Gross Domestic Product) is USD 2,256.6 with a Human Development Index of 0.63.

The Land border of India is shared with different countries such as Pakistan, Afghanistan, Bangladesh, Bhutan, Myanmar, Nepal and China. These countries could be termed as India's immediate neighbours. The land border runs into 15,106 Kms while the coast line is around 7,516 Kms. The land border is not a mere simple line but is a mixture of different terrain and topology which includes mountains, hilly areas, forests, deserts and marshy lands. With the presence of hostility due to disputes arising out of territorial issues, monitoring such vast and complex border is an issue.[2]

Whatever is applicable to the land border is valid for the Coast Line. India has a coast line of 7,517 Kms of which 5,423 Kms belongs to main land India while 2,094 Kms coastline represented by the chain of islands pertaining to Andaman, Nicobar, and Lakshadweep.[3]

This complex situation is aggravated further as India's maritime boundaries are shared with seven countries Pakistan, Maldives, Sri Lanka, Indonesia, Thailand, Myanmar and Bangladesh. Since Independence India has constantly faced trouble at the Western and North Western Sector front and perennial border dispute with China on the North East side as well as on the high altitude Ladakh sector. Geopolitics is a trinity of the relationship between Geography, History and Strategy (Sloan, 2017 as cited in Devaki Nandan, et. al, 2022)[4]. The geographical location of India is of real significance as it connects to South East and Far East Asia, West Asia and Africa through sea. India is an important trade and business partner with her neighbours and plays an important role in regional as well as international geo-economic and geo-strategic dynamics. The Indian Ocean Region has rapidly become one of the foremost policy priorities for India's foreign policy. The Indian Ocean Region which is currently one of the world's busiest sea routes carrying nearly fifty percent of the global container cargo, two thirds of the oil shipments and home to many developing and emerging economies. The current turbulent geo-political environment leads to geo-political risks which are affecting the Indian Economy and business. In the last 30 years India rose substantially on the global business landscape with many Indian companies having access to the international markets. The international geo-political developments act as business disruptions affect the performance of Indian companies through the transmission of global shocks and effects. The history of the troubled neighbourhood makes things difficult for the Indian companies who operate in the region. The following words by the former Indian Prime Minister Late Shri Atal Bihari Vajpayee "We can change history but not geography. We can change our friends but not our neighbours." clearly expresses the state of environment in which Indian companies operate. Today due to the advent of technology and digital transformation, India is able to develop good relations with far flung economies considered as distant neighbours such as the USA, Japan, and Australia to name a few.

**Table No 1: India's Immediate & Distant Neighbours**

| Sr. Nos. | Accessibility | Neighbours and Neighbourhood |
|---|---|---|
| 1. | **By Road** | Nepal, Pakistan, Bhutan, China, Myanmar, Bangladesh |
| 2. | **By Road & Sea** | China, Pakistan, Sri Lanka, Africa, Maldives, Bangladesh Iran, and GCC. |
| 3. | **By Multimodal Transport (Road, Sea, Rail & Air)** | Afghanistan, CIS, Central Asia and Eurasia |

| | | |
|---|---|---|
| 4. | **By Sea & Air** | Europe, Africa, Global South |
| 5. | **Digitally Connected** | USA, UK, Europe, Australia, Japan, and ASEAN, |

*Source:* Desk and Library research done by the Authors.

The Table No. 1 explains the connectivity of India's Immediate, Distance, Extended and Digitally connected neighbours and neighbourhood. In today global business environment, the connectivity plays a major role in facilitating commerce, economics and trade between the countries.

**Table No. 2: India & Her immediate Neighbours at a Glance**

| Sr. Nos. | Particulars | India | Sri Lanka | Pakistan | Bangladesh |
|---|---|---|---|---|---|
| 1. | GDP in USD (billions) | 3176.30 | 88.93 | 348.26 | 416 |
| 2. | Population estimate (million 2021) | 1407.56 | 22.16 | 231.40 | 169.38 |
| 3. | GDP Per Capita (USD in thousands) (2021) | 2277.43 | 3814.72 | 1537.94 | 2503.04 |
| 4. | Human Development Index (2020 Report) | 0.633 | 0.782 | 0.544 | 0.661 |
| 5. | Total Exports (Billion USD) (2020) | 660.50 | 14.99 | 34.57 | 44.39 |
| 6. | Total Imports (Billion USD) (2020) | 725.55 | 21.39 | 69.04 | 71.02 |
| 7. | Total reserves (includes gold, current US$ in billion) (2020) | 638.48 | 3.14 | 22.81 | 46.17 |
| 8. | Market Capitalization in USD (Trillions) | 2.59 | 0.016 | 0.033 | 0.089 |
| 9. | Global Innovation Index Rankings | 40 | 85 | 87 | 102 |

*Source:* Desk and Library research done by the Authors[a]

**Table No. 3: India & Her immediate Neighbours at a Glance**

| Sr. Nos. | Particulars | India | Nepal | Bhutan | Afghanistan |
|---|---|---|---|---|---|
| 1. | GDP in USD (billions) | 3176.30 | 36.29 | 2.54 | 14.79 |
| 2. | Population estimate (million 2021) | 1407.56 | 29.67 | 0.78 | 40.10 |
| 3. | GDP Per Capita (USD in thousands) (2021) | 2277.43 | 1222.88 | 3000.78 | 516.75 |
| 4. | Human Development Index (2020 Report) | 0.633 | 0.602 | 0.666 | 0.478 |
| 5. | Total Exports (Billion USD) (2020) | 660.50 | 1.89 | 0.69 | 0.36 |

| | | | | | |
|---|---|---|---|---|---|
| 6 | Total Imports (Billion USD) (2020) | 725.55 | 14.01 | 1.08 | 0.46 |
| 7 | Total reserves (includes gold, current US$ in billion) (2020) | 638.48 | 9.66 | 1.06 | 9.75 |
| 8 | Market Capitalization in USD (Trillions) | 2.59 | 0.021 | 375 million | NA |
| 9 | Global Innovation Index Rankings | 40 | 111 | 96 | - |

*Source:* Desk and Library research done by the Authors[b]

**Table No. 4: India & Her immediate Neighbours at a Glance**

| Sr. Nos. | Particulars | India | China | Myanmar | Maldives |
|---|---|---|---|---|---|
| 1. | GDP in USD (billions) | 3176.30 | 17734 | 65.09 | 5.14 |
| 2. | Population estimate (million 2021) | 1407.56 | 1412.36 | 54.81 | 0.52 |
| 3. | GDP Per Capita (USD in thousands) (2021) | 2277.43 | 12556.33 | 1317 | 8994.64 |
| 4. | Human Development Index (2020 Report) | 0.633 | 0.768 | 0.585 | 0.747 |
| 5. | Total Exports (Billion USD) (2020) | 660.50 | 3548.55 | 1498 | 1.85 |
| 6. | Total Imports (Billion USD) (2020) | 725.55 | 3089.62 | 1314 | 2.56 |
| 7. | Total reserves (includes gold, current US$ in billion) (2020) | 638.48 | 3427.93 | 7.27 (Gold Reserve) | 0.81 |
| 8. | Market Capitalization in USD (Trillions) | 2.59 | 13.21 | 0.032 | 0.0017 |
| **9.** | Global Innovation Index Rankings | 40 | 11 | 127 | - |

*Source:* Desk and Library research done by the Authors[c]

The Table Nos. 2, 3 and 4 highlights some of the Socio-Economic parameters of India's neighbouring countries. Except China, Pakistan and Bangladesh, the other neighbouring countries are relatively smaller in size with some of the mentioned parameters that are not substantially significant as against India. The Following Tables no. 5 and 6, explains that despite India's historical connect and linkages through trade relations with neighbouring countries, in comparison with China it is still a very negligible number.

**Table No. 5: INDIA's Bilateral Trade and Investment with her immediate Neighbours**

| Particulars | Srilanka | Pakistan | Bangladesh | Nepal | Bhutan |
|---|---|---|---|---|---|
| Trade in USD Billion | 5.45 | 0.516 | 18.2 | 11.005 | 1.422 |

*Source:* Desk and Library research done by the Authors

**Table No. 6: INDIA's Bilateral Trade and Investment with her immediate Neighbours**

| Particulars | Afghanistan | China | Myanmar | Maldives |
|---|---|---|---|---|
| Trade in USD Billion | 0.72 | 135.98 | 1.894 | 0.323 |

*Source:* Desk and Library research done by the Authors

From Table No. 5 and 6, it is evident that except for China and Bangladesh, India's trade and investments with its immediate neighbours is not significant. There may be many reasons for relatively low level of investment and trade of India with its immediate neighbours as against distant neighbours such as USA and Europe. Though India enjoys deep historical, cultural, and linguistic ties with each neighbouring country yet the knowledge deficit about neighbours, China's increasing footprint, negativity about India, long festering bilateral issues and serious governance deficits leading to instability and regime change, affects India's relationship with neighbouring countries (Chandra, 2020)[5]. This results into low level of trade and investment by Indian companies especially those are part of Nifty-50 Index in India's immediate neighbours

The current study made an attempt to understand the geo-political risks faced by some of the Indian companies which are a part of National Stock Exchanges Nifty-50 Index. The acknowledgement of such risks would help Indian companies to devise and define the Risk mitigation strategies so as to minimize the shocks and losses arising out of the volatile, uncertain, complex and ambiguous-VUCA environment and BANI ('brittle', 'anxious', 'nonlinear' and 'incomprehensible) world

## Literature Review and Conceptual Framework of the Study

Geopolitics is a complex term with multiple meanings and definitions. It is the study of the diverse fields such as geography, politics, strategy and history combined to generate the rise and fall of the great powers and wars among states. (Benner, 2010)[6]. The geopolitical events have an immense impact on the economic development which is reflected in the definition of geopolitics suggested by Werner J. Cahnman (1943)[d] as "Historic forces operating within a geographic framework are supposed to condition political action which, in turn, is to determine the course of economic development.

Throughout history it is observed that geopolitical events affect economic development and capital markets. It has not only affected the way in which business has been conducted but also impacted the place of economic activity. The Amsterdam stock exchange lost its premier status to the London Stock exchange in the late 17th and 18th century owing to the series of wars Netherland had with Britain and France. The London stock exchange and the city lost its status of importance in the field of International Finance post the international crisis and the onset of World War-I, The Eurocurrency market and Eurodollar came into the existence in late fifties as due to political reasons, as former Soviet Union preferred to hold the dollar funds in London instead of being in USA (Joshi, 1998)[7]. The first oil price rise shock of 1973 was the result of OPEC proclaim embargo which was targeted at nations that had supported Israel during the Yom Kippur War. The fall of the former Soviet Union in 1991 and the liquidation of the socialist bloc resulted in economic and political liberalization, open competition and increased mutual cooperation for development, which gave rise to a new economic activity in international relations.[e]

The events of 9/11 changed the world much in terms of safeguarding the safety and security and also impacted certain sectors such as Aviation, Automobiles and supply chain logistics. (Rice, 2018)[8]. The head of TATA Group which has its business presence in many countries, Mr. Ratan Tata acknowledged India's firm stand post Uri Terror Attack in which 18 Indian Soldiers - Jawans were killed, to boycott SAARC summit which was supposed to be held in Islamabad, Pakistan in November 2016. It is worth noting that, The Mumbai Terror attack on 26/11 one of the targets was TAJ Mahal Hotel (Indian Hotels) which is a part of TATA Group.

The Russia-Ukraine War which started in February 2022 has severely impacted the world economy in terms of Rise in Fuel, Food and Fertilizer Prices that resulted in Inflationary pressures in many economies and subsequent hike in Interest Rates which hampers the economic growth.

Due to the invasion by Russia, in March 2022 the US and the EU cut off seven Russian banks from SWIFT. A country whose banking system is cut off from SWIFT has a very difficult time moving money, and thus goods, in or out, and can thus suffer significant economic pain.[f]

The Classical Geopolitical Risks is expressed by CEND-Confiscation, Expropriation, Nationalization and Deprivation (Toksöz, 2014)[9], yet in recent times following risks are pertaining to the field of Politics and Geo-Politics as explained in the Table No. 6 below:

**Table No. 7: Different Types of Political Risk**

| Sr. Nos. | Type of Risks | Description |
|---|---|---|
| 1. | Geopolitics | Interstate wars, great power shifts, multilateral economic sanctions and interventions |
| 2. | Internal Conflicts | Social unrest, ethnic violence, migration, nationalism, separatism, federalism, civil wars, coups, revolution |
| 3. | Laws, regulations, policies | Changes in foreign ownership rules, taxation, environmental regulation, national laws |
| 4. | Breaches of Contract | Government engaging on contracts, including expropriations and politically motivated credit defaults |
| 5. | Corruption | Discriminatory taxation, systemic bribery |
| 6. | Extraterritorial reach | Unilateral sanctions, criminal investigations and prosecutions |
| 7. | Natural resource manipulation | Politically motivated changes in supply of energy, rare earth minerals |
| 8. | Social activism | Events or opinions that "go viral", facilitating collective action |
| 9. | Terrorism | Politically motivated threats or use of violence against person, property |
| 10. | Cyber Threats | Theft or destruction of intellectual property, espionage, extortion, massive disruption of companies, industries, governments, societies |
| 11. | Global Energy | Politically decided supply and Demand Issues |
| 12. | Unknown/Uncertainty | Effects of Global warming, Effects of demographic changes and Political events that cannot be foreseen |

*Source:* Sr. Nos. 1 to 10 Condoleeza Rice and Amy B. Zegart (2018)
Sr. Nos. 11 & 12 Bremmer and Keat (2010)

The Table no.7 indicate that their different events which shapes the Geopolitical risks, which makes them very difficult to understand and measure as it builds over a period of time. These risks tend to be underpriced by the financial markets. Geopolitical risk is a constant, but in the midst of a pandemic, a war in Europe and a climate transition that is not nearly as advanced as it needs to be, the nexus between geopolitics, economics and business seems to have tightened. The U.S. remains the largest power economically, militarily and diplomatically, but China is rising and may threaten each of these. All this is against a backdrop of poor global economic performance, with a recession looming in the U.S. and Europe and with China set to post its weakest growth in decades[10].

The collapse of empires and long-running autocratic regimes are also linked with increased level of Geopolitical and Political risks (Toksöz, 2014). The exceptional economic growth of a particular country or a continent increases the demand for natural resources such as oil, gas, water, food, fertilizer and even land mass, this increases the geopolitical risk further. In recent time's weaponization of Trade, Energy, Food, Oil and Financial markets & Systems, Blocking of the Channel of Communication and Supply Chain are also posing a great threat in terms of geo-political risk.

Some of the most dangerous geo-political risks that are emerging currently are,

1. The Tension Between China and Its neighbours over border dispute
2. The Trade disagreement between China and its Trading Partners
3. The High Sky and Deep & Distant Sea surveillance activities of China
4. Russia and Ukraine Dispute
5. The Rogue and Failed states
6. The Emergence of Non-State actors causing potential havoc.

In this context, geopolitical risk has a clear meaning for business: It is the potential for international political conflict to threaten the financial and operational stability of companies around the world. To develop a framework to mitigate this risk, MNCs must understand the specific nature of the relationship between corporate globalization and geopolitics, map the "sites of risk" for corporations in their activities, and adopt forecasting tools to enhance their enterprise resilience with respect to threats from conflict and terrorism. CEO leadership is crucial to advancing this process.[11]

**Table No. 8: India's Immediate Neighbourhood Issues and Concerns**

| Neigh-bouring Country | Bordering States of India | Current Geopolitical Issues faced by neigh-bouring country | Repercussions to India |
|---|---|---|---|
| **Afghanistan** | Jammu and Kashmir | Disputed border due to illegal activities carried out by POK & has strategic control over their trade routes. | Natural gas is supplied through Trans-Afghan gas pipeline through Afghanistan & Pakistan in India from Turkmenistan (has largest underdeveloped oil & natural gas) through Afghanistan & Pakistan.[g] |

| | | | |
|---|---|---|---|
| | | | Due to this geopolitical, geo-economic, and geostrategic rivalry, there is a lack of synergy to peace, prosperity, stability and humanitarian development in this region<br>India has vital economic, strategic, cultural interests and seeks to maintain energy needs and connectivity. |
| **Bangladesh** | West Bengal, Mizoram, Meghalaya, Tripura,and Assam | Rohingya refugee crisis.<br>Chinese investment on various infrastructural developments.<br>River water disputes (Teesta River water sharing), aiding illegal immigrants, and drug trades | Border Security Issues |
| **Bhutan** | Arunachal Pradesh, Assam, Sikkim, and West Bengal | Border Dispute between China and Bhutan over Doklam located near their tri-junction with India | Very Important for India's security due to incidents like as Doklam |
| **China** | Jammu & Kashmir, Himachal Pradesh, Uttrakhand, Sikkim, and Arunachal Pradesh | China & Taiwan tension, Belt & Road Initiative, Sino-Indo rivalry. | India- China border issue in Ladakh region. India is fearful about the regional security and rise in terror activity, separatism & extremism as China joins hand with Afghanistan to help develop political structure.[h] |
| **Myanmar** | Arunachal Pradesh, Manipur, Mizoram, and Nagaland | Rohingyas issue | India's outreach to Myanmar risks its relations with Bangladesh. |
| **Nepal** | Sikkim, West Bengal, Bihar, Uttar Pradesh, and Uttrakhand | Porous Border | Chinese footprints in Nepal, a cause of concern. |
| **Pakistan** | Jammu and Kashmir, Punjab, Gujarat, and Rajasthan | Deep economic and political crises. | Threat of Terrorists activities in the Indian Territory |
| **Sri Lanka** | Separated from India by Gulf of Mannar | Facing Economic Crisis and Internal tensions. | India is also dependent on the Colombo port for global trade as 60 per cent of India's trans-shipment is handled by the port. |

| | | | |
|---|---|---|---|
| **Maldives** | The south-west part of the Indian Ocean below the Lakshadweep Island | Climate Change and an existential crisis. Amplifying the India Out campaign. | Issues pertain to the safety and security and a strategic location in the Indian Ocean |

*Source:* Desk and Library research done by the Authors.

In today's turbulent context every nation has a set of geo-economic goals and objectives and another set of non-geo economic goals and objectives, which it seeks to attain. (Chauhan, 2022)[12] It is important to note that there are linkages between geography and geopolitical turbulence (Braithwaite, 2007)[13] and India's geographical location justifies it.

Neighbours will be sensitive towards India by creating effective and enduring foreign policy based on incentives. India has many bilateral issues with its neighbouring countries, still India can be a significant player by revised Foreign Policy, less intervention and taking advantage of political shifts. India can utilize its strengths to its fullest by increasing efficient cross border connectivity for seamless transit of people and goods, opening more to trade and transport which will lead to stronger dependency on India (Saran, 2022).[14]

As the business community faces a lot of challenges in Sri Lanka, CEOs of Indian companies point to "enormous scope" for foreign direct investment in various sectors including information technology, tourism and renewable energy. Mr. Prakash, President of the Indian CEO Forum which includes 70 companies out of which 38 are Indian companies and others are multinational corporations led by Indian based in Sri Lanka, stated though there is uncertainty but there are opportunities also. During the crisis running business including Indian companies was not smooth along with the import restrictions laid down by the government to save foreign exchange and soaring production cost but the Indian investments carried on, at times with support from their parent companies in India to continue operations (Srinivasan, 2023).[15]

India is planning to construct a petroleum refinery in Myanmar by investing USD 6 billion. The two nations have a strong collaboration and acknowledge the advantages of further sectoral integration in the energy industry. Both the nations will work together in refining, storage, mixing and retail sectors. There is a joint working group on oil & gas, a structure for guiding bilateral cooperation in the energy sector, led at the Secretary level. Indian firms are operating in the upstream and midstream segments of the oil and gas industry in Myanmar. Indian Oil Company Limited (IOCL), GAIL, and ONGC Videsh Limited (OVL) have previously established offices in Yangon. Petrochemical goods are being exported to Myanmar by GAIL (Siddiqui, 2020).[16]

The contents of the Table no. 8 and some of the issues which are linked to the geo-economic /non geo-economic goals and objectives pertaining to the Indian context and its location plays a very significant role in shaping the different Risk mitigation strategies that would be helpful for Indian Multinationals in recent future times. Thus it is evident from the literature surveyed that the Geo-political & Political risk should be an increasingly important component of any multinational corporation's strategic global perspective.

**Table No. 9: Selected Geopolitical Events since 1990**

| Sr. No | Geopolitical Event | Year |
|---|---|---|
| 1. | Collapse of USSR Unification of East and West Germany and opening of Indian Economy | **1990-92** |
| 2. | World Trade Center bombing of 1993, terrorist attack in New York City on February 26, 1993, in which a truck bomb exploded in a basement-level parking garage under the World Trade Center complex. | **February 1993** |
| 3. | Bombay bombings were a series of 12 terrorist bombings that took place in Bombay, Maharashtra, on 12 March 1993. | **March 1993** |
| 4. | AFGHANISTAN Taliban militia appeared in full control of Kabul after it announced it was setting up an Islamic state and executed the former president, Mr Najibullah, as one of its first acts. | **September 1996** |
| 5. | The Pokhran-II tests were a series of five nuclear bomb test explosions conducted by India at the Indian Army's Pokhran Test Range in May 1998. USA imposed economic sanctions on India for its series of underground nuclear tests. | **May 1998** |
| 6. | East African Embassy Bombings- simultaneous bombs blew up in front of the American embassies in Nairobi, Kenya, and Dares Salaam, Tanzania, in Africa | **August 1998** |
| 7. | The Kargil War, also known as the Kargil conflict, was fought between India and Pakistan from May to July 1999 in the Kargil district of Jammu and Kashmir and elsewhere along the Line of Control. | **May-July 1999** |
| 8. | The USS Cole bombing was a suicide attack by the terrorist group al-Qaeda against USS Cole, a guided missile destroyer of the United States Navy, on 12 October 2000, while she was being refueled in Yemen's Aden harbor. | **October 2000** |
| 9. | 9/11 USA Under Attack, USA Attacks Afghanistan | **September 2001** |
| 10. | The 2001 Indian Parliament attack was a terrorist attack on the Parliament of India in New Delhi, India on 13 December 2001. | **December 2001** |

| | | |
|---|---|---|
| 11. | Major military conflicts in Ukraine, Syria, Iraq and Afghanistan continue | **2001-Onwards** |
| 12. | Terrorists wage attacks in more than thirty countries, including Belgium, France, Germany, India, Indonesia, Peru, Thailand and United States | **2001-Onwards** |
| 13. | Bali bombings occurred on 12 October 2002 in the tourist district of Kuta on the Indonesian island of Bali. | **October 2002** |
| 14. | U.S. forces invaded Iraq vowing to destroy Iraqi weapons of mass destruction (WMD) and end the dictatorial rule of Saddam Hussein. The Iraq War was a protracted armed conflict in Iraq from 2003 to 2011 | **March 2003-Onwards** |
| 15. | Madrid train bombings were a series of coordinated, nearly simultaneous bombings against the Cercanías commuter train system of Madrid, Spain, on the morning of 11 March 2004—three days before Spain's general elections. | **March 2004** |
| 16. | The 2005 Bali bombings were a series of terrorist suicide bomb and a series of car bombs and attacks that occurred on 1 October 2005, in Bali, Indonesia. Bombs exploded at two sites in Jimbaran Beach Resort and in Kuta 30 km away, both in south Bali. | **October 2005** |
| 17. | China builds thirty-two hundred acres of land and military installations atop contested atolls in the South China Sea, raising regional tensions. | **2005-Onwards** |
| 18. | Mumbai train bombings were a series of seven bomb blasts on 11 July. They took place over a period of 11 minutes on the Suburban Railway in Mumbai, the capital of the Indian state of Maharashtra and the nation's financial capital. | **July 2006** |
| 19. | The "Panama Papers" scandal prompts international investigations, regulatory reforms, and the resignation of Iceland's prime minister | **2008** |
| 20. | 26/11 Terrorist Attack in Mumbai | **November 2008** |
| 21. | Islamist violence and protests shake Kazakhstan, Central Asia's most tranquil nation. | **2009-Onwards** |
| 22. | Russia-Ukraine Conflict | **2014-Onwards** |
| 23. | More than 350,000 migrants enter Europe | **2015** |
| 24. | Joaquin Guzman, known as "El Chapo," the world's most powerful drug trafficker, is recaptured following his escape from a Mexican maximum-security prison | **2015-16** |
| 25. | Iran and Saudi Arabia sever diplomatic ties | **3rd January, 2016** |
| 26. | China's stock market crashes, leading regulators to halt trading | **4th January, 2016** |
| 27. | Brazil's president, Dilma Rousseff, is impeached | **17th April, 2016** |
| 28. | Brexit- The United Kingdom votes to leave the European Union on 31 January 2020, the biggest blow to the European unification project since World War II. | **June-2016** |

| | | |
|---|---|---|
| 29. | Rodrigo Duterte becomes president of the Philippines, vowing rapprochement with China and straining the U.S. relations | **June 2016** |
| 30. | An attempted coup in Turkey leads to a crackdown and democratic backsliding. | **July, 2016** |
| 31. | Colombia strikes a peace deal with the FARC, ending a 50 year old conflict with the Marxist guerrilla group. | **24th August, 2016** |
| 32. | Major cyber-attacks hit the Democratic National Committee, Yahoo!, domain name service provider Dyn, and LinkedIn | **September, 2016** |
| 33. | North Korea conducts its fifth nuclear test | **9th September, 2016** |
| 34. | The Zika virus outbreak in Brazil spreads to every countries before Rio Olympics | **April 2015 to November 2016** |
| 35. | Donald J. Trump is elected president of the United States | **November 2016** |
| 36. | Italy's prime minister, Matteo Renzi, resigns after voters reject his plan to revamp Italy's political system, leaving Italy among the weakest links in the EU | **December-2016** |
| 37. | South Korea's President, Park Geun-hye, is impeached | **9th December 2016 – 10th March 2017** |
| 38. | Food riots erupt in Venezuela | **31st March 2017—12th August 2017 (134 days) December 2017 (sporadic)** |
| 39. | Heightened tension between North Korea and the United States | **2017** |
| 40. | Balakot airstrike -A bombing raid conducted by Indian warplanes on February 26, 2019, in Balakot, Pakistan against an alleged terrorist training camp. | **February 26th,2019** |
| 41. | Trump Meets North Korea's Kim Jong Un and says Nuclear Negotiations will resume | **June 2019** |
| 42. | Trump quits the Iran nuclear deal. Tension between United States and Iran | **2018-2020** |
| 43. | Outbreak of Covid-19 in China and its impact on the World | **November 2019 onwards** |
| 44. | Joe-Biden is elected president of the United States | **2020** |
| 45. | Chinese and Indian troops engaged in aggressive melee, face-offs, and skirmishes at locations along the Sino-Indian border, including near the disputed Pangong Lake in Ladakh and the Tibet Autonomous Region, and near the border between Sikkim and the Tibet Autonomous Region | **2020-2021** |
| 46. | The United States Armed Forces completed their withdrawal from Afghanistan | **August 2021** |
| 47. | Outbreak of War Between Russia and Ukraine | **February 2022** |
| 48. | Xi Jinping secured a third term as CCP General Secretary | **October -2022** |

| | | |
|---|---|---|
| 49. | Economic Collapse in Sri Lanka and Pakistan | **2021-23** |
| 50. | All diplomatic relations between Iran and Saudi Arabia have been restored due to China-Iraqi brokered talks | **March 2023** |
| 51. | The BRICS Countries has Overtaken The G7 In Global GDP* | **March 2023** |

*Source:* Rice and Zegart (2018) and Desk Library and web research done by the Authors

* see https://www.silkroadbriefing.com/news/2023/03/27/the-brics-has-overtaken-the-g7-in-global-gdp/ Date Assessed April 9th, 2023

The Table No. 9 illustrates the selected geo-political events since 1990 till March 2023 which has affected the global business environment. The listed event takes place across continents with wide ramifications on International Relations, Politics, Trade and Economics. These effects also translate into a geopolitical risk, that can be defined as the threat, realization, and escalation of adverse events associated with wars, terrorism, and any tensions among states and political factors that affect the peaceful course of international relations. (Caldara, Dario and Matteo Iacoviello ,2022).)[17] The Geopolitical Risks is significantly affects the business and economic activities. The Bank of England includes geopolitical risk—together with economic and policy uncertainty—among an 'uncertainty trinity' that could have significant adverse economic effects (Carney, 2016)[18]

The result of the geo-political risk could be the adverse impact on the Economic Performance of the businesses which operate in such environment. The inter-linkages of Geopolitical Events, Risks and their impacts are shown in the Figure No. 1 below.

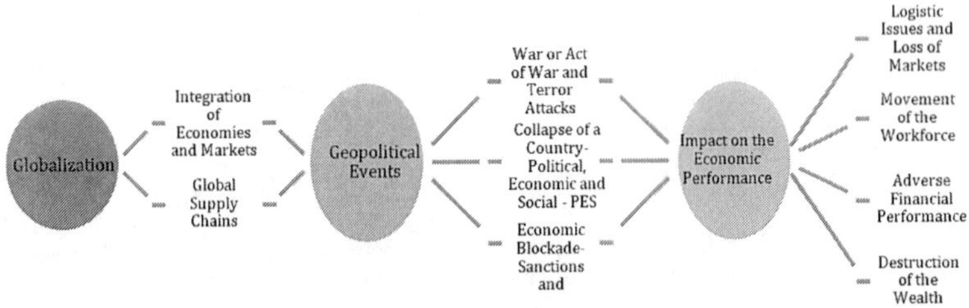


**Figure No. 1: Conceptual Framework of the Study**

The Figure No. 1 explains the conceptual framework for the current study. It highlights the linkages between the Globalization, Geo-political events and their impact on the Multinational companies' especially Indian ones in terms of the economic performance. It is important to note that identifying geo-political risks are not enough but correct analysis of it is imperative. The analysis leads to crafting the mitigation strategies for geopolitical and political risks. Last three decades saw emergence of many Indian companies and corporations doing business in different parts of the world. Some of these parts are sensitive to geopolitical risks hence it is the time that Indian companies first understand and identify these risks and with proper analysis shall construct proper mitigation strategies.

## Data Collection and Analysis

For the current study the companies which are having some global presence in terms of business and trade are selected. The study has considered the sample companies which are not only listed in the Indian Stock Markets but also part of the Stock indices.

India has two premier stock exchanges, Bombay Stock Exchange BSE one of the oldest stock exchanges of the world while the other is National Stock Exchange NSE which was formed in the 90's. The Index of BSE is known as BSE-SENSEX which consists of 30 companies while the Nifty-50 is the Index of NSE. Indexes are crucial because they serve as a representation of a country's market and economy. For example, Nifty-50 is the benchmark index of the NSE (National Stock Exchange) of India. Benchmarks are indices that combine multiple securities to represent a specific aspect of the market.

The Nifty 50 index measures the performance of the top 50 blue-chip companies on the National Stock Exchange, as per their market capitalization. Even though the Nifty index only includes 50 of the 1600 companies that trade on the NSE, it accounts for up to 66% of the NSE's float-adjusted market capitalization (float-adjusted means when an index considers only the shares that are available for investors and not held by other companies or government). As a result, it is regarded as an accurate representation of the Indian stock market.

The Nifty 50 stock list consist of the Nifty 50 companies from different sectors (as per the month ending June 2021), including-

1. Financial services- this sector has a maximum weightage of 37.17%
2. IT- 17.54%
3. Oil and gas- 11.24%
4. Consumer goods- 10.85%
5. Automobile- 4.94%
6. Pharma- 3.66%
7. Metals- 4.07%

8. Construction- 2.83%
9. Cement and cement products- 2.71%
10. Telecom- 1.94%
11. Power- 1.68%
12. Services- 0.73%
13. Fertilizers and pesticides- 0.65%

The current study considered the Nifty-50 index which comprises the stocks of 50 Companies with a combined market capitalization of Rs. 14,125,284.71Cr. (Equals to USD 1.72 trillion) .as at February 9th, 2023 as against the Total Market Capitalization of NSE of Rs. 27,567,268.13 Cr. (equals USD 3.40 trillion) as at 31st December, 2022. The Nifty-50 index is considered as at 31st December 2022.

The Study considered the Annual Reports of these Nifty-50 companies for the Year 2022, which is covering the Financial Year 2021-22. It is observed that out of 50 companies, 48 companies' annual reports were available while two company's reports were not available for the year 2022.

**Table No. 10: Nifty-50 Companies Data Availability**

| Sr. Nos. | Particulars | Number of Companies |
|---|---|---|
| 1. | Data Available in terms of Annual Reports for the Year 2022 (FY 2021-22) | 48 |
| 2. | Data Not Available in terms of Annual Reports for the Year 2022 (FY 2021-22) | 02 |
| | **Total** | **50** |

After analyzing and reading the 48 reports, it is observed that 41 companies reported or mentioned Geo-Political Risk while 07 companies did not mention it.

Composition of Companies which yet to mention the geopolitical risks or data not available sector-wise

1. Financial services- 03
2. IT- 01
3. Consumer goods- 02
4. Automobile- 01
5. Others -02

The Data from the 48 companies in terms of the mention of Risks pertaining to Business Operations with special reference to the Geo-

Political Risk and related risk was captured from the Annual Reports of the Nifty-50 companies. The Data was selected from the sections such as Letter from the Chairman, Management Discussion & Analysis and Risk Management Practices. The Total Data collated was about 10,000 words which was online fed to the **https://www.freewordcloudgenerator.com/generatewordcloud**,This is a free word cloud generator[19], from the vast data selected 2,000 words and created the Word Cloud as shown in Figure No. 2

*Source:* https://www.freewordcloudgenerator.com/generatewordcloud

**Figure No. 2: The Generated Word Cloud indicating Risks**

The Words which were common in these Nifty Companies along with their frequency of occurrences with minimum of 45 is displayed in the Table no. 11 below,

**Table No. 11: Summary of the Result generated by word cloud generator**

| Sr. Nos. | Words | Frequency of Occurrence |
|---|---|---|
| 1. | risk | 102 |
| 2. | global | 81 |
| 3. | inflation | 62 |
| 4. | supply | 56 |
| 5. | growth | 55 |
| 6. | geopolitical | 52 |
| 7. | risks | 50 |
| 8. | economic | 50 |
| 9. | prices | 49 |
| 10. | business | 49 |
| 11. | pandemic | 45 |

It is clear from the Table No. 11 that the Nifty-50 companies frequently use word such as Risk, Global, Inflation, Supply and Geopolitical in their Annual Reports while reporting their adverse impact on the Global Business Environment as well as Individual Financial performance.

Source : Table No. 12 and https://www.freewordcloudgenerator.com/generatewordcloud

**Figure No. 3 : The Generated Word Cloud for the Nifty-50 and their Markets/Country of Operations**

The Figure No. 3 explains the presence of selected Nifty-50 companies around the globe including India's immediate Neighbourhood. Some of the places where Indian companies are working are the part of conflict zones with turbulent business environment.

**Table No. 12: Selected Nifty 50 Companies and their global presence**

| Sr. Nos. | Name of the Nifty-5o Company | Area of Global Operations |
|---|---|---|
| 1. | Tech Mahindra | Pacific Regions- China, Hong Kong, Indonesia, Japan, Malaysia, Philippines, Singapore, South Korea, Taiwan, Vietnam,<br>America- North & South America, USA, Australia, New Zealand<br>Europe: Austria, Belgium, Denmark, Finland, France, Germany, UK, Sweden, Switzerland<br>Africa: Kenya, Nigeria, Rwanda, South Africa, Egypt, Uganda & Zambia<br>Middle East; Bahrain, Israel, Oman, Qatar, Saudi Arabia, Turkey and UAE |
| 2. | Hero Motors Company | Manufacturing Facility: Colombia, Bangladesh<br>Sales: Asia – Sri Lanka, Bangladesh, Nepal, Myanmar<br>Central & Latin America, Africa and Middle East, UAE |

| | | |
|---|---|---|
| 3. | Infosys | India, South Africa, USA, Canada & Mexico,<br>Asia Pacific & Middle East; Armenia, Saudi Arabia, Qatar, United Arab Emirates, Malaysia, Mauritius, Singapore, Australia, Philippines, Hong Kong, Taiwan, Japan, South Korea, China, New Zealand<br>EUROPE: The Netherlands, United Kingdom, Ireland, Belgium, Czech Republic, Switzerland, France, Portugal, Jersey, Spain, Italy, Croatia, Austria, Greece, Turkey, Germany, Lithuania, Latvia, Bulgaria, Romania, Hungary, Slovakia, Poland, Russia, Denmark, Norway, Sweden, Finland, Luxembourg. |
| 4. | Sun Pharma | USA, Canada, South America, Bangladesh, India, Japan, Malaysia, Myanmar, Sri Lanka, Thailand, France, Germany, Hungry, Italy, Netherlands, Poland, Romania, Spain, United Kingdom, Denmark, Finland, Norway, Sweden, Morocco, Nigeria, South Africa, Australia and New Zealand |
| 5. | Ultra-Cement | India, UAE, Bahrain and Sri Lanka |
| 6. | Cipla | India, Australia, Europe, Kenya, Malaysia, Morocco, Nepal, South Africa, Spain, Sri Lanka, Uganda, United Kingdom, USA |
| 7. | Maruti | Colombia, Chile, South Africa, Philippines, Egypt, Middle East, Australia, France, Italy |
| 8. | Bharti Airtel | Sri Lanka, Africa, Republic of the Congo, Rwanda, Seychelles, Tanzania, Uganda, Zambia, Guernsey, Jersey |
| 9. | Grasim | China, Canada ,Sweden, Indonesia |
| 10. | BPCL | India, Dubai, Oman, Kannur, Singapore and Mozambique |
| 11. | Apollo Hospital | Netherlands, USA, UK, Middle East, South East Asia<br>The hospitals have successfully attracted large number of patients from countries like Pacific Islands, Afghanistan, Bangladesh, Iraq, Kenya, Nigeria, Ethiopia, Oman, Yemen, Sri Lanka, Uzbekistan, Myanmar and Nepal. |
| 12. | Larsen &Toubro | Asia, UAE, Kuwait, Saudi Arabia, Oman, Qatar, Japan, China, Kurdistan, Sri Lanka, South Korea, Bangladesh, Africa, Kenya, Morocco, Algeria, Egypt, Ethiopia, Tanzania, USA, Canada, UK, Italy, France, Germany, Denmark, Sweden, Netherlands |
| 13. | Divi's Lab | America, Asia, Europe, Rest of the world, USA, Switzerland |
| 14. | Reliance | RIL is the 1st Indian company to be a partner in an Israel Innovation Authority (IIA) |
| 15. | Britannia | More than 60 countries across the globe.<br>Nepal, North America, Europe, Africa, South East Asia, Middle East- UAE & Oman & GCC countries. |
| 16. | United Phosphorus Ltd | China, Tokyo, , South Korea, UK, Belgium, Netherlands, France, Spain, Pennsylvania, Ivory Coast, South Africa, Durban, USA, Mexico, Guelph, Pennsylvania, North Carolina, Saltillo, Costa Rica, Colombia, Brazil, Argentina |
| 17. | Hindalco Ltd. | USA, Canada, Brazil, Germany, UK, Switzerland, Italy, China, South Korea |
| 18. | JSW Steel | USA |

| | | |
|---|---|---|
| 19. | Nestle India | UK, Canada, Australia, New Zealand, Nepal & Bhutan, Middle East, Indonesia, Philippines, Mauritius |
| 20. | Asian Paint | Asia, Indonesia, Nepal, Bangladesh, Sri Lanka, Middle East, South Pacific, Africa. |
| 21. | Hindustan Unilever Ltd | USA, Africa, Asia Pacific, Europe, Middle East, |
| 22. | Eicher Motors | Sweden, UK, Colombia, USA, Indonesia, Thailand, Philippines, Australia, New Zealand, Portugal, Malaysia, Brazil, Vietnam, South Korea, Japan, Argentina, Colombia, Thailand , UK |
| 23. | Tata Steel | Thailand, Malaysia, Europe, USA |

*Source:* Annual Reports of the selected Nifty-50 companies and Desk Research

After Analyzing the Annual Reports of the Nifty-50 companies, it is observed that these companies are taking a note of geo-political events which are mainly affecting the global supply chain and logistics along with procurement of raw materials especially from China, and then devising their risk mitigation strategies. Some of these efforts and strategies are listed as follows,

## Few Mitigation Strategies of Nifty-50 Companies

- Developing Scenarios, doing Risk Mapping and Establishing Risk Control Matrix.
- Adopt forecasting tools to enhance their enterprise resilience with respect to threats from conflict and terrorism
- Building a strong local base for sourcing, increasing safety stock levels.
- Leveraging alternate channels of distribution, broad basing manufacturing partners and activating alternate suppliers of key materials thereby increasing the resilience of supply chain.
- Avoid investing only in China and diversify the businesses to alternative destinations. Also, de-risking the supply chain from China
- Emphasis on the Cyber Security risk management and foreign exchange risk management

**Table No. 13: Selected Nifty 50 Companies and their geopolitical risk mitigation strategies**

| Sr. Nos. | Name of the Nifty-5o Company | Summary of the Risk Mitigation Strategies |
|---|---|---|
| 1. | Apollo Hospital | In the years 2021, 2022, pandemic had hampered global economic activity with healthcare having significant impact on global economy. However, supply disruptions continued into the subsequent year while a resurgence in COVID cases in certain geographies, challenges in China and the outbreak of the Russia-Ukraine War have set back the momentum of the global recovery.<br>Reviewing risks and initiating mitigating actions including scrutinizing cyber security and risk ownership as per a pre-defined cycle.<br>**Mitigation**- Defining a framework for identification, assessment, monitoring, mitigation, and reporting of risks. |
| 2. | L & T | L&T has a comprehensive Enterprise Risk Management (ERM) Framework- Identification, Assessment, Treatment and Reporting of risks.<br>**Geopolitical Risk-** As the company operates in multiple geographies it is exposed to risks on account of protectionist policies, political dynamics, trade barriers, sanctions, and geopolitical conflicts-Russia-Ukraine, has impacted the world in terms of disruption in supply chain and inflation.<br>**Mitigation of Geopolitical Risk – Mitigation strategies-** Country clearance approval procedure, monitoring of changes in sanction regimes, diversification of Order Book, counter party risk assessment, alternative strategic sourcing, etc. The Company engages periodically with external experts and Government Authorities to assess potential impacts of geopolitical conflicts on new investments, supply chain, logistics, and commodity prices.<br>**Cyber Security-** The Company is undergoing a digital transformation. Vulnerabilities like targeted attacks, ransomware threats, and phishing have enhanced the importance of protecting the information technology infrastructure and data of the Company.<br>**Mitigation of Cyber Security-** The Chief Information Security Officer of the Company, under the guidance of the Risk Management Committee, oversees the implementation of strong enterprise-wide cyber security practices. These practices are grouped into people, processes, and technology control areas under a company-wide Cyber Security Assurance Framework.<br>**Foreign Exchange and Commodity Price Risks**<br>The businesses of the Company are exposed to fluctuations in foreign exchange rates and commodity prices. Additionally, it has exposures to foreign currency denominated financial assets and liabilities. With the increasing tendency to access sanctions to combat geo-political issues, there have been reports of attempts to develop alternate payment systems to support trade and capital flows. The rise of cryptocurrency may pose additional challenges in this regard. |

| | | |
|---|---|---|
| 3. | Reliance | **Cybersecurity Risk- Risk Description-** COVID-19 pandemic has accelerated the digital transformation. This has subsequently increased RIL's dependence on digital technologies. While Reliance continues to focus on large scale digitization, it brings a lot of concerns around Cyber Security with the use of new technologies, open-source software, adoption of cloud, etc. Consequently, cyber-attack surfaces also increase substantially which increases the cyber security risks. Digital services being technology driven, there is an inherent risk of errors, bugs, or security vulnerabilities in products and internal systems.<br>**Risk Response of Cybersecurity Risk-** Measures taken by the Company include shift-left strategy in ensuring that security is completely integrated into the DevOps pipeline, highest order of security automation and orchestration to attain efficiency in its cyber defense, and validation of its cyber posture by third party experts. Increased cyber security awareness through employees' mandatory trainings and trainings for RIL's service providers are important controls and the Company considers this as a 'Human Firewall'. Reliance has also developed an anti-phishing platform in-house viz R-Phish, through which Reliance conducts regular phishing simulation to make sure that all its users are phishing resistant. A mature cybersecurity program based on NIST (National Institute of Standards and Technology) Cybersecurity Framework has been adopted. All systems and security tools are monitored for any cyberattacks via a 24x7 Security Operations Centre.<br>**Safety and Environmental Risks During Transportation-** With most of the crude being supplied to RIL by sea vessels, and the overwhelming majority of refined products being exported by sea, road and pipeline, the Company faces the risk of HSE incidents, oil spills and so on, leading to disruption in business activities. Events like technical integrity failure, natural disasters, extreme weather, human error and other adverse events or conditions could lead to loss of containment of hydrocarbons or other hazardous materials, as well as fires, explosions or other personal and process safety incidents. RIL operates a fleet of tugs, port service vessels and operations of port and terminal infrastructure and is exposed to a complex and diverse range of marine risks, with respect to exploration vessels, oil tankers, chemical tankers, gas tankers, and dry cargo vessels.<br>**Risk Response Safety and Environmental Risks During Transportation-** RIL has a strong vessel vetting, incident monitoring and emergency response system. A robust ship vetting programme ensures the vessels that are contracted to carry RIL cargo or those calling Sikka port to load products 'Free-on-board' are screened based on risks prior to their induction. The third- party ship vetting system, based on extensive data analysis, provides a risk rating benchmarked against other similar vessels. This allows a clear picture of the quality of the vessel and whether it is acceptable to RIL.<br>**Physical Security and Natural Calamity Risks-** Due to the geographical spread of operations, both onshore as well as offshore, Reliance is vulnerable to manmade and natural disasters. It is an attractive target for activities related to terrorism, criminal and violent protests, which could cause harm to people, infrastructure and disrupt business operations. Pandemic conditions can also have a severe impact. Therefore, it is important to proactively focus on safeguarding people and infrastructure from all internal and external threats. |

| | | |
|---|---|---|
| | | **Risk Response of Physical Security and Natural Calamity Risks-** Global Corporate Security (GCS) focuses on adopting pre-emptive de-risking strategies to safeguard and secure the Company. GCS has robust business continuity management plans and capability to handle disasters, natural calamities, and any other disruptions or incidents. Digital Services have developed and implemented an Integrated Disaster Recovery and Emergency Response Process. It has also implemented measures for prevention and detection of any physical security threats which includes patrolling the vulnerable areas, Real-time situational awareness by deploying alarms management and monitoring through centralised Networks Operations Centre (NoC). Disaster recovery processes and drills are also conducted for managing unscheduled downtime. Security & Loss Prevention (SLP) and Field Operations teams proactively support in reducing pilferage, theft and losses, alarm alerts, video based surveillance, GPS based trackers and consumption monitoring. |
| 4. | United Phosphorus Ltd | **Cybersecurity**- Global operations lead to greater reliance on internet-based applications. This increases the risks of breaches in data privacy and integrity.<br>**Impact on-** Database, Profitability, Day-to-day operations, Reputation Mitigation **Measures-** Investment in latest IT security systems, setting of adequate firewalls & disaster recovery system.<br>Environmental Health and Safety risk (EHS)- Changes in EHS rules and regulations<br>• Explosion and fire hazards<br>• Failure of mechanical, process safety and pollution control equipment.<br>• Contamination, chemical spills and other discharges or release of toxic or hazardous substances.<br>**Impact on-** Reputation, Market share, Regulatory shut down, Imposition of fine/penalty.<br>**Mitigation Measures**- staying updated on proposed changes in environment laws. Ensure adequate allocation and upgradation of safety tools, ensure regular checks for spills and chemical discharge & develop robust awareness initiatives, foster EHS focused culture |
| 5. | Hindalco Ltd. | **Cyber Security and Data Protection risks- It affects** Intellectual Capital Social and Relationship Capital Mitigation-Focus on formulation of industry standard policies, frameworks along with adopting best practices such as Information Security, Disaster Recovery & Business Continuity Management, IT Risk Management, etc. helps to strengthen the current systems. Periodic assessment of entire IT systems landscape and governance framework from vulnerability and penetration perspective through reputed expert agencies and addressing the identified observations in a time-bound manner. |
| 6. | Bajaj Finserv | During the year under review, a revised risk management policy/ framework was adopted by the Board. This framework, inter alia, includes identification of internal and external risks faced by the Company, including financial, operational, sectorial, sustainability, information, cyber security, strategic or any other risk as may be determined by the Risk Management Committee and the measures for risk mitigation, reporting of critical risks within the Company and Business Continuity Plan. |

| 7. | HDFC Life | Enterprise Risk Management (ERM) is embedded within our strategic and organizational framework.<br>Emerging Risks- New or developing risks that can affect the Company's financial strength, competitive position, viability, or reputation over the medium to long-term. Emerging risks may present a threat or an opportunity for the enterprise as a whole or a specific business unit or geography. The key categories of emerging risks are:<br>• Economic<br>• Geopolitical<br>• Regulatory/Legal<br>• Environmental/Societal<br>• Technological |
|---|---|---|
| 8. | JSW Steel | In FY 2021-22, external risks such as the COVID-19 pandemic have had a reducing impact while the geopolitical risks posed by the Russia-Ukraine conflict had far reaching effects on the Company's strategic and operational scope too. Overall, its strategic and operational risks were well-mitigated and did not disproportionately affect overall competitiveness. |

*Source:* Annual Reports of the selected Nifty-50 companies

**Figure No. 4 : The Generated Word Cloud for the selected Nifty-50 companies for their Risk Mitigation Strategies**

*Source:* Data from the Table No. 13 and https://www.freewordcloudgenerator.com/generatewordcloud

It is clear from the Figure No. 4 that the selected Nifty-50 companies are using words such as Security, Mitigation, monitoring, framework, measurement, impact and cyber security in understanding as well as appreciating geo-political risks so to devise the mitigation strategies for it.

## 3. Conclusions

From the analysis and discussion from the section 3, Data collection and analysis, following pointers emerged pertaining to the Geo-Political Risk Identification, Analysis and the Mitigation by the selected Nifty-50 companies. They are as follows,

- The Nifty-50 companies, though recognized the Geopolitical Risks, yet it is generic in nature and does not cover country specific risks.
- It also gives less attention pertaining to the risks associated with India's immediate neighbours and neighbourhood.
- The Nifty-50 companies also do not substantially highlight the financial turmoil in Sri-Lanka and Pakistan.
- The Nifty-50 Companies have not adequately taken a note of the dispute between India and China
- These companies' gives emphasis is given on the Russia-Ukraine War and after effects of the same such as disruption of supply chains, increased oil price and the business growth concerns.
- The selected Nifty-50 companies also laid emphasis on the Cyber security and emergence crypto currencies. These companies are taking efforts in mitigating the cyber security risk.
- Many of the companies are developed their Enterprise Risk Management Framework so to address and mitigate the geo-political and other risks.

It is evident from the study results that Nifty-50 companies need to pay more attention to the wide geopolitical events and geopolitical risks arising out of it. The more emphasis is currently given on the Russia-Ukraine war crisis which resulted in disruption of global supply chain and logistics. One of the reason that Indian companies not giving enough attention in their vicinity i.e. India's immediate neighbourhood could be because other than China, the trade and investment of these companies in the immediate neighbourhood is not that significant, hence in their plan of action, the Indian neighbourhood may be taking a back seat. It is also evident from the study though the Indian companies are now identifying the geo-political risks but they are still yet to analyze these risks fully as against their western counterparts so to do devise proper mitigation strategies for geopolitical events and their adverse effects on the economic performance. The Study also highlights the further scope in the same topic by quantifying the Impact of Geopolitical Risks and other related risks on the financial performance of the Nifty-50 companies. The Variables which could be analyzed in further studies, drawn from the conceptual framework mentioned in the current study with specific reference to the adverse impact of these geopolitical events on the economic performance. Currently The BRICS countries have overtaken the G7 economies in Global GDP and India is significant contributor in the BRICS GDP composition.[20] In the forthcoming years more Indian companies would be operating and dotting different places on the world map, hence it is imperative that Indian companies shall focus first on the Geo-Political Risks which are emanating from India's immediate neighbourhood in contiguity with the Geopolitical events and Risks arising out from India's extended and distant neighbourhood. The Geopolitically sensitive regions of the world are Middle East and South China Sea, in both these spot are dotted with presence of Indian companies. Considering the current geo-political scenario, the Pivot of Geopolitical Risks may shift to Indian Ocean Region which not only important for world and trade but close to Indian Culture and Economic Integration with the world. Hence it is important for Indian Companies to create suitable framework in order to identifying, measuring and mitigating the geo-political risk that would help them to minimize the adverse impacts of such events and risks on their economic performance.

## Notes

(a) World Bank, Internet, https://www.statista.com, https://www.wipo.int/global_innovation_index/en , https://tradingeconomics.com/

https://www.theglobaleconomy.com/India/, https://www.wipo.int/edocs/pubdocs/en/wipo_pub_2000_2022/lk.pdf and https://www.wipo.int/edocs/pubdocs/en/wipo_pub_2000_2022/pk.pdf

(b) World Bank, Internet, https://www.statista.com, https://www.wipo.int/global_innovation_index/en, https://www.indexmundi.com/facts/indicators/CM.MKT.LCAP.CD/rankings

https://www.wipo.int/edocs/pubdocs/en/wipo_pub_2000_2022/np.pdf

(c) World Bank, Internet, https://www.statista.com , https://www.wipo.int/global_innovation_index/en, https:/en.wikipedia.org/wiki/List_of_countries_by_Human_Development_Index

(d) See Werner J. Cahnman (1943), "Concepts of Geopolitics", American Sociological Review,Vol.8,No.1 February, p.56 in (Benner and Keat, 2010), p.37

(e) See https://www.yourarticlelibrary.com/history/collapse-of-ussr-and-its-impact-on- international-relations/48505

(f) See https://www.washingtonpost.com/business/why-swift-ban-is-such-a-potent-sanction-on-russia/2022/06/03/a6809b30-e340-11ec-ae64-6b23e5155b62_story.html)

(g) See https://www.sciencedirect.com/science/article/pii/S2352484717303219

(h) See https://internationalrelations-publishing.org/articles/1-1

## References


1. World Bank https://www.worldbank.org/en/country/india Accessed 10 November 2022
2. https://books.openedition.org/obp/4561?lang=en, Accessed 10 November 2023
3. Kumar et.al (2006) https://web.archive.org/web/20090908141613/http://drs.nio.org/drs/bitstream/2264/350/1/Curr_Sci_91_530.pdf). Accessed 9th November 2022
4. Devaki Nandan, Bharti Chauhan and Rahul Kumar, (2022), "The Geopolitical Importance of Afghanistan for India in the 21st century, JOURNAL OF THE ASIATIC SOCIETY OF MUMBAI, Vol. XCV, No.28
5. Chandra, S. (2020). India's Relations with Its SAARC Neighbours. In A. G. Wadhwa, *INDIA'S Foreign Policy Surviving in a Turbulent World* (pp. 194-216). New Delhi: Sage Publications India Pvt.Ltd.
6. Benner Ian and Keat Preston (2010). The Fat Tail- The Power of Political Knowledge in an Uncertain World. Ney York: Oxford University Press.
7. Joshi, P. R. (1998). Global Capital markets-Shopping for Finance. New Delhi: Tata Mcgraw Hill Publishing Company Ltd.
8. Rice Condoleezza and Zegart Amy (2018). Political Risk in the Age of Multinational Corporations. New York: New York: Twelve (Hachette Book Group).
9. Toksöz Mina (2014). Guide to Country Risk. USA and Great Britain: The Economist in Association with Profile Books Ltd. and Public Affairs.
10. See https://www.kroll.com/en/insights/publications/10-biggest-geopolitical-risks-by-likelihood-and-impact, Accessed 9th February, 2023
11. See https://www.strategy-business.com/article/03308#:~:text=In%20this%20context%2C%20geopolitical%20risk,of%20companies%20around%20the%20world
12. Chauhan, P. (2022). Geopolitics, Maritime Connectivity and Cultural Heritage. In N. K. Pandey, *Roads, Winds, Spices in the Western Indian Ocean-The Memory and Geopolitics of Maritime Heritage* (pp. 44-45). New Delhi: MacMillan education and Indian Council of World Affairs.
13. See Braithwaite Alex, (2005)," Location, location, Location…Identifying Hot Spots of International Conflicts", in the Journal *International Interactions*, Vol.31,pp. 251-273,published online on 26 January 2007, as Quoted in Chauhan, P. (2022). Geopolitics, Maritime Connectivity and Cultural Heritage. In N. K. Pandey, Roads, Winds, Spices in the Western Indian Ocean-The Memory and Geopolitics of Maritime Heritage (pp. 44-45). New Delhi: MacMillan education and Indian Council of World Affairs. pp.50
14. Saran, S. (2022), "Don't lose sight of the neighbourhood". *Hindustan Times News*, April 23rd https://www.hindustantimes.com/opinion/dont-lose-sight-of-the-neighourhood-101650717038818.html Accessed 9th February, 2023
15. Srinivasan Meena,(2023), "Despite crisis, it's good time to invest in Sri Lanka, say Colombo-based Indian CEOs", The Hindu business Line ,February 27th, https://www.thehindubusinessline.com/news/despite-crisis-its-good-time-

to-invest-in-sri-lanka-say-colombo-based-indian-ceos/article66557117.ece Accessed 9th March, 2023

16. Siddiqui, H. (2020), "Neighbourhood First: India to invest USD 6 billion for setting up a Petroleum refinery in Myanmar", Financial Express October 6th, https://www.financialexpress.com/business/defence-neighbourhood-first-india-to-invest-usd-6-bn-for-setting-up-a-petroleum-refinery-in-myanmar-2099145/ Accessed 19th February, 2023
17. Caldara, Dario and Matteo Iacoviello (2022). "Measuring Geopolitical Risk," International Finance Discussion Papers 1222r1. Washington: Board of Governors of the Federal Reserve System, https://doi.org/10.17016/IFDP.2022.1222r1.
18. Carney, M. (2016): "Uncertainty, the Economy and Policy," Bank of England. Cited in Caldara, Dario and Matteo Iacoviello (2022). "Measuring Geopolitical Risk," International Finance Discussion Papers 1222r1. Washington: Board of Governors of the Federal Reserve System, https://doi.org/10.17016/IFDP.2022.1222r1.
19. https://www.freewordcloudgenerator.com/generatewordcloud Accessed 9th February, 2023
20. see https://www.silkroadbriefing.com/news/2023/03/27/the-brics-has-overtaken-the-g7-in-global-gdp/ Accessed 9th April, 2023

# 11

# India-Russia Multifaceted Cordial Strategic Partners

**Dr. R. G. Gidadhubli**

There is chemistry of close, cordial and consistent relations between India and Russia and there is continuity from the Soviet era. It needs to be further added that there is no conflict of interest between India and Russia. An effort has been made in this paper to highlight multidimensional cordial relations between India and Russia as the relations encompass political, economic, security, energy and defence issues.

Firstly, it needs to be mentioned that there is continuity of close and cordial political bilateral relations between India and Russia. This is evident from the fact that 6th February 2023 marked the 30th Anniversary of India-Russia Friendship Treaty which was signed in 1993. India and Russia are 'Trusted Partners' as rightly stated by Russia's Ambassador to India Mr Denis Alipov in New Delhi. He also stated that Russia and India are strategic partners and are on the 'same page'.

Secondly, it needs to be mentioned that during the last few decades India-Russia relations are strengthened by organising several regional organisations namely RIC (Russia, India and China), BRICS (Brazil, Russia, India, China and South Africa) and SCO (Shanghai Cooperation Organisation). Leaders of India and Russia promote relations at the highest levels during the Summit Meetings held from time to time. Decisions taken at the Summit meetings are implemented at the state to state levels. India has played an active part in the regional organisations. For instance, in 2016 India assumed Chairmanship of BRICS and BRICS Bank which is an influential bloc. BRICS constitutes over 45 percent of world population and combined GDP of over $ 20 Trillion.

Thirdly, India has taken over the Presidency of G20 in 2023. The objective of India is not only to further enhance political and economic relations with Russia but also with other member countries of the G20 Group. On the 1st March 2023 the Heads of Foreign Relations of G20 countries met in New Delhi during which several issues concerning were discussed.

Fourthly, India's External Minister Mr S. Jaishankar held talks with the Russian counterpart Mr Sergei Lavrov in New Delhi on 1st March 2023 during which they discussed both bilateral and global issues. As reported by the media, the meeting focused on strengthening the bilateral partnership and the leaders of both the countries discussed ways to increase coordination at the global level especially at forums such as UN, G20 BRICS and SCO. Mr Lavrov emphasised that Russia supports India in the quest to strengthen genuine multi polarity.

It is important to note prior to the G20 Summit, India-Russia bilateral ties were strengthened by the visits to Moscow by the External Affairs Minister Mr. S. Jaishankar in November 2022 followed by the visit of National Security Advisor Mr Ajit Doval on 10th February 2023. Mr Doval called on Mr Putin during which wide-ranging bilateral and regional security issues were discussed. As per reports the leaders of both the countries agreed to continue to work towards implementing the Indo-Russian strategic partnership.

It is a matter of great significance that G20 meeting of Finance Ministers was held on 26th February 2023 in Bengaluru during which substantive dialogue on topical financial issues were held, and a wide range of demanded measures were agreed upon designed to give an additional impetus to the global economy and financial markets. The role of India and efforts made by India to achieve the objectives of G20 were appreciated by the representative of Russia. He has stated that the balanced approaches formulated in this context create a good foundation for responding to modern challenges in the area of global finance and related sectors.

## Energy Ties

India is not much endowed with hydrocarbon resources and hence is the major importer of oil. Russia is energy rich having huge oil and natural gas resources and is a major exporter of oil and natural gas in the world. While during the Soviet era, India imported over 30-35 percent of oil from the USSR, it has come down due to transportation problems after the Soviet breakup. However, Russia has been exporting oil to India which is the third largest consumer of crude oil in the world. On 3rd July

2019, India's Petroleum Minister Mr Dharmendra Pradhan discussed with the Russian Energy Minister Mr Novak for strengthening bilateral energy relations which was highlighted and supported by India's Prime Minister Mr Narendra Modi and the Russian President Mr Vladimir Putin. There are plans for undertaking joint projects and make investment in the energy sector. For instance, there is a roadmap for Indian investment in infrastructure development projects in Russia's Siberian and Arctic regions which have huge energy resources, which might help in increasing import of oil in the future. As opined by experts, Russia has been the single largest destination for Indian overseas investment in oil and natural gas projects, with cumulative investment exceeding $ 30 billion for promoting India's long term interest in energy sector. This will ensure India to strengthen ties with Russia and increase import of oil from Russia.

It is a matter of great significance that India has a long term strategy of transition of reducing dependence on oil to non-fossil fuels including nuclear energy. On this issue while the Western powers were reluctant, the former Soviet Union and post-Soviet Russia have been supporting India. This is evident from the fact that in 1988 the former Soviet Union supported India in setting up Kudankulam Nuclear Plant in Andhra Pradesh (KNPP). With the success of this project, there were specific plans to set up 25 nuclear power plants in various parts of India, some of which have been operational. Moreover, it needs to be mentioned that Russia has reinforced India's membership of Nuclear Supplier Group during the visit of the Russian President Mr Vladimir Putin to New Delhi in October 2018 at the 19th Annual Bilateral Summit Meeting. This has promoted India's role at global level.

## Bilateral Trade and Economy

India was a major trading partner of the former Soviet Union accounting for about 18-20 percent of India's total imports. But during the last couple of decades trade and economic ties between India and Russia have become a weak link due to several constraints. There is realisation of this issue on the part of the leaders of both India and Russia. In fact, the President of Russia Mr Vladimir Putin was candid in stating that trade turnover at present between Russia and India is too small and does not correspond to the potentialities. Mr Putin is hopeful and has a vision of 'Druzba Dosti' to take forward bilateral trade turnover with India to $ 30 billion by 2025 given close and cordial political and economic relations between the two countries. The Prime Minister of India Mr Narendra Modi having supported the vision of Mr Putin and has stressed that India is blessed with 3 Ds –Democracy, Demography and Demand. For promoting strong economic ties, he added $4^{th}$ D and that is Deregulation on the part of both the countries.

Bilateral meetings are held at the level of ministers of both India and Russia from time to time to implement policies undertaken by leaders of both the countries. For instance, bilateral meeting of the former India's External Affairs Minister Ms. Sushma Swaraj with her Russian counterpart Deputy Prime Minister Dmitry Rogozin on $22^{nd}$ October 2015 reinforced India's 'Special and Privileged Strategic Partnership' with Russia to implement Druzba Dosti vision of Mr Putin. As per reports the Russian minister assured that on its part of Russia was taking steps to create favourable conditions for developing trade, economic and investment cooperation, particularly free trade agreement and mutual stimulation and protection of investment for achieving the policies.

Some efforts have been made to implement the policies undertaken by the leaders of India and Russia. For instance, in June 2016 International Economic Forum was held in St. Petersburg which was attended by ten thousand participants from 70 countries including India for promoting Russia's foreign trade and economic ties. Russia and India new stage of economic partnership was held during the Economic Forum to boost bilateral trade and investment apart from setting up special economic zones and promoting startup companies.

As per reports, Russia has supported India to implement 'Make in India' policy of the Indian Prime Minister Mr Modi which is evident from the fact that several MOUs have been signed between Indian and Russian enterprises during the last few years. It is important to note that Development Corporation of the Moscow Region and Confederation of Indian Industries signed bilateral agreements to implement few turnkey projects in mining, metallurgy and oil and gas companies. Russia's Mosmetroy and India's Hindustan Construction Company bagged $ 372 million contract to construct underground metro in India.

It is important to note that few Chief Ministers of India have visited Russia to promote economic ties at state to state levels. For instance, Smt. Vasundhara Raje CM of Rajasthan visited Sverdlovsk in Russia in 2016 to promote economic ties in agriculture and heavy engineering. She also invited businessmen from Sverdlovsk to the exhibition that was held in Rajasthan. In fact, this was a part of bilateral meetings to be held from time to time at the local levels between the two countries. In this context mention may be made that agreements have been signed between the Development

Corporation of the Moscow Region and Indian Confederation of Indian Industry to promote industrial ties. As stated by Russian analyst Russia's Uralvagon Zavod has signed agreement with India's Kalyani Group to promote UVA products in India. Russia's Sukhoi Civil Aircraft Company has signed an agreement with India's Tata Group for manufacture spare parts for Sukhoi aircrafts.

In addition to what is stated above, there is scope and need for India to increase export of traditional goods to Russia including tea, tobacco, spices etc. In this regard it needs to be mentioned that Russia has played an important role in promoting external ties by forming and promoting Eurasian Economic Union comprising Russia, Belarus, Kazakhstan, Armenia and Kyrgyzstan which has emerged as a major market. Indian exporting groups can take advantage of this growing market.

As per reports India is one of the major producers and exporter of medicines in the world. In fact, more than 2000 medicines are exported by over 200 pharma companies. India is a major exporter of medicines to Russia and Central Asian countries. Indian major Pharma companies namely Glenmark, Lupin, Dr Reddy Labs are well known brand names and are major exporters of medicines to these countries. Hence as opined by some experts, considering growing demand for pharma products, there is immense scope for India for not only increasing exports from India but also setting up joint ventures in Russia with Russian pharma companies for producing certain pharma products to meet growing demand in Russia and in the Eurasian Economic Union and also Central Asian Countries. This will also help in enhancing bilateral economic ties and in achieving the vision of leaders of India and Russia.

## DEFENCE TIES

India and Russia share a 'Special and privileged strategic relationship' which is continuity from the Soviet era and that has helped India to strengthen defence capability in all branches namely Army, Navy and Air Force. At the outset it needs to be mentioned that while India imported about 65-70 percent of defence equipments during the Soviet era, the share of Russia accounts for about 50 percent at present. Moreover, India-Russia cooperation has helped India to achieve significant scientific and technological progress in the defence sector. In this regard the Russian ambassador in India Mr Denis Alipov speaking on the occasion of 30$^{th}$ Anniversary of Indo-Russian Friendship Treaty on 6$^{th}$ February 2023 mentioned that there is 'Trusted' relationship between Russia and India on security and defence issues.

Highlighting a few facts it is worth mentioning that BrahMos missiles are already operational which has immensely strengthened India's defence capability with consistent support from Russia during the last few decades. It is opined by some defence analysts, that India and Russia can co-produce and export supersonic BrahMos missiles to third countries. Apart from that as stated by Russia's defence experts, India is interested to purchase additional 40 multifunctional Su-30MKI fighters. It is important to note that these aircrafts are assembled from the Russian kits at the Indian HAL Corporation Plant which is competitive and costs less. Moreover, as opined by some defence analysts, there is cooperation from Russia to develop futuristic fifth-generation fighter aircrafts in India. In fact this promotes India's objective of 'Make in India' policy.

As opined by Russian representative of Rosoboronexport Mr Goreslavsky, strategic projects are undertaken on the basis of intergovernmental agreements between India and Russia with due participation of private sector in joint ventures. In fact there are close bilateral ties between Russia's Rosobornexport and India's HAL. He mentioned that pilot project that involves production of Russian Ka-226 helicopters in India will be the first to meet the requirements under this principle. Moreover, it is worth mentioning that Russia has keen interested in promoting ambitious joint ventures with India making it a major partner in the Asian region in the defence sector. Equally important is the fact that in 2016 India became the 35th country to be admitted to the Missile Technology Control Regime which is a major international group of which Russia is a key member. This has enhanced India's status in the world.

In lieu of conclusion it may be stated that India and Russia have succeeded in strengthening multi-dimensional relations for decades through political cooperation at bilateral and regional levels. Russia has appreciated India's role and leadership in ensuring the success of G20 Summit meetings held in India in February and March 2023. India has strongly supported 'Druzba-Dosti' vision of the Russian President Mr Vladimir Putin in enhancing trade and economic ties in the years to come. Russia has been consistent in promoting India on security and defence related issues.

## References

1. "Re-Emerging Russia and India Russia Relations" Dr R.G. Gidadhubli Book published by Kalpaz Publications, Delhi, 2020.
2. "Geo-Economics and Geo-Politics of Putin's Energy Policy for Russia" Dr R. G. Gidadhubli Article Published in NAM Today Monthly Journal, New Delhi, 12th December, 2021.

3. "Doval Calls on Putin, Talks Expansion of Strategic Ties." Times of India, 10th February 2023.
4. "Russia Praises India's Constructive Role in G20" Times of India, 27th February 2023.
5. "Indo-Russia Defense Cooperation. From Dependence to Dependability." In the Book Re-Emerging Indo-Russian Relations in the New World Order. Sanjay Deshpande and Chandrakant Yatanoor, G.B. Books, New Delhi, 2019.

# 12

# Indonesia: Not Distant Neighbour but Sibling of India, a Member of the Indic Family

**Mr Pulind Samant**

## India's Neighbours

Although the phraseology of 'immediate and distant neighbours' may not have been used exactly with that expression in the international relations scholarship extensively, the expression 'neighbourhood' has been in vogue for quite some time, especially for elaborating the challenges faced by the state of India since its inception, to point at what it means. In fact, the Government of India had used it in 2014 to pronounce its 'Neighbourhood First' policy, and initiate a few symbolic activities related thereto, which had included sending invites to all the heads of SAARC (South Asian Association for Regional Cooperation) states as guests of honour for the swearing in ceremony of Prime Minister Narendra Modi.

Although India had viewed SAARC nations as her own neighbourhood evidently in 2014, the same had undergone a significant review and change soon, when it decided to boycott the SAARC conference scheduled in November 2016 at Islamabad (Pakistan), a move which was supported by other member nations of SAARC, namely, Afghanistan, Bangladesh and Bhutan. Soon thereafter India had begun eyeing another regional grouping, namely, BIMSTEC (Bay of Bengal Initiative for Multi-Sector Technical and Economic Cooperation) as potentially a promising one within her neighbourhood, for furthering own as well as the region's interests. India's Minister of External Affairs Dr Jaishankar, soon after his appointment in the office in 2019, had justified such a review by underlining that India saw "energy, mindset and possibility" in BIMSTEC; he had simultaneously dismissed the possibility of continuing with SAARC, blaming it on the multiple and known problems of history and identity associated with it.[1] By virtue of that intentional review, India, however, had reviewed or rather reconstructed the definition of own neighbourhood too, by default. The very fact of the presence of Southeast Asian state of Myanmar in BIMSTEC, which had been an observer within the SAARC framework since 2008 (but not as a member), along with it further south-eastern neighbour Thailand, establishes that observation. India, thus, had effectively included a part of Southeast Asia in own neighbourhood, as perceived by it.

## Changing Scenario

Moving a step further in 2020, Prime Minister Modi spoke about the 'extended neighbourhood' of India, in his Red Fort address to the nation, on the 74th Independence Day of India. He had clarified India's review of her neighbourhood by asserting "Today, neighbours are not only those with whom we share geographical boundaries but also those with whom our hearts meet". Although he did not define the said term explicitly, he had addressed the ASEAN (Association of South East Asian Nations) nations as India's maritime neighbours, during the same speech.[2] PM Modi's said statement, by stressing upon the age-old religious and cultural ties of India with those nations, was made obviously with a view to publicly embracing them as friendly ones, the geography of which may not be perceived as India's neighbourhood in the general sense of their physical immediacy with India (except Myanmar), and more particularly with regard to the segregation of world's geography in certain straightjackets as done by the yesteryears' colonial powers, just as how the Indian subcontinent has come to be termed as South Asia, in the bargain. Secondly, in terms of sheer physical distance, the shortest distance between India (its south-western Lakshadweep Islands) and Maldives (its north-eastern tip, Kulhudhuffushi) which is considered India's neighbour, having been placed in 'South Asia', is at 413 kilometres. In comparison, the distance between India (Indira Point of the Nicobar Islands) and Indonesia (Sabang, the north-western tip of Sumatra province), is only 193 kilometres. In view of this comparative position of physical distances from Maldives to India in the west, and from India to Indonesia in the east, the claim, if any, for India's neighbourhood should actually tilt more in favour of Indonesia than Maldives.

## Meeting of Hearts

Going by the guideline of meeting of hearts as enunciated by PM Modi, in the context of identifying neighbours, a nation that is seen as fitting well in the extended neighbourhood of India is Indonesia, as India's maritime neighbour as well as a founder member of the ASEAN. India and Indonesia have been related with each other in many ways since the times going beyond the Common Era, and in the international relations terminology, almost two millennia before both the nations emerged as the modern nation states post the colonial period. Their relations can summarily be described as civilisational, encompassing the aspects of culture, ethnicity, and religion. So much so that, the Indonesian Archipelago was historically referred to as Indian Archipelago, East Indies etcetera by world historians of the nineteenth and twentieth centuries.[3] While the ancient Indians referred, collectively and generally, to the whole of Southeast Asia (including Indonesia, but possibly excluding parts of the Philippines), as Suvarna-bhumi (Sanskrit for 'land of gold')[4], many European historians referred to the same geography as Further India[5], Greater India[6] or Farther India.[7] The Southeast Asia region, more identified by the ASEAN tag of its regional grouping, is divided in two sub-regions, namely, mainland and maritime, consisting of five each of the total ten member states of ASEAN. While Cambodia is identified by scholars as the most India-influenced territory from within the mainland sub-regional lot[8], that identification in the maritime sub-region can be associated with Indonesia. While the indigenous Indonesians have traditionally referred to the land of their ancestors only as Nusantara (Bahasa Indonesia for 'archipelago'), the name Indonesia, meaning 'Islands of India' in Greek, had been coined by the European visitors, and was popularised by the German ethnologist Adolf Bastian through writing; the same name was accepted and used by the Indonesian nationalist groups in their struggle for independence from the Dutch colonial rule, and assigned it to the modern nation-state post-independence.[9]

## Indic Background of Indonesia

Having noted Indonesia's etymological connection with India as well as its inclusion by historians in the 'Greater India' of their perception, as above, it would be necessary to state certain background details that justify such perception. Before advent of Islam in Indonesia in the twelfth century, and even until it gained strength enough to become the dominant power there in the early sixteenth century C.E., Indonesia was known for the mighty and prosperous Buddhist and Hindu kingdoms of Sri-vijaya (c. fourth - eleventh century C.E.) as well as Shailendra (c. seventh – thirteenth century C.E.) and Majapahit (thirteenth – sixteenth century C.E.) respectively. Sri-vijaya, first independently and later as a part of the Shailendra Empire, regulated and prospered from the international trade flowing through the Malacca Straits under its control, being based in eastern Sumatra. While Malaysian Peninsula-based Shailendras were the strongest power of their times in the Southeast Asia region including a large part of Indonesia, the same status was enjoyed by Majapahit later. Before the beginning of the Dutch colonial rule in Indonesia, that is, three centuries before the common Indonesians started viewing their archipelago as the Indonesian nation, Majapahit had politically united more or less the same territory as one state, having vassal states in the vicinity. This historical fact being well known to Indonesians, especially the ruling class among them, it was a matter of pride as well as the rallying point in their struggle for independence against the Dutch. Sukarno, the first president of independent Indonesia, used to hang the Majapahit Empire map in his office, as the symbol of that feeling of pride.

The Hindu faith is considered to have travelled from India to Indonesia and got established there in the early centuries of the Common Era, the evidence of which is found in the form of inscriptions dated tentatively between the first and fourth century CE. The Buddhist faith, also from India, considered to have spread there in the fifth century CE, though it had reached the mainland Southeast Asia before the Common Era, during Mauryan Ashoka's reign in India. The entire socio-cultural life on the archipelago was modeled on that of India, including the arts, language, literature, architecture, statecraft etc., over centuries, a process which was called by renowned French historian George Coedes (1886-1969) as 'Indianisation'. Even Islam, which is the dominant religion in today's Indonesia, had entered there first, in western Sumatra, via India, though later it entered elsewhere, especially in Java, through other channels emanating from within the Southeast Asian region. The credit for the process of Indianisation goes to a number of Indians who visited the archipelago as adventurous sailors, enterprising traders, fortune-seeking princes as well as monks and priests who had been invited there for religious purposes, including solemnising the coronations of indigenous kings who were keen on benchmarking the Indian practice. While many of them stayed there for short durations, driven by various pursuits of their own, some of them settled there permanently, marrying locally and expanding their families. According to a local legend, one of the most prominent Indian names among such settlers is of sage Agastya, who is known and revered as Bhatara Guru by the local populace, especially of Java. This form bhatara stems from the Sanskrit word bhattara, both carrying the same meaning, that is, revered or venerable.[10]

The Indic sources for information pertaining to the civilisational affinity between India and Indonesia include Hindu texts like Valmiki's

Ramayana, Kshemendra's Ramayana-manjari, Harivamsha, a number of Puranas, namely, Vayu, Vishnu, Garuda, Markandeya, Vamana, Matsya and Brahmanda; Buddhist literature of Jataka, Milinda-panha and Niddesa, and collection of stories like Katha-saritsagara. The Hindu sources mainly locate places in Indonesia like Java and Sumatra, along with places in the adjoining geography of Peninsular Malaysia; others mainly render stories of travels of Indians there, and related or incidental information. All of them however, collectively corroborate the history of socio-cultural interaction of India with Suvarna-bhumi, that is, today's Southeast Asia; many of them locate Suvarna-dvipa and Yava-dvipa, which have been identified with today's Sumatra and Java of Indonesia respectively, by the modern age historians. The most interesting of the above facts emerges from the Valmiki Ramayana – when Rama was on the mission to locate Sita post her abduction by Ravana, the monkey-king in exile, Sugriva, sends out messengers in all directions for the purpose; one of those places had included Yava-dvipa (Java). This underlines the knowledge of the then Indians, Rama and his colleagues, of existence of Java and its vicinity, and their perception about those territories as their neighbourhood.

Scholarly work of historians, both Indians and others, has discovered the Indic influence over the languages of Indonesia, especially the Javanese, and also on its literature. The Old Javanese, the known oldest language of the Hindu-Javanese[11] society was heavily influenced by Sanskrit. Its literary version, called Kawi, was even more infused with Sanskrit vocabulary. A number of notable literary works like Ramayana, Arjuna-vivaha, Bharat-yuddha (Indonesian version of Mahabharata)[12] and Brahmanda-purana[13] were produced in Kawi. In fact, the national language of independent Indonesia is Bahasa Indonesia, where word "Bahasa" is nothing but bhasha (Sanskrit for language).

## Bilateral Relations between Modern States of India and Indonesia

The above account proves the civilisational status of Indonesia as a member of the Indic family, and thus a sibling of India as stated in the title of this paper. Now, whether this status has reflected in a brotherly political behaviour of the modern state of Indonesia remains to be examined. Such behaviour between India and Indonesia had started showing even during the time-period when both of them were struggling for their independence. In the 'Asian Relations Conference' organised in New Delhi between 23 March and 2 April 1947, Jawaharlal Nehru of India had announced withdrawal of Indian troops from Indonesia, who were fighting the Indonesian freedom-fighters, under their British commanders, as Britain had sided with the fellow European colonialists, namely, the Dutch.[14] But even much before this official position taken by India, the Indian troops present in Indonesia were reportedly supplying arms occasionally, presumably out of brotherly feelings, to the Indonesian freedom fighters surreptitiously, during the historical battle of Surabaya in 1945.[15] Thereafter in 1948, Indian pilot politician Biju Patnaik had risked his life in rescuing leaders of Indonesian freedom struggle Mohammed Hatta and Sultan Syahrir from their imminent arrest by the Dutch colonial authorities, and bringing them safely to India, on instructions from then Prime Minister (PM) Nehru. Later in 1950, Sukarno, the first President of newly independent Indonesia was invited as the guest of honour on the occasion of the first Republic Day of India on 26 January 1950. When the Tsunami earthquake took place in December 2004, Indonesia was the hardest hit, among the total of eleven affected nations that had included India too. The Indian Navy, however, was the first foreign navy to reach the Indonesian shores for the rescue and relief operations, and had launched 'Operation Gambhir' focusing on Indonesia, by deploying two warships there with 40 tons of relief aid including three tons of medical relief supplies. One of those warships was converted into a full-fledged 50 bed hospital ship, equipped with medical facilities such as X-ray and ICU. Indian Naval groups were able to start those operations within 12 hours from the time of the Tsunami-eruption. India was also among the first nations to provide assistance amounting to US$ 1 million in relief supplies to Indonesia following the said disaster.[16] During a later disaster spelled by Covid-19 virus, the humanitarian assistance was, however, from both the sides, to each other. Indonesia had sent 200 oxygen concentrators along with 1400 oxygen cylinders to India, in May 2021.[17] Indian reciprocation of this kind Indonesian gesture happened in July 2021, when India sent the aid of 300 oxygen concentrators, along with 100 metric tons of liquid medical oxygen to Indonesia, under 'Operation Samudra Setu'.[18]

Indonesia too, from the view-point of mutual understanding, has shown great consistency in maintaining healthy bilateral relations with India. India and Indonesia have forged robust cooperation in the area of defence and security. In May 2018, during the visit of PM Modi to Indonesia, a new Defence Cooperation Agreement was signed by both the nations, to reflect the elevation of relationship between them to a Comprehensive Strategic Partnership. Indonesia has also emerged as the second largest trading partner of India in the Southeast Asian region, in the year 2021-22[19].

Indonesia has extended its co-operation to India on various important occasions at international forums. It had opposed the moves within the Organisation of Islamic Co-operation (OIC) during the said body's annual meets, to issue strong statements on Kashmir.[20] Being the largest Muslim majority nation in the world, Indonesia had presumably used its position within the OIC to facilitate invitation to India as the guest of honour at the OIC meeting in March 2019, hosted by the United Arab Emirates (UAE). Its Foreign Minister Retno Marsudi had justified the said invitation by underlining the ethos of pluralism and the value of democracy commonly shared between India and Indonesia, and their joint effort to strengthen co-operation to create peace and tolerance in the world.[21] She had also asserted then the commonality of goals between India and Indonesia in their respective Indo-Pacific strategies, in support of the position taken.[22] More recently in 2020, Indonesia had refrained from commenting on abrogation of Article 370 of the Constitution by the Government of India, revoking the special status of the state of Jammu and Kashmir, when its immediate neighbour who shares religious, linguistic and ethnic ties with it, namely Malaysia, had taken an openly hostile position against India. This position of Indonesia, of not entertaining the Kashmir issue as a matter of dispute of international relevance, has been maintained by it steadfastly throughout. It can probably be seen as a continuing reciprocation of India's similar gesture in the past with regard to the southeastern island of the Indonesian Archipelago, named Timur, the eastern half of which eventually emerged as an independent nation by the name of East Timor in 2002, post armed struggle with Indonesia, followed by international intervention. India then had not only refrained from commenting on the issue against Indonesia, but had also declined the proposal of joining the United Nations Peacekeeping Force (UNPF) in that territory.[23]

More importantly, Indonesia, in the capacity of a non-permanent member of the United Nations Security Council (UNSC) and also as the head of the Sanctions Committee on Counter-Terrorism within the UNSC, had played a key role in 2019 in declaring Masood Azhar, a dreaded Islamic terrorist for India, as a global terrorist. Its Foreign Minister Marsudi, had referred to the rise in the radical ideas as well that in the acts of terror, as being the areas of common concerns between the two nations, in the said context. She had also said that terrorism could not be justified under the pretext of religion.[24], thus expressing solidarity with the Indian position.

Going by the construct of 'common goals in their respective Indo-Pacific strategies' and also under the 'shared vision of maritime co-operation in the Indo-Pacific' as identified during PM Modi's visit to Indonesia in May, 2018, India has been working on developing its maiden deep-sea port in partnership with Indonesia, on latter's Sabang Island, so as to help gain a strategic access to the region, as a counter-balancing force.[25] This

Sabang, positioned on the mouth of the Malacca Straits, is considered a key global choke point; it is around 90 nautical miles from India's Andaman and Nicobar Islands, which have been identified as "primary areas of interest" by the Indian Navy in the 'Indian Maritime Security Strategy' document.[26] These islands are uniquely positioned for India to undertake surveillance operations and monitoring in the Straits of Malacca, falling between Indonesia's Sumatra and Peninsular Malaysia.

The whole world is aware about China's aggressive postures with regard to its unilateral marking of own boundaries in the South China Sea (SCS), thereby restricting the movements, strategic as well as commercial, of the concerned littoral states of the Southeast Asia region. Indonesia, is not one of the claimants in the SCS related dispute, but it has gone through the experience of similarly identifiable territorial skirmishes with China in the past, with regard to its northernmost island of Natuna Besar in the SCS. It therefore started building up a military base on that island in December, 2018. This move on the part of Indonesia has a strategic relevance for India from its own security requirements, in view of the increasing presence of Chinese distant water fishing (DWF) vessels[27] as well as warships[28] in the Indian Ocean Region (IOR), on India's eastern flank. Any fortification, such as at Natuna as above, by strategically located Indonesia, is a step in the direction of helping strengthening India's own security as well as facilitating indirectly India's emergence as a net security provider in the region, by enabling it to focus on other critical fronts in the IOR, the point that was asserted by PM Modi while addressing the UNSC during India's month-long presidency in August 2021[29].

## Conclusion

India and Indonesia have shared between them a strong civilisational bond built over a couple of thousand years. Both nations have asserted their values of pluralism and democracy as modern nation states, and have also demonstrated consistent growth post gaining independence from their European colonizers, in a determined way. It is a cliché to say that you cannot choose your neighbours and you have to adjust your ways of cohabitation with them. India has been facing several issues of concern with its newly created 'immediate neighbours' post partition of 1947, reflecting in several ways including the bottlenecks experienced in the operations of the regional grouping of SAARC. At that backdrop, the record of the seemingly 'distant neighbour' Indonesia's political understanding as well as multifaceted cooperation with India is commendable. The root cause of this apparent contrast can be understood by simple analysis of the related history. Those immediate neighbours had attained their such status by willingly separating not only their territories from India but also severing the civilisational ties by giving primacy to their Muslim religion over anything else, and taking adversarial positions as a consequence, whereas Indonesia, though Muslim majority demographically, has always cherished own Indic civilisational past and the lasting bond created by the same. This sense of being a member of the Indic family, has apparently overwhelmed the sense of physical proximity or otherwise, and has also reflected consistently in the brotherly political behaviour throughout.

Indonesia is most strategically located in the Indo-Pacific, possessing the largest territory, the strongest economy and the biggest military power in the Southeast Asia region, a region considered as central to the construct of Indo-Pacific; it also houses the headquarter of the ASEAN, of which it is a founder member. Thus, it is in India's permanent interest to maintain and strengthen the bond, Indic as well as geo-strategic, with Indonesia, which is a fellow G20 member, from whom India took over the Presidency of the group just last year.

## Notes

1. The Economic Times, 07 June 2019, p. 2.
2. "India has deepened ties with all countries in 'extended neighbourhood: PM Modi", Times of India, 15 August 2020, https://timesofindia.indiatimes.com/india/india-has-deepened-ties-with-all-countries-in-extended-neighbourhood-pm-modi/articleshow/77562855.cms
3. "Suvarnadvipa", S.R. Goyal in India's Interaction with Southeast Asia (Vol. 1, Pt. 3), G.C. Pande (Ed.), centre for Studies in Civilisations, New Delhi, 2006, p. 262.
4. Southeast Asia is India's El-Dorado, R.K. Dube, in India's Interaction with Southeast Asia (Vol. 1, Pt. 3), G.C. Pande (Ed.), Centre for Studies in Civilisations, New Delhi, 2006, p. 87.
5. Letters from the Far East, Charles Eliot, Edward Arnold, London, 1907, p. 47.
6. Civilisation of the East (Vol. II), M. Rene Grousset, 1929 (quoted in Discovery of India, Jawaharlal Nehru, The John Day Co., New York, 1946, p. 201); Towards Angkor, H.G. Quaritch Wales, 1933 (quoted in Jawaharlal Nehru, op. cit., p. 203); Sumatra, Edwin M. Loeb and Robert von Heine-Geldern, 1935 (quoted in South Indian Influences in the Far East, K.A.N. Sastri, Hind Kitabs Ltd., Bombay, 1949, pp. 114-115).
7. See The Indianised States of Southeast Asia, George Coedes and Susan B. Cowing and Walter Vella, Honolulu East-West Centre Press, 1968.
8. "Indian Cultural Heritage in Cambodia", B.R. Chatterjee in India's Contribution to World Thought and Culture, 1970, and The Making of Southeast Asia, George Coedes, 1966 (quoted in "Hinduism in Southeast Asia: Burma, Champa, Kambuja, Ceylon, Bali and Indonesia", V.C. Srivastava in India's Interaction

with Southeast Asia (Vol. 1, Pt. 3), G.C. Pande (Ed.), Centre for Studies in Civilisations, New Delhi, 2006, pp. 636, 648.

9. Justus, M. van der Kroef (1951). "*The Term Indonesia: Its Origin and Usage*". *Journal of the American Oriental Society*. 71 (3): 166 71. doi:10.2307/ 595186. JSTOR 595186.
10. Sanskrit-English Dictionary, V.S. Apte, Motilal Banarasidas Publishers Pvt Ltd., Delhi, 2017, p. 452.
11. This term has been used by a number of historians to indicate the socio-cultural composition of then Javanese society. See India and Java, B.R. Chatterjee, Prabasi Press, Calcutta, 1933; K.A.N. Sastri (op. cit.); N.J. Krom and F.D.K. Bosch as quoted in Historians of South-East Asia, D.G.E. Hall (Ed.), Oxford University Press, London, 1961; Some Contribution of India to the Ancient Civilisations of Indonesia and Malaysia, H.B. Sarkar, Punthi Pustak, Calcutta, 1970.
12. Indian Influence on the Literature of Java and Bali, H.B. Sarkar, Greater India Society, Calcutta, 1934.
13. "South-East Asia and the Indian Ocean in the Puranas", S.N. Roy in India's Interaction with Southeast Asia (Vol. 1, Pt. 3), G.C. Pande (Ed.), Centre for Studies in Civilisations, New Delhi, 2006, pp. 143-158.
14. India's announcement in the Asian Relations Conference of 1947, https://en.wikipedia.org/ wiki/Asian_Relations_ Conference#:~:text=Organized%20by%20the%20Indian%20Council,and%20presided%20by%20Sarojini%20Naidu. Retrieved on 6 February 2023.
15. Asia Reborn, Prasenjit K. Basu, Aleph Book Co., New Delhi, 2017, p. 417
16. Press Release, Embassy of India, Jakarta, 24 December 2004. https://www.mea.gov.in/Portal/CountryNews/ 3398_Press_Release_Government_of_India_expresses_solidarity_with_the_Government_and_the_people_of_Indonesia_on_the_solemn_occasion_of_Indian_Ocean_Tsunami_Disaster_commemoration.pdf , retrieved on 6 February 2023.
17. "Indonesia Sends COVID-19 Pandemic Management Assistance to India", Office of Assistant to Deputy Cabinet Secretary for State Documents & Translation, 12 May 2021. https://setkab.go.id/en/indonesia-sends-covid-19-pandemic-management-assistance-to-india/ , retrieved on 6 February 2023.
18. Press Release, Embassy of India, Jakarta, 24 July 2021.

    https://www.indianembassyjakarta.gov.in/whats_new?id=eyJpdiI6IlpmN3BVU1dPSm5CRkp3NWZ2K0lnZ0E9PSIsInZhbHVlIjoicWZLcjl3W-Ec5d1JFd1EwS0pWZDFMdz09IiwibWFjIjoiNWVmNDRkMzYwMGM-1MDc1NTJlYzY3Y2NhMTdkODViZWMzYTc4MThiMjc2NGE0YWYzNmUxMjFhMmIzZTJjNmRkMCJ9#:~:text=Embassy%20of%20India%2C%20Ja-karta& text=Ambassador%20of%20India%20to%20Indonesia,wave%20of%20COVID% 2D19%20pandemic, retrieved on 6 February 2023.
19. India-Indonesia Bilateral Brief (Unclassified) as on 25 November 2022. https://www.mea.gov.in/Portal/ForeignRelation/Indonesia22nov.pdf retrieved on 7 February 2023.
20. The Economic Times, 25 February 2019, p. 2.

21. The Economic Times, 25 March 2019, p. 3.
22. *Ibid.*
23. India and Southeast Asia: The Security Cooperation, Lt. Gen. Yoginder Mohan Bammi (Retd.), New Delhi, Gyan Publishing House, 2006, p. 199.
24. The Economic Times, 25 March 2019, p. 3.
25. The Economic Times, 20 March 2019, p. 3.
26. "Andaman and Nicobar can lift India's Maritime Capacity", Harsh Pant and Sohini Bose, Hindustan Times, 14 January 2023, p. 12.
27. "Spurt in China's DWF Vessels in High Seas on Radar of Indian Security Set-up", Dipanjan Roy Chaudhury, The Economic Times, 6 February 2023, p. 2.
28. Admiral Karambir Singh's statement at the Raisina Dialogue 2020, Hindustan Times, 16 January 2020, p. 8.
29. "India Asserts its 'Net Security Provider role; in the Indian Ocean Region", Anirban Bhaumik, Deccan Herald, 10 August 2021. https://www.deccanherald.com/india/india-asserts-its-net-security-provider-role-in-indian-ocean-1017935.html, retrieved on 6 February 2023.

# 13

# Climate Change and Action: India and Neighbhourhood Response

**Mr. Prakash Almeida**

## Introduction

Climate change is real and a grave threat to progress and prosperity in South Asia which is facing a climate chaos. What happens in South Asia will clearly have a profound impact since the countries of this region are growing rapidly and are extremely vulnerable to climate impacts. All countries in South Asia are also working to address climate change at the national level.The impact and cost of climate change in South Asia will depend largely on how the leadership responds to the worsening crisis. Clearly the leadership in South Asia will need to act together. Working together can help whole of South Asia as a one geographic unit and regional economy to manage the adverse impacts of climate change. While the recent COP 26 and COP 27 have reached universal agreements on temperature reduction and decarbonisation goals there is an urgent need to reach South Asian agreement on facing the climate change impacts collectively. This will expand the capacities and resilience of countries in South Asia to adapt, mitigate, recover and manage the climate perils while protecting the highly vulnerable economies to extreme weather events which are increasing in number and intensity; and devastating livelihoods both in rural and urban areas. There is a need to take new visionary initiatives such as new frameworks specific to South Asia. To achieve a collective effort we need mindset change in South Asia. The experience of SAARC is not so encouraging and we have experienced time and again Pakistan is not playing the role expected of it as a mature country. Pakistan now in perilous state and becoming almost a satellite vassal State of China is a country of contradictions and time has come for South Asian countries to move ahead with or without Pakistan. India is better placed to provide the necessary leadership for climate change action in South Asian neighbourhood. The present leadership under Prime Minister Shri Narendra Modi has already taken lead at all fronts to face the challenge of climate change. Countries in South Asia will benefit from joining hands with India. They can hugely benefit from India's capabilities and resources. The world today looks at India for various visionary leadership roles and it would be a tragedy if South Asian countries do not take necessary steps in South Asian neighbourhood response to climate change. Various research studies have shown the urgent need to take these steps.

The climate crisis remains the biggest long-term threat facing humanity, according to the 2022 Global Risks Report. Let us take a brief view of the climate change threat to key areas. Overall, South Asia's forest carbon pool appears to increase by the 2080s, implying absorption of more carbon dioxide ($CO_2$), the most prevalent greenhouse gas. Meanwhile, net biome productivity—the difference between the amount of $CO_2$ taken up from the atmosphere by photosynthesis and that released by decomposition and forest fires—appears positive and increasing by the 2030s and 2050s, but will be negative and declining by the 2080s. This declining trend implies that forest ecosystems will be unable to compensate for the rising metabolic losses due to increasing temperature.

Global sea level could rise between 0.2 meter and 0.8 meter by 2100. However, the smallest resolution of predictive models at present is 1.0 meter and projections on that basis overestimate the extent of future flooding. Bearing that in mind, a 1-meter rise would cause widespread inundation in coastal areas: about 0.72 percent (20,932 square kilometers [$km^2$]) of drylands and 0.75 percent (3,694 $km^2$) of the wetlands in South Asia, affecting about 95 million people. This would increase to 3.17 percent of dryland and 5.50 percent of wetland areas, and more than 200 million people when extreme storm surge is also considered.

Some crops in parts of the region may benefit from future warmer temperatures, but the overall impact of climate change on agriculture is expected to be negative, posing a serious threat to regional food security. Early yield gains are predicted in rice, for example, in Bhutan and India but yields may begin to decline again by the 2050s. By the 2080s, rice production is forecast to increase by as much as 16 percent in Nepal's hills and mountains, but decline by as much as 23 percent in the extensive tropical and subtropical regions of Bangladesh, Bhutan, India, and Sri Lanka.

Climate and anomalous weather events will result in a rise of vector- and waterborne diseases in South Asia. Deaths from dengue, malaria, and diarrhoea are projected to increase with climate change. However, from the 2030s to the 2080s, the number of malaria cases will likely fall, while those of dengue and diarrhoea will probably rise. Water supply in Bangladesh, Bhutan, Nepal and Sri Lanka are likely to be higher due to the positive effects of partly increased rainfall. On the other hand, due to variations in intensity and distribution of rainfall, the region as a whole will experience water deficit, particularly in India where water deficit will be roughly 300 billion cubic meters ($m^3$) and 400 billion $m^3$ by 2030s and 2050s respectively. Increasing flooding, surges, storms, rainfall, sea-level rise, and human activity are all causes of worsening erosion in the region. Coastal areas, overgrazed rangelands, and denuded mountains are particularly affected. In India, 26 percent of the coastline is prone to erosion, with 450 hectares of land lost every year. Sri Lanka's coastline is subject to significant erosion in certain areas, while the hill country is prone to frequent landslides. In mountain communities in Bhutan, India, and Nepal, landslides are occurring with disturbing regularity. The loss of land is damaging economies, agriculture, and habitats, and constricting livelihood opportunities, particularly of the rural poor.

With more extreme weather events likely due to climate change, coastal and mountain soil erosion in South Asia will worsen over the next decades. The region's long and heavily settled coastlines are seriously threatened by sea-level rise. In Bangladesh alone, sea level is predicted to rise 45 centimetres by 2050, affecting 10 percent–15 percent of the land area and an estimated 35 million people.[4] Sea level is also projected to rise by around 15–38 centimetres in India by 2050, placing major cities driving regional growth at risk. South Asia is extremely vulnerable to natural disasters, and a significant portion is exposed to more than one type of hazard. Between 1990 and 2008, more than 750 million people—50 percent of South Asia's population—were affected by at least one type of disaster, resulting in almost 230,000 deaths and about $45 billion in damages.

South Asia has been one of the least urbanised regions in the world, with an urban population representing only about 28 percent of its total of 1.4 billion people. However, urban growth rates of 2.53 percent have eclipsed global and regional averages (UN Population Division 2007) and set its cities on a path to rapid expansion. Infrastructure gaps, social service deficits, and urban management issues, associated with the region's largely unplanned urbanisation, will be intensified by the sudden spikes in urban–

rural migration due to climatic changes and other drivers. Urban poverty incidence, already at 50 percent, is projected to increase. Climatic risks such as sea-level rise, rising temperatures, and extreme weather events will amplify the vulnerability of South Asian cities. About 14 percent of the region's urban population, totalling about 400 million, live in coastal and major river delta areas that are 10 meters or less above sea level.[8] Impacts will be most pronounced in the megacities of Delhi, Dhaka, Kolkata, and Mumbai.

Climate change will affect both energy generation and demand in South Asia. Changes in temperature and precipitation can diminish the capacity of power plants (e.g., hydropower plants) and efficiency of distribution systems, hence reduced energy supply. Meanwhile, aside from normal determinants such as population and economic development, climate change will place a higher demand for energy, due to higher requirements for heating and cooling. All these impacts will have an adverse effect on the economy. ADB's research shows that Climate change will affect South Asia more than most other regions. In economic terms, the region will lose nearly 2 percent of its gross domestic product (GDP) by 2050.

South Asia's weather is likely to become hotter than the global average, while monsoon rains and heavy storms will increase in most parts of the region. As well, the mountainous countries face increased flooding and landslides, while the coastal countries of the region are likely to be partly inundated by sea-level rise. The Global Climate Risk Index that **analyses to what extent countries and regions have been affected by impacts of weather-related loss events has shown through its reports that** *intense cyclones, excessive rainfall and severe floods make India and its neighbours among the worst affected countries in the world. In the 2019 Index,* India was ranked the 14th most vulnerable nation in a list topped by Puerto Rico, which was ravaged by Hurricane Maria in 2017. Sri Lanka was in second place after Puerto Rico. Nepal was ranked the world's fourth most vulnerable country in this latest edition of the index, while Bangladesh was ranked ninth. In the 2021 Index released by Germanwatch India ranks 7$^{th}$ most vulnerable globally. In 2019, monsoons lasted for an extra month and 110 percent of the normal rainfall occurred, which is most since 1994. The floods caused by these heavy and excessive rains were responsible for the death of over 1800 people across 14 states and led to the displacement of 1.8 million people. Overall, the economic damage of US$10 billion was caused by the intense monsoons in 2019 and affected around 11.8 million people. Eight tropical cyclones hit the country in the year 2019. The worst of which was *"Cyclone Fani"* which affected a total of 28 million people, killing nearly 90 people in India and Bangladesh and causing economic losses of US$8.1 billion.

By 2050, 64 percent of the population in Asia will be in cities, hence, we need to make cities climate resilient. More than 50 percent of urban residents in Asia live in low lying costal zones or flood plains. Rapid urban growth has also caused other environmental problems resulting from industrial activity and waste generation, which must be tackled. Without ambitious action against climate change, we are headed towards a global temperature increase of 4.4°C by the end of this century. Deserts are expanding in South Asian regions already experience severe, recurrent droughts. Millions of people are facing water stress.

Climate change requires not just governmental but multi-layered social response such as gender-specific response. For example, Climate Change Adaptation and Disaster Risk Reduction in Bangladesh, for example, is a women-centered initiative that helps communities in Bangladesh adapt to climate change by addressing extreme weather conditions. The initiative, implemented by Action Aid Bangladesh brings together groups of women who lead vulnerability assessments of climate risks, then identify and implement action plans. Making cooking eco-friendly can contribute substantially to greenhouse gas emissions. The cognitive behavioural shift needed to adapt and mitigate climate change certainly needs a concerted effort. The very nature of global warming and climate change demands a collective response and action plan. Emissions anywhere post a problem everywhere. As huge populations have high exposure to extreme weather events as seen in recent past. The UNFCC report says that almost over 40 percent of climate related disasters have occurred in Asia Pacific. As Asia is now becoming the economic engine for the global economy with rapidly expanding regional economies the environment and ecology in Asia Pacific are bound to face adverse impacts due to growing emissions related to growing industrialised production, demographic shifts, urbanisation and mobility.

Climate smart policies for sustainable resilient economic development is the need of the hour. There could be conscious efforts to promote environmental goods and services, nurturing green businesses, enhancing regional and international cooperation and regulations, collective decarbonisation and sustainable development strategies. If the economic development policies are aligned collectively to climate change action goals in South Asia, then the whole region will benefit substantially and as a result the adverse impacts of climate change on economies could be significantly reduced. Together South Asia can achieve more. For example, if South Asia develops a common market for solar panels, wind turbines, waste management technologies, green mobility solutions, eco-friendly agriculture solutions and other areas then there would be a huge economy with economies of scale in areas such as renewable energy, etc. These initiatives will lead to resource wastages and optimum utilisation in a sustainable way. There could be South Asian solar and wind energy grid benefitting all countries boosting energy security. Just imagine solar power from Rajasthan powering Dhaka. In COP 26 India envisioned grand Global Solar Grid Alliance and South Asian Solar Grid can be the right starting point. The whole trading system in South Asia could be made green and thus sustainable invariably benefiting all countries. With better interoperable regulations and coherence trade will get massive boosts in the collective green market in South Asia. Every country will be able to leverage one's own competitive and comparative advantages for mutual benefit.

Jointly planned river basin development will massively boost trade through inland water ways while reducing pressure on road transport, emission and costs. Dependence on fossil fuels could be collectively reduced. Every country in South Asia is facing climate change induced migrations, distressful environmental refugees who lose their livelihood security. As developmental projects could be environmentally managed better with regional cooperation, these problems could be mitigated.

The most severe impacts of climate change cut across boundaries. In response, South Asian developing member countries have reaffirmed their commitment to work together in addressing common challenges. In 2007, the South Asian Association for Regional Cooperation (SAARC) Council of Ministers adopted the SAARC Declaration on Climate Change calling on SAARC leaders to collectively assess and respond to climate change risks and impacts. In 2008, the SAARC Environment Ministers Dhaka Declaration on Climate Change included a 3-year action plan that urges the international community to promote partnership and provide additional finance to address climate change. In their 25th Jubilee Year, the SAARC Summit in 2010 concluded with the Thimphu Declaration on Climate Change, which sets an ambitious goal for South Asia to lead the world in furthering renewable energy, cutting carbon emissions, and reducing poverty while strengthening resilience to climate change. The SAARC had started with a vision of collective economic development but the scenario is rather clouded mostly due to the senseless belligerence of Pakistan and all other countries in South Asia become the losers. India can take leadership and move ahead joining hand with other countries in the neighbourhood for the necessary climate change action plan. If we peep into the history and see the way the European Union evolved, we see the vision of common markets with an overarching goal of peace through trade. Jean Monnet, the French economist after the end of Second World War and the beginning of the inevitable Cold War envisioned European collective coal and steel market to initiative dynamics of common market. We had the seeds of such vision – peace through trade in SAARC but every time Pakistan threw spanners in the momentum in these directions. We can envision collective renewable energy market for South Asia as a climate change action response and moving to other areas such as achieving nutrition security through Millets and so on? Through collective research and development effort we can solve many of our developmental challenges.

We will be able to handle many challenges related to water scarcity, soil security, biodiversity, etc through better mechanism and calibrated strategies. South Asia can certainly emerge a regional Carbon market well aligned with the international market and will have better negotiation levers. Surely regional electricity market can be beneficial to all. We will be better prepared for changing trade environment with global value chains. There could be massive regional human resource development initiatives for the regional green market with focus on skills development, gender equality issues, etc. Had such collective South Asian initiative had been in place we would have certainly responded better to the Covid crisis. We can unleash our regional developmental potential and energies. The full potential of our natural resources could be realised. For example, the full potential of renewable resources such as hydropower could be realised for regional growth and development. Countries in South Asia will be able to do better on ESG (Environment, Sustainability and Governance) compliances and this will boost foreign investment in the region benefitting all countries. There could be many noveler mutually rewarding opportunities for cooperation.

Funding climate action response will require funds. India is better placed economically to extend hand of help. A South Asian Climate Fund could be initiated. The 2010 Thimphu Declaration by SAARC heads of government called for a study to explore ways of providing capital for "projects that promote low-carbon technology and renewable energy". Such a Fund can help in adaptation and mitigation. This will reduce external dependence of the region. We can think of creative funding resources. India has seen numerous start-ups in climate change space. All other countries can benefit from these dynamics in India that has consistent shining track record of climate change action. Though countries have to work within their boundaries there would be a better accountability in the regional climate action cooperation framework there would be better scrutiny and accountability for environmental management in one's own country. Climate change has no nationality and doesn't have an agenda or a political affiliation, and can only be solved by cooperation. It's nature's wake-up call to us and shows how interconnected we are to nature. So, an interconnected climate action response is a common sense thing to do.

## Conclusion

Ignoring climate change, South Asian nations stand to lose the economic gains made till now. Fragmented national policies are not fit for the climate challenge. The arbitrary nature of national borders makes climate change hard to manage. We cannot neglect ecological boundaries and when glaciers melt the hydrological cycles in the whole region is impacted with floods. Like truth climate change involves us all and no country in South Asia can remain oblivious to its devastating impacts. Common sense demands a visionary collective regional response that can go a long way in systematically responding to the challenges of sustainable development. Prosperity requires peace. Peace is possible through trade and the rise of a collective South Asian green economy will vary substantially contributing to global efforts. South Asian countries need to find a common ground and build agreements and new frameworks. This will also enable individual countries to meet their international commitments in decarbonisation and other areas. Like truth, peace too involves us all. We must not be found waiting in our vision and mission. If various contentious issues and diplomatic bitterness could be kept in cold storage breaking the diplomacy deadlocks for a decade and fully focus on sustainable regional development then the whole South Asian neighbourhood will create a whole new futures for the people with better security and environment based on renewed trust and safety net in the collective South Asian climate change action. Separating geopolitics from climate change cooperation is certainly a challenge but it has to be achieved through new institutional foundations. We can begin with small and meaningful steps such as people to people interactions focussed on climate change response. Private sector can play a great role and their regional collaborations can bring immediate benefits to the economies. The youth could be mobilised in this direction. We need to infuse new spirit of climate change cooperation in SAARC. Together South Asia can achieve more to face climate change. Climate change action response could revive regional cooperation on a sound basis. Without South Asian cooperation many of the goals of climate action are beyond reach. All South Asian nations have mounting climate anxieties. Cooperation always delivers results. The crucial question is: While climate change is ravaging us will the statesmanship rise to the occasion in South Asia? The failure will fail the future of the whole region.

## References

The Global Risk Report, 2021.

Asian Economic Integration Report 2023, Asian Development Bank.

Climate Change South Asia Information Update, ADB, 2022.

Annual Report, NIDM, 2021-2022, NIDM, New Delhi.

### Websites:

www.unfccc.int

www.nidm,gov,in

www.thethirdpole.net

www.germanwatch.org

www.adb.org

# 14

# Education as a Factor in Promoting Good Neighbourliness

**Prof. Chintamani Mahapatra**

Trade, investment, defence cooperation, political understanding among governments are critical in maintaining good relations between India and its neighbours in South Asia. It is noteworthy that trade and investment among South Asian countries are limited, defence cooperation is almost non-existent and in the case of Pakistan mutual hostility informs the Indo-Pakistan relationship; and political misunderstanding is rampant between India and most of its neighbours.

One of the key factors that have shaped relationships between India and its neighbours is history; and how history is written and taught in the neighbouring countries. Children in most of the South countries learn early in their career either nothing or some general themes about India or narratives full of anti-India characterisations and rhetoric.

The children who grow to become leaders, bureaucrats, diplomats or businessmen and entrepreneurs in the neighbouring countries carry the impressions from their early education and their actions and behaviours show clearly in the kind of bad neighbourliness India experiences in South Asia.

What can New Delhi do to promote better understanding of India among the people of the neighbouring countries? Here comes the crucial role of education. Actually, time has come for us to consider education as a key component of national security. Academics and policymakers have securitised water, food, environment and several other issues in recent decades. But education too can be considered as an issue that can promote security or hamper complex security interests.

## Securitisation of Education: Need of the Hour

Education should be mainstreamed in the security discourse of India. The government needs to ensure education security for all at all levels, but particularly at higher education, to push the momentum of the country's march towards becoming an effective global player.

In recent years a vast number of issues has been securitised by the governments and the scholars in various countries, which include, among others, water security, food security, human security, environmental security, energy security, cyber security, and so on.

More recently, the United States under the Trump Administration has begun to consider women economic empowerment as a national security issue. Australia has viewed national security education as a prime area of teaching and research and 12 Australian universities offer national security courses distinct from disciplines, such as international relations and military studies. The Australian Department of Education and Training has listed 19 courses on National Security!

As education is fast becoming internationally competitive, it will most likely enter a phase of contestation reminiscent of the cold war era. Education policy of a country, especially related to financing educational institutes abroad, introducing certain preferred courses in foreign universities or colleges or seeking franchise to open campus extension in other countries might be fiercely contested.

The beginning has already been made in the United States, where large number of Confucius Institutes have been established and funded heavily by the Chinese government. The US legislators have suddenly woken up to realise that China has been trying to "indoctrinate American children" and promote "Communist government's propaganda" in the classrooms. As efforts are being made to close down some Confucius Institutes and block the non-transparent flow of Chinese funds in the name of education, China is likely to challenge this sooner than later. The Australian Government has also come up with a "foreign influence transparency scheme" to keep track on Confucius Institutes in the country.

In the backdrop of these developments, systematic marketing of education by countries, such as the US, UK, Canada, Australia, China, Germany, France and a few other countries will come under scrutiny by the target countries. Millions of students from the developing countries are annually spending billions of dollars in the above handful of countries for acquiring degrees, professional certificates and undergoing skill development trainings. The international ranking of universities and rate race that has begun among many universities to get a place in such rankings will also be scrutinised more and more and questioned in coming times.

Internationalisation of education these days is an oft-repeated concept in the lexicon of global education discourse. In April 2019, Egyptian government hosted the Global Forum for Internationalisation of Education and Scientific Research. International Association of Universities has been tracking developments related to internationalisation of education, promoting it and periodically publishing global survey reports.

However, for India, it is important to consider securitisation of education sector and making it a primary component of India's national security. First, India has a vast youth bulge that can bring strength to the country only if the youths are educated, employed and empowered. Second, today's global economy is marked by the fast emerging knowledge industry and securitisation of education will be timely to leverage India's potential. Third, internationalisation of curricula in the Indian educational eco-system can prepare the Indian youth to compete in the global employment market, and simultaneously earn foreign exchange by encouraging inbound student mobility and save foreign exchange by removing the need for Indian students to look for educational opportunities abroad. Fourth, social justice can be provided to marginalised section and the economically weaker sections of Indian society, who cannot afford foreign education, by making them available international-standard education in the home country.

It is time to ponder why a large number of Indian students are migrating to foreign countries by spending parental money to seek educational and professional training opportunities. It is time to debate whether the political leadership in India should not launch smart college and smart university programmes in addition to "smart city" initiative. Why is it that we have one of the largest education systems in the world and yet our universities are placed so low in international ranking in terms of quality education? Why is it that a large number of engineering graduates in India suffer from un-employability? Why is it that vast number of medical degree aspirants have to seek admissions into medical institutions of China, Russia, Azerbaijan, Poland and a few Central Asian countries?

Even after more than seven decades of independent existence, priority given to the education sector in India is abysmally low. People have to struggle hard to get a job in bureaucracy, private sector companies, educational institutions and journalism, yet we have not adequately debated setting educational eligibility for law makers. While the executive and judicial branches of our parliamentary system are peopled with highly qualified persons, law-making bodies have inadequate number of highly qualified leaders or representatives. The largest democracy in the world must consider evolving a system to back up numbers with quality. There is little doubt that the Indian political class is intelligent and articulate. But it can certainly be better.

In years to come, countries with better-educated, superior skilled and excellent innovators will find a rightful place in the global hierarchy of power. Weapons, bombs, missiles will certainly not loose their relevance to guard our borders. But level of education, science, technology, skill, innovation and public health will determine national power. India's aspirations for a rightful place in the global order requires more investment in, singular attention to and high priority for the education sector.

## Education as Tool for Trade

The Western developed countries for long have used education as a tool for promoting trade, business and other interests with countries around the world. Thousands of students from developing countries compete for scholarships and fellowships to study in educational institutions in the United States, Britain, France, Germany, Australia, Canada and many other countries. Gradually rich and elite families from the developing countries have begun to finance the education of their children in Western countries for acquiring certificates, diplomas or degrees, so that their children can be better placed in jobs in their respective home countries or even in the international market place.

But there is a flip side to this phenomenon. The foreign-educated students become the points of contacts for traders and businessmen of the countries they go to study. The Western industries, corporate houses, traders and investors deftly build contacts with foreign returned citizens of the developing countries to promote their respective interests. Some of the foreign educated students in their later career become political leaders holding high ministerial berths, top positions in the bureaucracy or entrepreneurs and industrialists. In the process, they facilitate trade and commerce with countries they went for higher studies or training.

## Education Promotes Understanding

It is also significant to note that education can promote mutual understanding between peoples of different countries and promote international cooperation. In the field of international relations studies, it is often observed that knowledge about foreign countries is inadequate and often marked by kaleidoscopic views and impressions. In a globalising world, half-baked knowledge or outright ignorance about other countries can be seriously counterproductive.

What has been the policy on such issues in India? What is the state of one good experiment India undertaking by establishing South Asian University? How many students of neighbouring countries come to study in India? Can it be improved further? Should the government of India adopt a more dynamic and innovative approach to use education as a tool to promote good neighbourliness policy? The paper attempts an explanation of all these issues.

## Foreign Students in India

India does not have any comprehensive and time tested policy to internationalise Indian educational institutes in India that should aim at bringing a large number of foreign students to get education in India. We all know the low priority given to education sector in the Indian social sector policy formulations. It is also a fact that with a huge population, India has been slow to educate the masses to a desirable extent. India needs first to educate every child and provide facilities to every student to acquire higher educational degrees.

Why has India that was once a Viswa Guru drawing learners from other civilisations to its educational institutions, not yet been able to draw foreign students in large numbers to its educational institutions? Instead a large number of students are going abroad in search of better educational opportunities from year to year. Even during the COVID-19 pandemic, more than 250,000 Indian students left India for study abroad. Their number saw more than 60 percent rise in 2021. And in 2022, about 750,000 students went to study abroad.[1] According to the date provided by the Ministry of Education to Lok Sabha, the lower house of the Indian Parliament, Cumulatively, more than 30 lakh Indians undertook their studies in foreign countries between 2017 and 2022[2].

Significantly, in response to a question in the Lok Sabha whether Indian students spend more for education abroad than India's education budget and whether the government has any plan to set up "International University of high standard" in India to save the funds, Subhas Sarkar, Education Minister of State, said that "as of now there is no proposal to set up International University in the country"[3].

Ironically, after a prolonged debate, proposal to allow foreign universities to open campuses in India was approved. The UGC prepared a draft Regulations to facilitate the establishment of campuses of Foreign

Higher Educational Institutions in India and circulated it to the public for comments. It was intended to increase access to higher education in satellite campuses in India of reputed Foreign Higher Education Institutions (FHEI). The UGC draft said: "A legislative framework facilitating such entry will be put in place, and universities will be given special dispensation regarding regulatory, governance, and content norms on par with other autonomous institutions of India[4]."

The opposition parties and critics pointed out that this regulation reflected inability of the government to provide best of education to Indians by establishing world-class universities in India. The UGC was of the view that it would bring advanced learning systems and pedagogy to India and in any case students mobility for study abroad is not an Indian, but a global phenomenon. Actually, almost half of all international students enrol themselves only in 14 countries; 54 out of 200 countries account for about 80 percent of foreign students[5]. The critics pointed out that India with 1,113 higher education institutions should be addressing the regulatory and administrative issues within its education system[6].

India should try to be a hub of world-class higher education institutions and centre of innovation and research where students from various parts of the globe can be provided with affordable yet high quality education. The critics have also pointed out that India should develop the capability to attract foreign students to India rather than push Indians to go abroad in search of better education. The country this way can not only save foreign exchange but also earn foreign exchange.

As of now, total number of foreign students enrolled in Indian universities is very limited. According to All India Survey of Higher Education "Foreign students come from 164 different countries from across the globe. The top 10 countries constitute 63.7 percent of the total foreign students enrolled. Highest share of foreign students come from neighbouring countries of which Nepal is 26.88 percent of the total, followed by Afghanistan (9.8 percent), Bangladesh (4.38 percent), Sudan (4.02 percent), Bhutan constitutes (3.82 percent) and Nigeria (3.4 percent)"[7].

In terms of number of countries from where students come to study in India, 163 is quite impressive. But the total number of foreign students in India is less than 50,000. Except Nepal, number of students from other South Asian countries are minimal or nothing. It contrasts with more than a lakh of Indian students who got visa to study in the United States in 2022 alone[8].

Even a smaller European country like Poland draws more foreign students. In the 2021/22 academic year, "89,420 foreign students from

180 countries were studying in Poland"[9]. Clearly, India needs to develop the required educational infrastructure not only for the benefit of Indian students but also to attract foreign students in large numbers. The high quality of physical infrastructure, credible academic profile, high-end research facilities and affordable fee structure must be in place to do so. While it will take years to get students in adequate numbers from Europe and North America, the beginning must be made to attract students from neighbouring countries to study in Indian institutions.

There is no doubt that the Indian Council of Cultural Relations, bilateral educational exchange programmes are in place for decades that facilitate internationalisation of Indian campuses. But compared to the scenario in many countries, internalisation of Indian campuses appears cosmetic. Connect to India and Study Abroad programmes initiated in India were good beginning, but outcome has been anything but satisfactory. South Asia University established by signing a charter with all SAARC member countries also had a good beginning, but its performance so far is lacklustre. It is headless for last several years, the new campus took years to be built and number of students from the neighbouring countries is unexpectedly less.

With the new education policy adopted by the government of India and the drive towards making Indian education system modern and as per the requirements of the twenty-first century in a globalised world, if implemented properly, will surely make India an education hub for at least the students of the Global South, particularly from India's neighbourhood—both immediate and extended.

It is gratifying that India on assuming the Presidency of the G20 has focused, among other issues of crucial importance, education as priority theme. India intends to narrow the wide gaps in quality education and skilling in collaboration with the G20 countries[10].

The G20 education working has been the task to deliberate on four priority subjects: "cnsuring foundational literacy and numeracy especially in context of blended learning, making tech-enabled learning more inclusive, qualitative and collaborative at every level and building capacities, promoting life-long learning in the context of future of work and strengthening research and promoting Innovation through richer collaboration and partnerships."[11] The working group has reportedly already discussed important issues, such as use of technology for educational universal access, dealing with challenges of digital divide, preserving data privacy, cyber safety etc.

## Concluding Observations

India has emerged as an important global actor. Hundreds of developing countries of the Global South look at India as a leader that can voice the demands and concerns of the Global South. G20 presidency has given an opportunity to India to put the problems and concerns of the Global South in the agenda of the G20 summit. Prime Minister Narendra Modi held a virtual summit with leaders of numerous countries of the Global South to hear them and articulate those in the G20 meetings.

India has taken the initiative to make India a Centre of Innovation of Research where the interests of the Global South will get priority and appropriate technology will be innovated for poverty alleviation and economic development. India has also launched an initiative to provide fellowships and scholarships to students of the Global South to study in India. Prime Minister Modi has openly supported shaping the globalisation in a way that would be Global South-sensitive.

It is in this spirit that Indian Ministry of External Affairs should have innovative education diplomacy aimed at making India an international education centre. Educational cooperation with neighbouring countries can a long way in strengthening political cooperation, building trade ties, facilitating mutual investments, combating non-traditional security threats and above all promoting mutual trust.

SAARC as a regional cooperation has failed to take off the ground largely because of the role of Pakistan that has destabilised the entire region and made it terrorism-ridden. Multiple sub-regional cooperative mechanisms have played a substantive role in peace, stability and development. Mega groupings of nations in the forms of East Summit and ASEAN Regional Forum have different mandates. But educational exchanges and cooperation between India and the countries in the Indo-Pacific region can go a long way in complementing the efforts of sub-regional groupings and mega institutions and multilateral activities for achieving peace and stability, growth and development.

While India can think of establishing a few world class universities where international students carefully chosen and study and research together, the existing reputed institutions, such as IITs and IIMs can also be leveraged to educate and train students from the Indo-Pacific countries. Existing universities should be encouraged and assisted to implement existing Memorandum of Understanding or conclude new ones with neighbouring countries.

Building new universities with quality faculty and resilient infrastructure take time. But a good beginning can be made by expanding or initiating Summer Courses in the universities, holding short-term workshops by think tanks, skill development courses by IIMs etc. can be useful for building a propitious regional environment for India to play its due role in peace building and realising Prime Minister's SAGAR Vision that calls for Security and Growth for All in the Region.

## Notes

1. This data was provided by the Ministry of Education, https://www.news18.com/news/education-career/more-than-7-5-lakh-indians-went-abroad-to-study-in-2022-up-by-68-from-2021-moe-7022509.html
2. https://www.livemint.com/education/news/more-than-30-lakh-indian-students-went-abroad-for-higher-studies-in-6-years-11675733737392.html
3. https://www.outlookindia.com/national/over-30-lakh-indians-went-abroad-during-2017-22-for-higher-education-govt-news-259973
4. https://www.forbesindia.com/article/take-one-big-story-of-the-day/foreign-university-campuses-in-india-is-the-move-practical/82871/1
5. https://www.universityworldnews.com/post.php?story=20230202105458 74
6. https://www.forbesindia.com/article/take-one-big-story-of-the-day/foreign-university-campuses-in-india-is-the-move-practical/82871/1
7. https://timesofindia.indiatimes.com/home/education/times-study-abroad/top-news/india-gets-maximum-foreign-students-from-nepal-karnataka-favourite-for-higher-edu-hrd/articleshow/71275896.cms
8. https://timesofindia.indiatimes.com/home/education/times-study-abroad/top-news/india-gets-maximum-foreign-students-from-nepal-karnataka-favourite-for-higher-edu-hrd/articleshow/71275896.cms
9. https://www.thefirstnews.com/article/number-of-foreign-students-in-poland-grows-36318
10. https://www.financialexpress.com/education-2/g20-education-working-group-to-focus-on-inclusivity/2963762/
11. For details see https://opportunityindia.franchiseindia.com/article/g20-ewg-to-focus-on-quality-education-for-all-35245

# 15

# India's Vaccine Diplomacy and Regionalism

**Dr Rajiv. M. Gupte and Prof Anand. N. limaye**

## Introduction

Even as India has established herself as "Pharmacy of the world", the claim has been proven once again. India helped the neighbouring nations and across the globe with COVID-19 vaccines during the pandemic. This is in tune with India's neighbourhood first policy and has indeed helped augment India's soft power. COVID-19 Pandemic had drastic impact on regional and global geopolitical architecture and India's image in neighbourhood and extended neighbourhood. In early 2021 India established "Neighbourhood First" policy and propagated her role as net security provider in the region.

India had already established as a major player in export of pharmaceuticals products to the extent of 23 billion dollars of export with target of 50 billion this year.

**Figure 1. Region-wise distribution of India's pharmaceutical product exports**

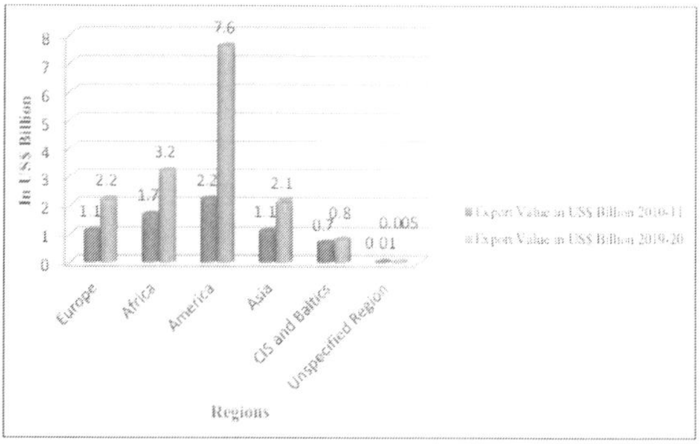


*Source*: Ministry of Commerce and Industry, Government of India.

During pandemic many countries have been perusing global health diplomacy (Lisk and Sehovic, 2020). India decided not only to vaccinate her people but also to assist neighbouring countries (Pattanaik, 2021). As such India's relationship with her neighbours had not been very cordial, given the internal and external dynamics, however one remained a peace-loving country. The *Vasudhaiva Kutumbakam* has a pivotal place in India's foreign policy (Mahapatra, 2016). India had supported her neighbourhood at times of calamities, tsunamis, floods, earthquakes and also helped in space technology. While the neighbouring countries were finding it difficult to contain COVID-19. India's neighbourhood first policy has certainly helped them. The Political, Socio Economic and strategic landscape in India's neighbourhood has been changing considerably.

India's diplomacy primarily centered on managing relations with the neighbours as can be traced back to Nehru's Panchsheel doctrine, to Gujral doctrine based on principal on non-reciprocity (Muni, 2017). Since 1914 India's foreign policy witnessed the shift from idealism to realism. 1990s decade was watershed moment in South Asian regional cooperation as the world witnessed economic reforms. India is conscious in promoting regional cooperation thru trade and technological cooperation during this changing geopolitical architecture (Behuria, 2012). The Gujral doctrine played a key role in India's neighbourhood policy enabling other countries to rise above the region security conundrum. India provided the neighbouring countries with unilateral concession with seeking reciprocity. Subsequent governments provided national democratic alliance (1989-2004) and united progressive alliance (2004-2014). As a result, the trade and security relation with SAARC countries witnessed a dramatic shift.

But the real implementation of neighbourhood first policy came in 2014. There have been many visits from the heads of SAARC and BIMSTEC countries. During the address in $69^{th}$ UNGA the Indian prime minister stated that a nations destiny is linked to the neighbourhood and that is why India's highest priority was advancing friendship and cooperation with the neighbours.

COVID-19 Pandemic emerged as a global health crisis. As a result, there was a serious threat to trade, global supply chain, health and other related aspects. There had to be collaborative efforts of regional organisations such as SAARC. Many South Asian countries reported a serious threat to health and economy. Despite the differences, Indian Prime Minister proposed a joint Emergency Fund based on health cooperation with an initial contribution of 10 million dollars, and with a pool of contribution it reached 21 million dollars (Jha & Jha, 2020). Accept for Pakistan all countries pledged to contribute directly to the SAARC COVID-19 emergency fund. Pakistan pledged three million dollars which would be deposited to SAARC secretariat. This action demonstrated the regional differences. As India is the biggest pharmacy in the world, the leadership realised the lead to play a significant role in health cooperation and vaccination. This was India's *Maitri* initiative.

**Table 1. India's COVID-19 vaccine supplies as for to its geographical neighbours as of May 2021.**

India's COVID-19 vaccine supplies so far to its neighbours (in lakhs)

| S. No. | Country | Grant | | | Commercial | | | COVAX | | | Total supplie |
|---|---|---|---|---|---|---|---|---|---|---|---|
| | | Quantity | Date of despatch | | Quantity | Date of despatch | | Quantity | Date of despatch | | |
| 1. | Afghanistan | 0.5 | 0.5 | 7 February | – | – | | 0.468 | 0.468 | 6 March | 0.968 |
| 2. | Bangladesh | 3.3 | 2.0 | 21 January | 7.0 | 5.0 | 25 January | – | – | | 10.3 |
| | | | 1.2 | 26 March | | 2.0 | 22 February | | | | |
| | | | 0.1 | 2 April | | – | – | | | | |
| 3. | Bhutan | 0.55 | 0.15 | 20 January | – | – | | – | – | | 0.55 |
| | | | 0.40 | 21 March | | | | | | | |
| 4. | Maldives | 0.2 | 0.1 | 20 January | 0.1 | 0.1 | 29 March | 0.012 | 0.012 | 6 March | 0.312 |
| | | | 0.1 | 19 February | | | | | | | |
| 5. | Myanmar | 1.7 | 1.5 | 22 January | 2.0 | 2.0 | 11 February | – | – | | 3.7 |
| | | | 0.2 | 11 February | | | | | | | |
| 6. | Nepal | 1.1 | 1.0 | 21 January | 1.0 | 1.0 | 20 February | 0.348 | 0.348 | 5 March | 2.448 |
| | | | 0.1 | 28 March | | | | | | | |
| 7. | Pakistan | – | – | | – | – | | – | – | | – |
| 8. | Sri Lanka | 0.5 | 0.5 | 28 January | 0.5 | 0.5 | 24 February | 0.264 | 0.264 | 6 March | 1.264 |
| Total Supplies to India's Geographical Neighbours | | | | | | | | | | | 19.542 |
| Total Supplies to 95 countries across the world, including India's Geographical Neighbours | | | | | | | | | | | 66.370 |
| Percentage share of India's Geographical Neighbours in India's total vaccine supply | | | | | | | | | | | 29.44% |

Source: Ministry of External Affairs, Government of India, 2021.

## India's Soft Power

This initiative positively affected India's Soft power not only in immediate neighbourhood but also globally.

## Bangladesh

In April 26, 2021 Bangladesh sealed the orders with India to contain the spread of COVID-19. In October 2020, Bangladesh had declined China's offer of corona vaccine due to the efficacy. And as the purchase would have involved a clause on sharing cost of clinical trials. Bangladesh turned to India, as India contributes to 60 percent of global Vaccine production. In the past few years' public opinion about India in Bangladesh had suffered. In January 2020, India adopted CAA (Citizen Amendment Act) which triggered Protest in Bangladesh. Failure to sign TEESTA river water agreement was another issue. Bangladesh was the first country to receive vaccine from India under the *Maitri* initiative. In January 2021, Dhaka received 3.3 million COVI-SHEILD vaccine's with further was raised to 10.3 million.

Beijing had been already making inroads with BRI (Belt and road initiative). China also sought military alliance with Bangladesh. Although it never happened Bangladesh tried to maintain cordial relations with both India and China.

**Figure 3**

| Country | Grant | Commercial | Total |
|---|---|---|---|
| India | 3.3 | 7 | 10.3 |
| China | 0.5 | 0 | 0.5 |

*Source*: MEA Website.

## Nepal and Bhutan

The mountain states faced heavy challenges during the pandemic. The vaccine *Maitri* initiative had a very positive effect on the relationship. India emerged a first responder to Bhutan and Nepal. Bhutan also reciprocated with a supply of 40 MTs of liquid oxygen. Nepal received 8 Lacs Doses from SINOPHARM, China in the past years had not so conducive relation with India, received about 100 million doses from India.

**Figure 4**

| Country | India | | | China |
|---|---|---|---|---|
| | Grant | Commercial | COVAX | Grant |
| Nepal | 1.1 | 1 | 0.34 | 0.8 |
| Bhutan | 055 | | | |

*Source*: MEA Website.

## Myanmar and Thailand

Myanmar is strategically important for India as a gate way to India's North-east region. Myanmar received 1.7 million doses from India, the military coup disrupted the trajectory of the Myanmar pandemic response. In Feb 2021 the healthcare workers and civil servants across the country launched a national civil disobedience movement. There was also public resentment against China, it has been the key to the shielding of Myanmar in UNSC.

**Figure 5**

| Vaccines provided by India (In million doses) | | | |
|---|---|---|---|
| Country | Grant | Commercial | Total |
| Myanmar | 1.7 | 2 | 3.7 |

| Vaccine provided by China (In million doses) | | | |
|---|---|---|---|
| Myanmar | 0.5 | 0 | 0.5 |
| Thailand | 0.5 | 5.5 | 6 |

*Source*: MEA Website.

India's other Southeast Asian neighbour, Thailand is also under pressure. There was public disapproval to the government decision to not join COVAX, which is subscribed to by almost the entire neighbourhood. Thailand was among one of the countries that sent relief to India during the second wave as a part of Thailand's look west policy and is regarded as a rising market. Here India needs to play a larger role.

## Sri Lanka and Maldives

These two nations where primarily looking at Russia and China for vaccines. As a part of China's debt diplomacy were they mainly under the influence of India's northern neighbour. The bail out packages from India started positive disposition towards India. These countries began their vaccination drives primarily by utilising donations from India. This led to a great deal of pro-India rhetoric, with presidents of both countries taking to twitter to thank India for her generosity. Hey also declared in Feb 2021 that Sri Lanka was likely to have only India's COVISHEILD. Both countries following India's donation placed direct orders with Serum Institute India. However, due to lag in supplies they sought to source vaccines from China and Russia.

**Figure 6**

| Country | India | China | Russia |
|---|---|---|---|
| Sri Lanka | 1,000,000 | 1,100,000 | 65,000 |
| Maldives | 30,00,000 | 2,00,000 | ------------- |

*Source*: MEA Website.

Sri Lanka also received 65000 doses from Russia. Both Sri Lanka and Maldives had been concerned with India's difficulties during second wave and often explained the situation to their own public.

## Pakistan and Afghanistan

As India commenced the vaccine diplomacy, in January 2021, till March, India did not receive any request for vaccine from Pakistan. Pakistan suffered a setback as it was highly dependent on COVAX.

Pakistan had to reengineer its entire vaccine strategy, As India halted the exports of vaccine. Islamabad received 1.6 million doses from China. Pakistan offered to send relief material to India during initial onslaught of send wave. The conditional offer was to release all the Kashmiri prisoners on humanitarian grounds.

**Figure 7**

| Country | India | China | Russia |
|---|---|---|---|
| Afghanistan | 500,000 | 0 | 0 |
| Pakistan | 0 | 10,60,000 | 50,000 |

*Source*: MEA Website.

Russia also supplied 50,000 doses of SPUTNIK V vaccines. While, Russia-Pakistan ties are not very strong, Russia could possibly look at the stakes in Afghanistan thru Pakistan.

India has a lot of interest in Afghanistan, pertaining to Central Asian energy markets and broader connectivity projects. Kabul received one Million doses in two phases. However, during second wave they looked at China and Russia as alternative suppliers. In March 2021, US Secretary of State official included India in the process thru a plan for the future of Afghanistan that outlined the crucial role of regional actors including India.

### *The Result*

Pew research data states that these Vaccine diplomacy efforts have sustainably improved the global views of India for enhancing India's soft power.

## Global View of India

**Figure 8**

| Country | Unfavourable | Favourable | After Pandemic |
|---|---|---|---|
| South Korea | 18 | 64 | +5 |
| Philippines | 21 | 58 | +2 |
| Japan | 24 | 8 | +2 |
| Indonesia | 23 | 57 | +15 |
| Australia | 33 | 57 | +10 |
| US | 23 | 50 | +15 |

*Source*- PEW data.

## Consequences

Vaccine diplomacy of India has immensely contributed to India's soft power. Such huge market, trained man power, advancements in Information Technology, robust Institutional framework and thriving democracy can be leveraged for regionalism. India's Neighbourhood is not devoid from regional frameworks in variousforms. SAARC, BIMSTEC and ASEAN are some of the established frame works. At this stage we suggest that this diplomacy needs to be extended to:

A. Regional Trade
B. Global Pandemic treaty
C. Asia Pacific charter

## A. Regional Trade

The improved soft power of India needs to be translated into advancing the trade benefits. The paper presents a Hypothetical Framework using game theory. The rise and fall of various institution are a result of states regional choices in terms of their membership preferences. We look at proposing inclusion of Japan in this framework and leave China at bay.

The role of the larger state depends upon the gains which are relatively large while the costs are also large. Long lasting question on whether sponsoring framework of institution is benefit or costly to the leader rests on benevolence or predatory hegemon, which side is emphasised.

**Figure 8(a)**

| | Number 1 State (leader) | Number 2 State |
|---|---|---|
| Benefit | Large (This becomes larger than the no.1 State considering Prestige to be critical) | Small |
| Cost | Large (This can be reduced by requesting the number 2 state to share the burden) | Small (this can be increased if the number 2 state is required to share the burden) |

*Source:* Shintaro Hamanaka (Asian development Bank - Regionalism Cycle in Asia (-Pacific) p. 2)

## JAPAN

**Figure 8 (b)**

| | No framework | Asia- only framework | Japans active participation | Japans active participation |
|---|---|---|---|---|
| Benefit | None | Extremely Large | Small | Small |
| Cost | None | Large | Large | Medium |
| Net benefit | None (0) | Positive (2) | Negative (-2) | (-1) |

*Source:* Shintaro Hamanaka (Asian development bank - Regionalism Cycle in Asia (-Pacific) p. 3)

## CHINA

**Figure 9**

| | **No frame-work** | **Asia- only framework** | **Japans active participation** | **Japans active participation** |
|---|---|---|---|---|
| Benefit | None | Negative | Medium | Medium |
| Cost | None | None | Very small | Large |
| Net benefit | None (0) | Negative (-2) | Positive (2) | (-1) |

*Source:* Shintaro Hamanaka (Asian development bank - Regionalism Cycle in Asia (-Pacific) p. 3)

**Figure 10**

| **China / Japan** | **Participation** | **Non-participation** |
|---|---|---|
| **Participation** | **-4,4** | **2,-2** |
| **Non-participation** | **-2,2** | **0,0** |

*Source*: MEA Website.

Thus, it can be seen that inclusion of extra regional partner like Japan would add value to both the parties. We further suggest that India continues non-participation in RCEP (Regional Comprehensive Economic Partnership).

### B. Global Pandemic Treaty

It has been proposed by WHO (World Health Organisation) that regional pandemic treaty should be negotiated by the member states. We suggest that this treaty should be adopted under Article 21 instead of Article 19. Also, there may be public hearings and different stake holders including government, Industry representation, heathcare experts and legal opinion makers. This instrument needs to be binding under international law and:

1. Ensure higher, sustained and long-term government engagement.
2. Early detection and prevention of pandemic.
3. Resilience and response mechanism.
4. One health approach.

There should also be a compulsory licensing provision.

### C. Indo-Pacific Charter

As the hegemonic designs of some regional players punctuate the peace and security of other nations, it would be appropriate for India to take lead in developing Indo-Pacific Charter. At the juncture when India is preceding over three important institutions- G20, SCO, UNSC, it would only be appropriate if India spearheads this.

(a) Resilience of global supply chain.
(b) Respect for peace and sovereignty of their nations.
(c) Respect for Multilateral framework.
(d) Protecting Sea Lines of Communication.
(e) Transparency in Data Sharing.
(f) Regional Arms race.

## Conclusion

During pandemic India has been a great contributor in vaccination programmes in the region. The vaccine diplomacy juxta positioned with debt diplomacy has resulted into enhancement of India's Soft Power. While India has been a responsible power in the Indo-Pacific region and enjoying strong soft power status, should take lead in developing regional trade framework, Global Pandemic Treaty and Indo-Pacific Charter.

## References

http://aric.adb.org/pdf/workingpaper/WP42_Regionalism_Cycle_in_Asia.pdf

https://econpapers.repec.org/RePEc:ris:adbrei:0042

https://www.investindia.gov.in/siru/india-pharmacy-world

https://www.pmindia.gov.in/en/news_updates/english-rendering-of-the-pms-statement-at-the-general-debateof-the-69th-session-of-the-united-nations-general-assembly-unga/

https://www.trtworld.com/magazine/is-india-s-neighbourhood-first-policy-unable-to-win-regional-allies-50492

https://commerce.gov.in/international-trade/

https://www.thehindu.com/news/national/coronavirus-how-different-is-the-pm-cares-fund-from-the-pmsnational-relief-fund/article31546287.ece

https://journals.sagepub.com/doi/10.1177/00219096221079310

https://www.historydiscussion.net/history-of-india/indias-relationship-with-her-neighbours/1685

https://thediplomat.com/2021/05/dont-write-off-indian-vaccine-diplomacy-yet/

https://www.geo.tv/latest/355115-pakistan-pakistan-requests-to-procure-5-mn-doses-of-russian-sputnikvaccine

# 16

# India's Cultural Diplomacy: An Effort Toward Strengthening Neighbourhood Ties

**Prof Prashant Shamrao Amrutkar**

The political, economic and strategic landscape of India's immediate neighbourhood has shifted radically. PM Narendra Modi's appealing personality and strong political position within the country have given him leverage to carve out a new direction in the Indian foreign policy. Consequently, we see digression from prior Indian foreign policy in some areas, while deepening and broadening existing partnerships in others. (Ganguly, 2017:131-143.) True to our history, the 'Neighbours First' policy, has been a standout component of the Modi administration's diplomatic strategy. According to the government's strategic vision, India must reconcile its disagreements with its small neighbours, portray a more positive image, and create more connectedness (Kaura and Meena, 2020:10-27).

## Culture as a Binding Force

Power is important in international politics; traditionally, power has been defined in terms of military capability and outcomes in wars and conflicts. With the advent of the worldwide democratic movement, which culminated in the second half of the twentieth century, the concept of power has undergone fundamental alterations, with power being interpreted in terms of growing influence not from the point of victory in war but from the point of peace. The concept of soft power has gained importance in this context; a critical component of soft power is cultural diplomacy, which is calling the shots in the field of diplomacy and has experienced colossal transformation with the evolution of soft power (Shome).

In the Indian Subcontinent, Indian culture and civilisation serve as the foundation for communities that span nations and geographical boundaries. The various common characteristics of culture and civilisation in South Asian countries can help to bridge cross-border populations and bring them together on a common platform to develop diplomatic relations. Globalisation has contributed to the use of culture as an important tool of diplomacy by strengthening the idea of a borderless world in which citizenship has grown increasingly cosmopolitan in nature.

## Cultural diplomacy

Cultural diplomacy is a type of public diplomacy and soft power that encompasses the "exchange of ideas, information, art, language and other aspects of culture among states and their peoples in order to create mutual understanding" (Waller, 2009:74). The goal of cultural diplomacy is to help people in a foreign country understand their country's principles and institutions in order to get widespread support for economic and political goals (Maack, 2001:59).

Culture is a set of values and activities that provide meaning to society. This includes both high culture (books, art, and education for the elite) and popular culture (appeals to the masses) (Nye, 2004:22). Through cultural diplomacy, countries strive to demonstrate this to worldwide audiences. It falls under the umbrella of soft power "The ability to acquire what you want by appeal rather than compulsion or money. It is impacted by the culture, political ideals, and policies of a country" (Nye, 2004:18). This demonstrates the importance of culture in attracting visitors to a country. Cultural diplomacy is a kind of public diplomacy. Public diplomacy is boosted by a bigger society and culture, while simultaneously public diplomacy helps to "amplify and broadcast that society and culture to the globe at large" (Carnes, 2006:15).

## India's Cultural Diplomacy

India has inherited a civilisation which is over 5,000 years old and is rightly called the melting pot of the ancient and the medieval world. Culture forms an integral part of the national power profile of India. India is the birthplace of four major religions in the world. It is undoubtedly the abode of cultural diversity which is rightly articulated in Jawaharlal Nehru's magnum opus work '*The Discovery of India*'.

In this context, governments since independence have promoted cultural diplomacy and the Modi government is deploying soft power diplomacy. The Modi government's soft power is tied to old Indian ideas such as *"Vasudhaiva Kutumbakam"* (the whole world as a family). Some broad types of soft power expression are the relationship between ancient heritage and civilisation relations (Buddhism, Yoga, Sanskrit, Ayurveda and Zero). Ancient heritage and civilisational links mainly appeal to Panchamrit's culture and regional security features. The two main forces under the ancient banner are Buddhism and Yoga. India is strongly influenced by Buddhism and yoga, making it recognised as the spiritual capital of the world (Uttam 2019:898). Some examples include the Buddhism tourism circuit in the eastern parts of India, the conscious promotion of Hindu tourism circuit throughout India, especially the southern part of India which consists of majestic temples like the Tirupati temple, Brihadeshwara temple, Dakhineshwar temple to name a few. Other examples include the Islamic holy sites of Ajmer Sharif dargah and Hazratbal Shrine of Kashmir.

Over the past decade, the Indian Council for Cultural Relations (ICCR) has organised several Buddhist conferences in Asian countries, such as Thailand (April 2010), South Korea (May 2010), Nepal (May 2016) and Nalanda, India (March 2017). The Indian Council for Cultural Relations, an independent foreign service, has developed a cultural diplomacy programme that organises seminars in Buddhist countries. In Ladakh, the Indian council for cultural relations held a festival with scholars and representatives from China, Mongolia and South Korea. In September 2015, Fudan University in Shanghai held a conference on India-China Buddhist ties, the first of its kind. In October 2016, the "Fifth International Buddhist Conference" was organised by the ministry of tourism and the committee on cultural relations in Varanasi, attended by more than 240 representatives from 39 countries. The "Buddhism in the 21st century" conference was held in Rajgir in 2017 (Scoot, 2016; Sundar, 2015).

In 2015, the Vivekananda International Foundation and the Tokyo Foundation held the India-Buddhism conflict avoidance initiative in Bodh Gaya, which was inaugurated by Prime Minister Narendra Modi. Modi explicitly stated that "this century cannot be the century of Asia without the Buddha" (Pethiyagoda, 2015).

Modi spends a day at Buddhist temples during his visits to Buddhist countries. The essence of Buddhism was effectively propagated. Modi's visit to Kathmandu was a speciality of his 4-CS agenda, such as cooperation, engagement, culture and constitution, and he gave Nepal a gift of bodhi tree, repeating cultural views. Modi called for the ancient

India-Sri Lanka Buddhist link, which was completed under king Ashoka of Mauryan Empire. He made a strategic choice to visit Sri Lanka's ancient capitals, Anuradhapura and Jaya Shri Mahabodhi, symbolising the place where India-Sri Lanka relations are being witnessed. In addition, he started the Indian-funded Jafana cultural center and visited the Mahabodhi temple in Colombo (De Silva, 2015).

Modi's visit to China is closely watched by the people of both countries. With China undergoing a Cultural Renaissance under President Xi Jinping, Modi took the appropriate time during his visit to make Buddhism a topic for discussion. During Modi's visit, 24 agreements were signed mainly in trade agreements, establishing sister cities and scientific research cooperation (Aneja, 2015; De Silva, 2015).

Modi's government is launching Buddhist diplomacy for two major foreign policy goals; the first is strategic and the second is economic. Buddhism is seen as the main vehicle for rebalancing flows in east and Southeast Asia. India is issuing visas to Buddhist tourists visiting the country on religious Tours. With the help of the World Bank, India's ministry of tourism and culture is also developing a fast Buddhist tourism route. Besides Buddhism, Modi's government is using other religions to articulate strong ties with these countries (https://mea.gov.in; Sharma 2014).

## Indo-Sri Lanka

The deep people-to-people connect and shared Buddhist heritage between India and Sri Lanka has been observed. In July 2020, the Government of India declared the Kushinagar Airport in India, the place of Lord Buddha's Mahaparinibbana, as an international airport, to allow Buddhist pilgrims from around the world to visit the revered site associated with Lord Buddha with ease. Given the pre-eminence of India-Sri Lanka Buddhist ties, both countries have agreed that the first inaugural flight to this airport will be from Sri Lanka. Prime Minister Modi during the Virtual Bilateral Summit held between India and Sri Lanka on 26 September 2020, announced a USD 15 million grant assistance for protection and promotion of Buddhist ties between India and Sri Lanka.

## Indo-Nepal

Nepal and India share special closeness and similarity in cultural tradition. They are so closely and strongly interlinked by social life and cultural tradition that nobody can imagine to separate them. Both have made great contributions to enriching religious and cultural heritage in this region, and beyond. Lord Buddha, born in Nepal, has left his footprints not only in South Asia but all over the world. Sita, the daughter of Nepal, who was married to Ram, the crown prince of Ayodhya in India, has made special place in the hearts of Hindus living anywhere in the world. The contributions made by Indian philosophers and saints need no further elaboration. It is these great personalities of this region that have helped evolve, develop and spread the cultural heritage that is proudly known today as the South Asian culture. (https://in.nepalembassy.gov.np/socio-cultural/).

The cultural links between Nepal and India have many facets. Religion is perhaps the most important factor, and plays a predominant role in shaping the cultural relations between these two countries. This is manifested in the large number of peoples from both countries visiting each other's countries for pilgrimage. Thousands of Nepalese nationals visit pilgrimage sites in India every year. The char dham yatra (visit of four dhams in India, viz. Badrinath/Kedarnath in Uttarakhand, Jagannath (Puri) in Orissa, Rameshwaram in Tamil Nadu, and Dwarka in Gujrat) is a life-time aspiration of almost all Hindus. There are many other places in India which are considered sacred sites by Nepalese people. They include Haridwar, Rishikesh, Varanasi, Gaya, Vaishnodevi, and many more. Similarly, there are a number of religious sites in Nepal which are considered very sacred and important, and are attractions as 'must visit' religious destinations for Indian nationals. Such sites include Pashupatinath in Kathmandu, Lumbini (the birth place of Buddha) in Rupandehi district, Ram-Janaki temple in Janakpur (the birth place of Janak and Sita), and many more. As the peoples of both countries share common religious faiths and philosophies, and revere and worship same gods and incarnations, their cultural ties are really very strong and inseparable (https://in.nepalembassy.gov.np/socio-cultural/).

Despite these efforts, Modi has yet to adopt an institutional approach to integrating religion into his foreign policy. Ramayana is highly respected in ASEAN countries such as Thailand, Cambodia and Indonesia. The Ramayana project team from these countries also came to India, and Indian artists also visited these countries, which will showcase their art throughout the country. This is not a contemporary effort, but an extension of the historical truth of the civilised dialogue between these countries and India, which emerged more than a thousand years ago. Angkor Wat in Cambodia, Borobudur in Indonesia, Wat Phu and Mayson valley in Laos, Rama temple in Thailand, and Hindu temple in Vietnam are typical examples of cultural and civilised relations between India and these countries (Basrur, 2017).

Another major aspect of India's cultural diplomacy is yoga. After successful lobbying at the UN general assembly, Modi government institutionalised the annual International Yoga Day, the first of which took place on June 21, 2015. Modi claimed that yoga is India's gift to the world, bringing peace and reconciliation to the body and mind "with self-examination and exploration of the sense of oneness with the world" (India Today, 2014).

Cultural diplomacy is also used as a means to burnish India's credentials of being a *moralpolitik* and a great power which is strongly opposed to the traditional notion of power i.e. hard power and is committed to the use of soft power to heal a world deeply divided by divisive issues ranging from climate change and the pernicious effects of neo-liberalism, such as mindless consumerism and the problems of global inequality and inequity arising from it. India is committed to the emergence of a more peaceful, tolerant and inclusive moral and secure world order where there will be no exploitation of fellow human beings and where all individuals can develop their moral and intellectual faculties to the fullest.

Modi has used certain soft power assets - Buddhism, Culture connections, Economic Aid, Indian Diaspora and Yoga. It is credited to Prime Minister Modi that how India communicates with other countries and how to increase relations, on this issue, Modi has increased the confidence of the country and has empowered it.

## Modi's Cultural Initiatives

Modi's government relies heavily on cultural and civilised relations to promote India's soft power. Since independence, India's foreign policy has formulated and benefited a lot from the five principles of peaceful coexistence (Panchsheel), which was first proposed by Nehru. But the Modi government's national executive council decided to change the foreign policy "five principles of peaceful coexistence" to "Panchamrita" or "5S". The four-page draft resolution, prepared by Ram Madhav, general secretary of the Bharatiya Janata Party, never uses the word "India" but uses India's Sanskrit name, Bharat, throughout. The title of the document reads: our national ambition is for Bharat to become a strong and respected world power. The Modi government has developed its foreign policy label "Panchamrita"- Samman dignity and honour; Samvad increased participation and dialogue; Samriddhi prosperity; Suraksha regional and global security; Sabhyata and Sanskriti culture and civilisation. These five themes have become the "Panchamrita" principle. It claims that Modi's government is "not influenced by any third party" and has single-handedly made "geopolitics" irrelevant. "Our participation is independent in thought and action, and confident in drawing strength from our traditions," the resolution said. It said India's national ambition was "Bharat's emergence as a strong and respected world power", for which the government had adopted "Panchamrita". The government has restored Bharat's place in international affairs with a speed and determination never before seen in our foreign engagement, fully re-established the partnership, and crossed new borders in our diplomatic relations. (https://www.telegraphindia.com 2015; https://defenceforumindia.com 2015)

The Modi government has expanded its first neighbourhood policy and reached out to Iran, China and Myanmar. Some of the catalysts seem more influential than ever to extend to India's neighbours: geography, regional integration such as three-dimensional pulses, and geo-economics; the inevitability of development; Security. In this regard, the two sides stressed bilateral relations, health, education, technology, economy and development in the region. (Chaturvedy, 2014; https://www.gatewayhouse.in 2014)

Under the Modi administration, India has made relations with its East Asian neighbours a foreign policy priority at a time when the United States is committed to a "pivot to Asia." In November 2014, at the Indo-ASEAN summit held in Myanmar, Indian prime minister Narendra Modi announced to upgrade India's previous "look East Policy" to a more action-oriented "Act East" strategy. It has accelerated these efforts to strengthen India's connection to the east through physical infrastructure projects, trade and investment agreements and regional institutions. (Hemant Singh, 2018; Palit, 2016; Uday Singh, 2018)

## Conclusion

The Modi government has launched an initiative to use cultural elements as a soft power in foreign policy. The use of soft power in foreign policy has not been done under Modi government for first time in Indian history but it is certainly stronger when it comes to launches and deployments. While previous administrations have used soft power to support foreign policy, their efforts have been relatively unfocused, poorly designed and consistent. Modi government one has indeed had more success in institutionalising and developing a more coherent and strategic approach to soft power than previous governments.

It is clear from the discussion so far that India's neighbourhood first policy since 2014 has had a mixed record. If India's relations with Pakistan deteriorated, and China expanded its strategic footprints in Nepal, the

Maldives, Sri Lanka and Pakistan, India's cooperation with Bangladesh, Bhutan, Afghanistan and Myanmar showed positive trends. India's diplomatic attention has consciously shifted from SAARC to BIMSTEC, giving an eastward shift to India's neighbourhood policy.

## References


Amitendu Palit. "India's Act East Policy and Implications for South-East Asia" Southeast Asian Affairs (2016), pp. 81-85, ISEAS, Yusof Ishak Institute.

Aneja, Atul. "Soft Power Set to Define Prime Minister Narendra Modi's China Visit", 11 May 2015, The Hindu, http://www.thehindu.com/news/international/social-media-bollywood-and-yoga-to-dominate-modis-chinavisit/article719 4559.ece

Basrur, Rajesh. "Modi's foreign policy fundamentals: a trajectory unchanged" International affairs 93-1(2017), Oxford University Press, https://www.chathamhouse.org/sites/default/files/publications/ia/INTA93_1_02_Basrur.pdf

Carnes, Lord. Losing Hearts and Minds? Public Diplomacy and Strategic Influence in the Age of Terror (Westport, CT: Praeger Security International, 2006, 15.)

Chaturvedy, Rajeev Ranjan 2014. "'Neighbourhood First': Modi's Foreign Policy Mantra", Institute of South Asian Studies, No. 346, 3 October 2014, https://www.files.ethz.ch/isn/184416/ISAS_Brief_No__346_Neighbourhood _First_03102014141625.pdf)

De Silva, Bandu. "Emerging Cultural Emphasis in India's Foreign Policy Under Modi", 29 May 2015, Colombo Telegraph, https://www.colombotelegraph.com/index.php/emerging-cultural-emphasis-in-indias-foreign-policy-undermo di)

De Silva, Bandu. "Emerging Cultural Emphasis in India's Foreign Policy Under Modi", 29 May 2015, Colombo Telegraph, https://www.colombotelegraph.com/index.php/emerging-cultural-emphasis-in-indias-foreign-policy-under modi/)

Ganguly, S. (2017a). Has Modi truly changed India's foreign policy? The Washington Quarterly, 40(2), 131–143.

Hemant Singh. "Act East Policy" of India: Meaning and Objectives", Jagran Josh, 25 May 2018, https://www.jagranjosh.com/general-knowledge/meaning-and-objectives-of-the-act-east-policy-of-india-1527251668-1

https://defenceforumindia.com 2015, "Panchsheel gives way to Panchamrit- New pillars of foreign policy" DFI, 4 March 2015,https://defenceforumindia.com/forum/threads/panchsheel-gives-way-to-panchamrit-new-pillars-of-foreignpolicy 67418/

https://in.nepalembassy.gov.np/socio-cultural/

https://www.gatewayhouse.in 2014, India, Modi and Neighbourhood" Gaitway House, 25 August 2014, https://www.gatewayhouse.in/india-modi-andthe-neighbourhood/)

https://www.telegraphindia.com 2015, "Modi Government Plans Buddhism Blitz in Cultural Diplomacy Refocus", The Telegraph, 31 August 2015, https://www.telegraphindia.com/india/modi-govt-plans-buddhism-blitz-in-cultural-diplomacyrefocus/cid/1512830)

https://mea.gov.in; Sharma 2014

India Today 2014. "Modi asks world leaders to adopt International Yoga Day", 27 September 2014, India Today, https://www.indiatoday.in/international-yoga-day/story/narendra-modi-asks-world-leaders-to-adopt-international-yogaday-301197-2014-09-27.

Kaura, Vinay and Rani Meena, India's Neighbourhood Policy During 2014– 2019: Political Context and Policy Outcomes, Indian Journal of Public Administration 66(1) 10–27, 2020 © 2020 IIPA.

Maack Mary N. "Books and Libraries as Instruments of Cultural Diplomacy in Francophone Africa during the Cold War," Libraries & Culture 36, no. 1 (Winter 2001): 59.

Nye Joseph S., Soft Power: The Means to Success in World Politics (Cambridge: Perseus Books, 2004), 22.

Pethiyagoda Kadira. "Modi Deploy his Culture Skills in Asia", Brookings, 1 June 2015, https://www.brookings.edu/opinions/modi-deploys-his-culture-skills-in-asia-2/.

Scoot, David, "Buddhism in current China-India Diplomacy", Sage Journals, 1December 2016, https://doi.org/10.1177%2F1868102616045003O5 )

Sharma, Ashok B. "India and East Asia: Prime Minister Narendra Modi's "Buddhist Diplomacy"", 5 November 2104, Global Research, https://www.globalresearch.ca/india-and-east-asia-prime-minister-narendra-modis-buddhist diplomacy /5412129

Shome, Pranay Kumar. Soft Power and Cultural Diplomacy in the Contemporary World, in Diplomacy and Beyond Plus A Journal of Foreign Policy & National Affairs, https://diplomacybeyond.com/soft-power-and-cultural-diplomacy-in-the-contemporary-world/)

Uday Vanu Singh. "Significance of India's Act East Policy and Engagement with ASEAN", Institute of Defence Studies and Analyses, 4 December 2108, https://idsa.in/backgrounder/significance-india-act-east-policy-andengagement-with-asean-ubsingh_041218

Uttam Anand. India's soft power diplomacy under Modi Govt. First, in International Journal of Research and Analytical Reviews, June 2019, Volume 6, Issue 2, p. 898)

Waller Michael J. (ed.). "Cultural Diplomacy, Political Influence, and Integrated Strategy," in Strategic Influence: Public Diplomacy, Counterpropaganda, and Political Warfare, (Washington, DC: Institute of World Politics Press, 2009), 74.

# Index

## C



## D



## E

## F



## G



## H



## I

## J



## K

## L



## M

## Q



## R



## S

## T



## U

## V



## W



## Y



## Z